First World War
and Army of Occupation
War Diary
France, Belgium and Germany

56 DIVISION
Headquarters, Branches and Services
General Staff
1 April 1917 - 30 April 1917

WO95/2933/4

The Naval & Military Press Ltd
www.nmarchive.com
Published in association with The National Archives

Published by

The Naval & Military Press Ltd

Unit 10 Ridgewood Industrial Park,

Uckfield, East Sussex,

TN22 5QE England

Tel: +44 (0) 1825 749494

www.naval-military-press.com

www.nmarchive.com

This diary has been reprinted in facsimile from the original. Any imperfections are inevitably reproduced and the quality may fall short of modern type and cartographic standards.

© **Crown Copyright**
Images reproduced by permission of The National Archives, London, England, 2015.

Contents

Document type	Place/Title	Date From	Date To
Heading	War Diary of General Staff-56th Division from 1st May 17 to 31st May 17 Vol 16		
Miscellaneous	War Diary Appendices.		
War Diary	Arras.	01/05/1917	21/05/1917
War Diary	Warlus	22/05/1917	24/05/1917
War Diary	Habarcq	25/05/1917	31/05/1917
Heading	App I O.O.		
Miscellaneous	A Form. Messages And Signals.	04/05/1917	04/05/1917
Operation(al) Order(s)	56th Division Order No. 90	04/05/1917	04/05/1917
Operation(al) Order(s)	56th Division Order No. 91	05/05/1917	05/05/1917
Operation(al) Order(s)	56th Division Order No. 92	09/05/1917	09/05/1917
Operation(al) Order(s)	56th Division Order No. 93	11/05/1917	11/05/1917
Miscellaneous	56th Division-Relief Table.		
Operation(al) Order(s)	56th Division (Warning) Order No. 94	16/05/1917	16/05/1917
Operation(al) Order(s)	56th Division Order No. 95	17/05/1917	17/05/1917
Operation(al) Order(s)	56th Division Order No. 96	17/05/1917	17/05/1917
Map			
Miscellaneous	A Form. Messages And Signals.		
Operation(al) Order(s)	Addendum No. 1 to 56th Division Order No. 96	17/05/1917	17/05/1917
Operation(al) Order(s)	56th Division Order No. 97	17/05/1917	17/05/1917
Miscellaneous	March Table To Accompany 56th Division Order No. 97		
Operation(al) Order(s)	56th Division Order No. 98	18/05/1917	18/05/1917
Operation(al) Order(s)	56th Division Order No. 99	22/05/1917	22/05/1917
Miscellaneous	Issued With 56th Division Order No. 99 Appendix "A"		
Miscellaneous	Issued With 56th Division Order No. 99 Appendix "B"		
Miscellaneous	A Form. Messages And Signals.	04/05/1917	04/05/1917
Miscellaneous	A Form. Messages And Signals.		
Miscellaneous	A Form. Messages And Signals.	01/05/1917	01/05/1917
Operation(al) Order(s)	56th Division Order No. 100	30/05/1917	30/05/1917
Heading	App II		
Miscellaneous	56th. Division No. G.3/177.	01/05/1917	01/05/1917
Miscellaneous	56th. Divn. G.3/204.	02/05/1917	02/05/1917
Miscellaneous	Signal Communication During Forthcoming Operations.	01/05/1917	01/05/1917
Miscellaneous	56th Division No. G.3/164.	01/05/1917	01/05/1917
Miscellaneous	VI Corps No. G.X. 1/H/140.	30/04/1917	30/04/1917
Miscellaneous	56th Divn. G.3/262.	11/05/1917	11/05/1917
Heading	56th Divn. Tactical Progress Reports (which in VI Corps) War Diary Copies. App III		
Miscellaneous	56th Division Tactical Progress Report No. 21 from 5 p.m. 19th May to 5 p.m. 20th May 1917	20/05/1917	20/05/1917
Miscellaneous	56th Divisional Tactical Progress Report No. 20 from 5 p.m. 18th May to 5 p.m. 19th May 1917	19/05/1917	19/05/1917
Miscellaneous	56th Divisional Tactical Progress Report No. 19 from 5 p.m. 17th May to 5 p.m. 18th May 1917	18/05/1917	18/05/1917
Miscellaneous	56th Divisional Tactical Progress Report No. 18 from 5 p.m. 16th May to 5 p.m. 17th May 1917	17/05/1917	17/05/1917
Miscellaneous	56th Divisional Tactical Progress Report No. 17 from 5 p.m. 15th May to 5 p.m. 16th May 1917	16/05/1917	16/05/1917

Miscellaneous	56th Divisional Tactical Progress Report No. 16 from 5 p.m. 14th May to 5 p.m. 15th May 1917	15/05/1917	15/05/1917
Miscellaneous	56th Divisional Tactical Progress Report No. 15 from 5 p.m. 13th May to 5 p.m. 14th May 1917	14/05/1917	14/05/1917
Miscellaneous	Annexe To 56th Divisional Tactical Progress Report No. 15		
Miscellaneous	56th Divisional Tactical Progress Report No. 14 from 5 p.m. 12th May to 5 p.m. 13th May 1917	13/05/1917	13/05/1917
Miscellaneous	56th Divisional Tactical Progress Report No. 13 from 5 p.m. 11th May to 5 p.m. 12th May 1917	12/05/1917	12/05/1917
Miscellaneous	Annexe To 56th Divisional Tactical Progress Report No. 13		
Miscellaneous	56th Division Tactical Progress Report No. 12. from 5 p.m. 10th May to 5 p.m. 11th May 1917	11/05/1917	11/05/1917
Miscellaneous	56th Division Tactical Progress Report No. 11 from 5 p.m. 9th May to 5 p.m. 10th May 1917	10/05/1917	10/05/1917
Miscellaneous	56th Division Tactical Progress Report No. 10 from 5 p.m. 9th May to 6 p.m. 10th May 1917	09/05/1917	09/05/1917
Miscellaneous	56th Division Tactical Progress Report No. 9 from 5 p.m. 7th May to 5 p.m. 8th May 1917	08/05/1917	08/05/1917
Miscellaneous	56th Division Tactical Progress Report No. 8 from 5 p.m. 6th May to 5 p.m. 7th May 1917	07/05/1917	07/05/1917
Miscellaneous	56th Division Tactical Progress Report No. 7. from 5 p.m. 5th May 1917 to 5 p.m. 6th May 1917	06/05/1917	06/05/1917
Miscellaneous	56th Division Tactical Progress Report No. 6 from 5 p.m. 4th May 1917 to 5 p.m. 5th May 1917	05/05/1917	05/05/1917
Miscellaneous	56th Divisional Tactical Progress Report No. 5. from 5 p.m. 3rd May to 5 p.m. 4th May 1917	04/05/1917	04/05/1917
Miscellaneous	56th Divisional Tactical Progress Report No. 4 from 5.0 p.m. 1st May to 5.0 p.m. 2nd May 1917	02/05/1917	02/05/1917
Miscellaneous	56th Division Tactical Progress Report No. 3 from 5 p.m. 30th April to 5 p.m. 1st May 1917	01/05/1917	01/05/1917
Map	Defence Scheme		
Map	Trenches Corrected To 1-4-17.		
Miscellaneous	Glossary.		
Operation(al) Order(s)	Addendum No. 2 to 56th Division Order No. 96	17/05/1917	17/05/1917
Map			
Miscellaneous	Location Table.		
Diagram etc	Defence Scheme Appendix "B"		
Heading	App VI Miscellaneous		
Miscellaneous	C Form Messages And Signals.		
Miscellaneous	C Form (Duplicate). Messages And Signals.		
Heading	War Diary of General Staff Branch 56th Division from 1st June 1917 to 30th June 1917 Vol 17		
Heading	Cover for Documents. Nature of Enclosures.		
War Diary	Habarcq	01/06/1917	11/06/1917
War Diary	Arras.	11/06/1917	30/06/1917
Miscellaneous	56th Division. Narrative of Operations from 28th April to 21st May 1917.	22/05/1917	22/05/1917
Map	51B S.W.		
Map	Defence Scheme		
Miscellaneous	Defence Scheme for the Cambrai Road or Right Divisional Sector of the VI Corps Front.	22/06/1917	22/06/1917
Miscellaneous			
Miscellaneous	General Description Of The Divisional Front.		
Miscellaneous	Appendix "A" Location Of Strombos Horns.		

Heading	56th Division Tactical Program Reports. War Diary Copies		
Heading	Papers for G.S.O I		
Miscellaneous	56th Divisional Tactical Progress Report No. 1 from 12 noon 11th June to 12 noon 12th June, 1917	12/06/1917	12/06/1917
Miscellaneous	Preliminary Examination Of Man Belonging To 3rd Bn. 458th Infantry Regt. 236th Div.		
Miscellaneous	56th Divisional Tactical Progress Report No. 2. from 12 noon 12th June to 12 noon 13th June 1917	13/06/1917	13/06/1917
Miscellaneous	56th Divisional Tactical Progress Report No. 3 from 12 noon 13th June to 12 noon 14th June 1917	14/06/1917	14/06/1917
Miscellaneous	56th Divisional Tactical Progress Report No. 4 from 12 noon 14th June to 12 noon 15th June 1917	15/06/1917	15/06/1917
Miscellaneous	56th Division Tactical Progress Report No. 5. from 12 noon 15th June to 12 noon 16th June 1917	16/06/1917	16/06/1917
Miscellaneous	56th Division Tactical Progress Report No. 6 from 12 noon 16th June to 12 noon 17th June 1917	17/06/1917	17/06/1917
Miscellaneous	56th Division Tactical Progress Report No. 7. from 12 noon 17th June to 12 noon 18th June 1917	18/06/1917	18/06/1917
Miscellaneous	Re 56th Div. T.P.R. No. 8		
Miscellaneous	56th Division Tactical Progress Report No. 8 from 12 noon 18th June to 12 noon 19th June 1917	19/06/1917	19/06/1917
Miscellaneous	56th Divisional Tactical Progress Report No. 9 from 12 noon 19th June to 12 noon 20th June 1917	20/06/1917	20/06/1917
Miscellaneous	56th Divisional Tactical Progress Report No. 10. from 12 noon 20th June to 12 noon 21st June, 1917	21/06/1917	21/06/1917
Miscellaneous	56th Divisional Tactical Progress Report No. 11 from 12 noon 21st June to 12 noon 22nd June 1917	22/06/1917	22/06/1917
Miscellaneous	56th Divisional Tactical Progress Report No. 12 from 12 noon 22nd June to 12 noon 23rd June, 1917	23/06/1917	23/06/1917
Miscellaneous	56th Divisional Tactical Progress Report No. 13 from 12 noon 23rd June to 12 noon 24th June, 1917	24/06/1917	24/06/1917
Miscellaneous	56th Divisional Tactical Progress Report No. 14, from 12 noon 24th June to 12 noon 25th June 1917	25/06/1917	25/06/1917
Miscellaneous	56th Division Tactical Progress Report No. 15. from 12 noon 25th June to 12 noon 26th June 1917	26/06/1917	26/06/1917
Miscellaneous	56th Division Tactical Progress Report No. 16. from 12 noon 26th June to 12 noon 27th June 1917	27/06/1917	27/06/1917
Miscellaneous	56th Division Tactical Progress Report No. 17. from 12 noon 27th June to 12 noon 28th June 1917	28/06/1917	28/06/1917
Miscellaneous	56th Division Tactical Progress Report No. 18. from 12 noon 28th June to 12 noon 29th June 1917	29/06/1917	29/06/1917
Miscellaneous	56th Division Tactical Progress Report No. 19. from 12 noon 29th June to 12 noon 30th June 1917	30/06/1917	30/06/1917
Operation(al) Order(s)	56th Division Order No. 101.	06/06/1917	06/06/1917
Miscellaneous	Relief Table to accompany 56th Division Order No. 101		
Map	Map B		
Operation(al) Order(s)	56th Division Order No. 102.	07/06/1917	07/06/1917
Miscellaneous	56th Divn. G.3/424.	10/06/1917	10/06/1917
Miscellaneous	56th Divn. G.3/440.	12/06/1917	12/06/1917
Miscellaneous	56th Division. G.3/439.	13/06/1917	13/06/1917
Operation(al) Order(s)	56th Division Order No. 103	11/06/1917	11/06/1917
Operation(al) Order(s)	56th Division Order No. 104	14/06/1917	14/06/1917
Operation(al) Order(s)	56th Division Order No. 105	17/06/1917	17/06/1917
Operation(al) Order(s)	56th Division Order No. 106	26/06/1917	26/06/1917
Operation(al) Order(s)	56th Division Order No. 107	29/06/1917	29/06/1917

Miscellaneous	Relief Table To Accompany 56th Division Order No. 107		
Miscellaneous	Location Table.		
Heading	56th Division General Staff Jan-Jun 1917		
Heading	This Seems to be a duplicate copy of 56 Div Gs diary for April 1917		
Miscellaneous	A the national archives		
War Diary	Beaumetz-Les-Loges	01/04/1917	08/04/1917
War Diary	Agny.	09/04/1917	19/04/1917
War Diary	Couin	20/04/1917	25/04/1917
War Diary	Hauteville	26/04/1917	26/04/1917
War Diary	Warlus	27/04/1917	30/04/1917

Army Form W. 3091.

Cover for Documents.

Nature of Enclosures.

CONFIDENTIAL

WAR DIARY
of
GENERAL STAFF - 56th DIVISION

From 1st May '17 to 31st May '17

Notes, or Letters written.

WAR DIARY

Appendices

1. O.O
3. T.P.R
4. Location tables
5. Narrative of operations
6. Miscellaneous
2. Instructions for operations

Army Form C. 2118.

WAR DIARY
or
INTELLIGENCE SUMMARY
(Erase heading not required.)

Instructions regarding War Diaries and Intelligence Summaries are contained in F.S. Regs., Part II. and the Staff Manual respectively. Title Pages will be prepared in manuscript.

Place	Date	Hour	Summary of Events and Information	Remarks and references to Appendices
ARRAS.	May 1st	a.m. 4.0	A practice barrage was put down on S.O.S. Line. Enemy's reply was slow and well behind our front line.	APPENDIX II
		p.m. 2.45	Morning Report. - Hostile Artillery was active throughout the night on forward areas. VI Corps instructions for forthcoming Operations issued. 56th Division Instructions - Signal Communications issued. Orders for shelling of BOIS DU VERT with gas shells on night Y/Z issued Amendment to O.O.No.88 issued, cancelling orders for further advance from RED Line. Evening Report. Intermittent shelling of back areas especially MARLIERE & GUEMAPPE.	do. APPENDIX I
	2nd	a.m. 2.30	Movement of Battalions of 167th Brigade into concentration area complete. Morning Report. A quiet night, except for a considerable use of gas shells on back areas Zero hour received and distributed. Evening Report. A quiet day.	APPENDIX II
		p.m. 9.15	Move of 168th Infantry Brigade into Reserve Assembly Area completed. Our Back Areas were heavily shelled with gas shells during the night.	
	3rd	a.m. 3.45.	Zero hour. The attack commenced in the dark, and no reports were received for a considerable time.	
		5.54	7th Middlesex Regiment reported that at the commencement of the attack heavy M.G. and rifle fire had prevented them reaching the first objective.	
		6.0	169th Brigade reported heavy hostile M.G. fire from 0.15.b. but that it was impossible to obtain information as to the situation.	

2449 Wt. W14957/M90 750,000 1/16 J.B.C. & A. Forms/C.2118/12.

Army Form C. 2118.

WAR DIARY
or
INTELLIGENCE SUMMARY
(Erase heading not required.)

Instructions regarding War Diaries and Intelligence Summaries are contained in F. S. Regs., Part II. and the Staff Manual respectively. Title Pages will be prepared in manuscript.

Place	Date	Hour	Summary of Events and Information	Remarks and references to Appendices
	3rd	a.m. 6.15	F.O.O. reported that our men could be seen digging in in front of ROHART FACTORY, and that 14th Division appeared to have reached its objectives.	
		6.40	Report from wounded Officer; 1st Londons made two attacks but each time were driven back by M.G. fire and were now in original trenches. This was confirmed by report timed 4.55 a.m.	
		7. 0	169th Brigade reported that 2nd Londons had two platoons in trench S.E. of CAVALRY FARM with 4 M.Gs. Enemy appeared to be holding TOOL TRENCH. 2nd Londons holding portion of LANYARD TRENCH. 2nd Londons and L.R.B. both in trench N.15.a.0.5. to CAMBRAI ROAD. L.R.B. in front of pit West of ROHART FACTORY.	
		7.10	G.O.C. ordered 168th Brigade to move two Battalions to WANCOURT LINE, and two battalions to THE HARP.	
		7.45	F.O.O. reported 14th Division had captured Wood in 0.21.d. and that 169th Brigade had captured LANYARD TRENCH, but that hostile M.Gs. were between LANYARD and TOOL Trenches.	
		8.55	167th Brigade reported casualties were very heavy in assaulting battalions from M.G. fire. 7th Middlesex held line of shell holes 80 yards West of TOOL TRENCH. Heavy hostile barrage at present prevented the Reserve Bn. moving up.	
		9.25	7th Middlesex reported large number of Germans moving up to TOOL Trench. Artillery instructed to stand by to barrage TOOL Trench.	
		9.30	Div. M.G.O. ordered to arrange to enfilade TOOL Trench from 0.19.b.	
		9.55	Germans reported to be massing for counter-attack in STIRRUP LANE - Corps H.A. informed.	
		10. 0	3rd Division reported that they were in the N. end of TOOL TRENCH and bombing Southwards. POLE Trench strongly held by the enemy.	
		10.25	F.O.O. reported at least four companies of Germans retiring on the road in 0.10.a. & b.	
		10.30	In view of above report 167th Infantry Brigade were told to move Reserve Battalion forward as close as possible.	

Army Form C. 2118.

WAR DIARY
or
INTELLIGENCE SUMMARY
(Erase heading not required.)

Instructions regarding War Diaries and Intelligence Summaries are contained in F.S. Regs., Part II. and the Staff Manual respectively. Title Pages will be prepared in manuscript.

Place	Date	Hour	Summary of Events and Information	Remarks and references to Appendices
	3rd	a.m. 10.45	169th Brigade reported bombers of 9th Londons had rushed Cavalry Farm after T.M. bombardment and all dug-outs bombed. 22 prisoners taken. Bombing up S. end of TOOL Trench progressing.	
		10.50	3rd Division asked for our guns to lift off TOOL Trench.	
		11.0	Move of 168th Brigade complete.	
		11.35	3rd Division reported situation - Right Brigade held Northern end of TOOL TRENCH East of COPSE at 0.8. Central - along HILL Trench - 0.2.c.0.0. - P.2.d. Central - East of BOIS des AUBEPINES.	
		11.50	14th Division reported S.O.S. signals from both Brigades.	
		p.m. 12.30	14th Division reported both Brigades heavily counter-attacked and now back in original trenches.	
		12.35	169th Brigade reported that they had no troops North of the CAMBRAI Road, but they still held the trench immediately W. of the Pit in 0.15.c.	
		3.50	VI Corps ordered all Divisions to consolidate ground, and 56th Division to occupy TOOL Trench. No action taken pending Conference of Divisional Commanders.	
			167th Brigade reported 7th Middlesex in touch with the 3rd Division in our original line - enemy holding the whole of TOOL Trench; many of our men in shell holes in front of TOOL Trench.	
		4.0	This report was confirmed by 3rd Division.	
		5.45	168th Brigade ordered to place 1 Battalion at disposal of 167th Brigade and 1 Battalion at disposal of 169th Brigade. 167th and 169th Brigades order inter-battalion reliefs to take place during the night.	
			Prisoners to 6 p.m. - 2 Officers, 5 N.C.Os. 29 Other ranks.	
		8.10	F.O.O. reported 50 of our men seen going East from North part of LANYARD TRENCH without arms.	

Army Form C. 2118.

WAR DIARY
or
INTELLIGENCE SUMMARY
(Erase heading not required.)

Instructions regarding War Diaries and Intelligence Summaries are contained in F. S. Regs., Part II. and the Staff Manual respectively. Title Pages will be prepared in manuscript.

Place	Date	Hour	Summary of Events and Information	Remarks and references to Appendices
	3rd	p.m. 8.15	169th Brigade reported that they were holding LANYARD TRENCH S. of CAMBRAI Rd. thence a line to CAVALRY FARM inclusive, about 100 yards South of the main road.	
		11.15	169th Brigade reported that after 1 hour's intense bombardment the enemy counter-attacked and drove our troops out of CAVALRY FARM.	
		11.45	169th Brigade report 2nd and 5th Londons had pushed forward again and re-occupied all ground won during the day except CAVALRY FARM.	
			During this advance 1 Officer & 15 O.Rs. were captured by 169th Brigade.	
			These gains were held till 1 hour before sunrise when troops were withdrawn according to orders.	
	4th	a.m. 2.0	Inter-battalion reliefs in both Brigade areas completed.	
			Morning Report - Fairly quiet night.	
		11.45	Warning Order No. 89 for relief of 167th and 169th Brigades in the line by 168th Brigade issued.	APPENDIX I.
		p.m. 1.15	O.O.No. 90 issued with details for this relief.	do.
			During the day hostile heavies were active at intervals.	
			VI Corps ordered RED Line to be reached by 15th.	
	5th	a.m. 2.10	Relief of front area by 168th Brigade complete.	
			Morning Report - There was a good deal of indiscriminate shelling during the night by hostile H.A. and with gas shells.	
		7.0	A heavy barrage was put down from WANCOURT TOWER to KNIFE Trench for 10 minutes, but no infantry action followed.	
			A conspicuous absence of movement about TOOL TRENCH, and hostile shelling of CAVALRY FARM led to /suspicion	

Army Form C. 2118.

WAR DIARY
or
INTELLIGENCE SUMMARY

(Erase heading not required.)

Instructions regarding War Diaries and Intelligence Summaries are contained in F.S. Regs., Part II. and the Staff Manual respectively. Title Pages will be prepared in manuscript.

Place	Date	Hour	Summary of Events and Information	Remarks and references to Appendices
	5th	7.0 (cont)	suspicion that this might not be held, and patrols were pushed forward to ascertain the situation, but they were checked by heavy M.G. and rifle fire.	
		p.m. 5.0	A quiet day. VI Corps order for readjustment of Divisional boundaries received. O.O. No. 91 issued for Division to extend its boundary Northwards.	APPENDIX I
		10.20 to 11.50	A heavy hostile barrage went down along the whole front and was vigorously replied to by our Artillery.	
	6th		Morning Report - Patrols again attempted to enter TOOL Trench, but were met by M.G. fire. There was slight shelling of batteries during the day. An observed shoot by our H.A. on Tool Trench caused a large number of Germans to evacuate it across the open.	
	7th		Evening report - Hostile artillery active during the night, especially on Oy. Some gas shells on FOSSES FM. Our patrols were active during the night.	
		5am	Readjustment of divisional front complete. During the day rail ways + Battery positions were shelled. Another observed shoot on TOOL Trench was very effective. Our patrols entered CAVALRY FM and its copse in O & carried out [?] them both unoccupied. TOOL Trench was found to be strongly held.	
	8th		Hostile artillery was much less active by day and night, but fire was carried out on communication [?] [?] [?]	

2449 Wt. W14957/M90 750,000 1/16 J.B.C. & A. Forms/C.2118/12.

Army Form C. 2118.

WAR DIARY
or
INTELLIGENCE SUMMARY
(Erase heading not required.)

Place	Date	Hour	Summary of Events and Information	Remarks and references to Appendices
ARRAS	9th	9-	Our patrols were active during the night. Hostile artillery was again rather normal during the day. Much work has been done during the last few days on deepening trenches, improving communication, wiring.	
			Preliminary instructions were received for VI Corps for a series of small attacks along the Army front. 51 Div. to capture Tool Trench on evening of 11th inst.	
		9-	O.O. No 92 issued for carrying out this operation.	APPENDIX I
	10th	-	Hostile artillery was active on our Front during the night. Much work was done on improving existing trenches, digging new CTs and strong points, especially in O.8.a. Patrols reported CAVALRY FARM and trench SE of JN unoccupied.	
			During the day Rattle Wood area was active as was BULLET trench & GORDON Alley. Our Field guns carried out destructive fire on TOOL trench according to programme. Hostile artillery was very active during the night, but confined itself to desultory shelling of back areas during the day.	
	11th			

Army Form C. 2118.

WAR DIARY
or
INTELLIGENCE SUMMARY
(Erase heading not required.)

Instructions regarding War Diaries and Intelligence Summaries are contained in F. S. Regs., Part II. and the Staff Manual respectively. Title Pages will be prepared in manuscript.

Place	Date	Hour	Summary of Events and Information	Remarks and references to Appendices
ARRAS	May 11th			
		8-30 p.m.	Zero hour. By the time the attack took place owing to smoke and approaching darkness visibility on TOOL TRENCH was bad. No definite news was received for some time as to the progress of the attack.	
		9pm	O.O. 93 fw relief of 168 Bde. issued. Instructions re the overall attack along the front round	APPENDIX II
		9-7 p.m.	168th Bde. Reported that a heavy barrage had been put down at zero plus 3 well behind our attacking troops.	
		10-5 p.m.	168th Bde. reported that all three Companies of Left Bn. were in TOOL TRENCH, that about 50 Germans were seen running away from TOOL TRENCH and that Lewis Guns were used very effectively against them. Many dead were found in the trench and 9 prisoners of 128 I.R. had arrived at Battalion Headquarters.	
		10-25 p.m.	Corps H.A. reported German barrage practically ceased.	
		10-30 p.m.	G.O.C. told Divisional Artillery that barrage fire was no longer required.	
		10-45 p.m.	168th Bde. reported that Left Bn. were in touch with Right Bn. in TOOL TRENCH, but that no news had been received from the Right Bn.	
		11-15 p.m.	The 4th London Regt. reported that they had taken the whole of their objective and were in touch with the London Scottish on their Left.	
	May 12th			
		2-0 a.m.	168th Bde. reported that Right Bn. had taken its objective with little resistance, that Left Company of Left Bn. had come under heavy M.G. fire while advancing. Both Battalions now consolidating on their objectives, that 12 prisoners and 3 M.G"s had been taken. A bombing fight was in progress in TOOL TRENCH some distance N.E. of the COPSE and 0.8 Central.	
		5-0 a.m.	Morning Report. Situation fairly quiet. Three C.T's dug to new Front Line and a good block formed on our left flank in TOOL TRENCH.	
		5-50 a.m.	Corps H.A. asked to deal with TOOL TRENCH North of our block as enemy seemed determined to bomb down the trench. One attack had already been repulsed with the assistance of L.T.M's just W. of COPSE in 0.8 Central.	
			During the day hostile Artillery was active on Support Battalion areas and batteries /in	

Army Form C. 2118.

WAR DIARY
or
INTELLIGENCE SUMMARY
(Erase heading not required.)

Instructions regarding War Diaries and Intelligence Summaries are contained in F. S. Regs., Part II. and the Staff Manual respectively. Title Pages will be prepared in manuscript.

Place	Date	Hour	Summary of Events and Information	Remarks and references to Appendices
	~~13th May.~~ 13th May.		in N.11 and N.17. Total captures in this operation were 1 N.C.O. and 9 men of the 128 I.R.; 1 N.C.O. of the 5th Grenadier Regt. and 6 M.G's. In addition at 3-30 a.m. an Officer and Orderly of the 5th Gren. Regt. came up to TOOL TRENCH not knowing it had been captured. The Officer was killed and the Orderly wounded and taken prisoner. During the night the 1st Londons relieved the 9th Londons in reserve. Morning Report. Except for heavy shelling of RAKE TRENCH and battery positions in N.18.a hostile Artillery was less active than usual. During the night the 3 new 7 C.T's and TOOL TRENCH were deepened and the advance posts strengthened. Our left flank in O.8.a was wired up and wiring was also commenced along the whole front. During the day hostile Artillery was active on Back Areas especially on GORDON ALLEY. Our Stokes Mortars did effective shooting just North of the block in TOOL TRENCH and our snipers claimed to have killed 13 Germans out of a number who attempted to leave the trench.	
	14th May. 4.15 am		Relief of the front line complete. Hostile artillery was active during the night — Two deserters of the 5th GRENADIER Regt. came into Rifle Brigade before dawn. Much digging & wiring was carried out on the forward line	
		10 a	by 18de. took over command of the line from 1st Rfle. During the day hostile artillery was quieter than usual but a very heavy trench mortar bombardment was opened at 2 pm in reply to the Germans attack on our left.	
	15th May		Night and day passed without incident — Relief of the support battalions by 2 batt ½/16 Ldn. completed.	

2449 Wt. W14957/M90 750,000 1/16 J.B.C. & A. Forms/C.2118/12.

Army Form C. 2118.

WAR DIARY
or
INTELLIGENCE SUMMARY.
(Erase heading not required.)

Instructions regarding War Diaries and Intelligence Summaries are contained in F. S. Regs., Part II. and the Staff Manual respectively. Title pages will be prepared in manuscript.

Place	Date	Hour	Summary of Events and Information	Remarks and references to Appendices
ARRAS	15th May		Normal artillery fire during the night. Prisoners' information from prisoners that reinforcements were contemplated caused us to push well forward. Our line was found to be held in strength. Considerable work in repairing trenches was found necessary & consolidation continued at Aquiel Farm.	
			O.O. No. 94 for relief of Division by 29 Div. issued. (Appendix)	APPENDIX I
		9pm	An attempt was made to ensure that MANY MEN Rested during the night. But it was found to be strongly held.	
		Midnight	Little or no rifle or MG fire incidents noted. Owing to extreme inactivity on part of hostile troops, orders were given for strong patrols forward to ascertain the situation. By the enemy lines were found to be manned. Still	
			During the day the following orders were issued	
	2.15p		O.O. No. 95 with orders for action in case of the enemy's attack.	APPENDIX
	3.30p		O.O. No. 96 with 2 Addenda with orders for attack on HOOK & LONG TRENCHES	
			O.O. No. 97 - Orders issued that tomorrow july 5th to be duration of the 37th Division	

Army Form C. 2118.

WAR DIARY
or
INTELLIGENCE SUMMARY.
(Erase heading not required.)

Instructions regarding War Diaries and Intelligence Summaries are contained in F. S. Regs., Part II. and the Staff Manual respectively. Title pages will be prepared in manuscript.

Place	Date	Hour	Summary of Events and Information	Remarks and references to Appendices
ARRAS	18th May		Morning report. Patrols pushed out which Battle Troops distributed normally. During the evening of the 17th the Light Battalions were held in reserve. The enemy shelled during the night and considerable damage was done. Patrols during the night pushed forward toward LANY ROAD TRENCH without making any hostile known. During the day our snipers obtained some hits — the neighbourhood of the Block — Too Trench & an L.T.M. came into action there.	
		9.30 a.m.	An attempt was made by the 8th MIDDLESEX Reg to reach the remaining Tool Trench by the Block was found to be occupied. The men attempting failed to reach their objective and pulled back.	
		11 a.m.	51st Div. O.O. No.98 received.	APPENDIX I
			Morning report. Patrols reported enemy consolidating on a line of shell holes 200 yards E. of TOOL trench.	
			April day. During the day 168 & 167 Bde were relieved in support & reserve respectively. At the 2.9th Div on the left, 4th MIDDLESEX Reg attacked HOOK and LONG trenches — HOOK trench was captured except on the right where on the phone line the enemy attack however failed — The division on the left was driven in prisoners — the	

Army Form C. 2118.

WAR DIARY
or
INTELLIGENCE SUMMARY.
(Erase heading not required.)

Instructions regarding War Diaries and Intelligence Summaries are contained in F. S. Regs., Part II. and the Staff Manual respectively. Title pages will be prepared in manuscript.

Place	Date	Hour	Summary of Events and Information	Remarks and references to Appendices
ARRAS	20th May		patrols in the back area looked for by Bttn Hdqtrs + had but little of a all officers + the majority of the men being casualties. During the day much movement in the enemy lines afforded well with by artillery & rifle fire. During the night by Bn we relieved in the line	
WARLUS	21st May	10—	Bn H.Q. opened at WARLUS + by Bn was with 21st bn DAINVILLE.	APPENDIX I
	22nd	7.30—	Bn O.O. No 99 with orders to move to HABARCQ received	
	23rd		G.O.C. inspected 16th Bde.	
	24th	11am	Bn H.Q. opened at HABARCQ + brigade moved into billets there	
HABARCQ	25th		Sports, rest + refitting. Medical and Lewis Gun courses held three days	
			programmes. Field ... the men	
	26th		2 Officers + 91 O.R.s	
			2.O.15	
	27th		1 coy & 12 LONDONS did work on Ath Echelon at FICHEUX — O.T.C. attached	

Army Form C. 2118.

WAR DIARY
or
INTELLIGENCE SUMMARY.
(Erase heading not required.)

Instructions regarding War Diaries and Intelligence Summaries are contained in F. S. Regs., Part II. and the Staff Manual respectively. Title pages will be prepared in manuscript.

Place	Date	Hour	Summary of Events and Information	Remarks and references to Appendices
HABARCQ	28th May		G.O.C. inspected remaining two Battalions of 167 Bde.	
		5 pm	Conference of Brigade commanders C.R.E. A.A. & Q.M.G. in Bn HQ	
	29th May		Orders received for 2 Coys 5th CHESHIRE Regt and 1 Field Coy RE to proceed to ARRAS for work in the line.	
	30th May		G.O.C. inspected two Battalions 167 Bde. OO No.100 road-forming scheme	APPENDIX I
	31st May		G.O.C. inspected two Battalions of 167 Bde.	

"A" Form.
MESSAGES AND SIGNALS.

Army Form C.2121 (in pads of 100).

TO: To all recipients of Order No 90.

Sender's Number.	Day of Month.	In reply to Number.	AAA
G. 184	4/5		

Reference 56th Division Order No. 90, para. 6 for 167th and 168th Infantry Brigades read 167th and 169th Infantry Brigades. AAA Addsd to all recipients of Order No. 90.

From 56th Divn.
Time 3.15 pm

J.K. Maitland Capt
General Staff

SECRET. *War Diary*   Copy No. 25

56th DIVISION ORDER NO. 90.   4th May 1917.

1.   168th Infantry Brigade will relieve 167th and 169th Infantry Brigades in the line to-night. G.O.C. 167th and 169th Infantry Brigades will each leave their best Battalion at the disposal of G.O.C. 168th Infantry Brigade, who will arrange to accommodate them not further East than the WANCOURT line.

2.   168th M.G. Coy. will take over from both 167th and 169th M.G. Coys.

3.   193rd Div. M.G. Coy. will remain as at present, keeping 8 guns at the disposal of G.O.C. 168th Infantry Brigade, and arranging for their relief within the Coy. as may be necessary.

4.   All details of relief will be arranged between Brigadiers concerned.

5.   On relief, areas are allotted as follows :-

    <u>167th Infantry Brigade</u> (less 1 Bn.)

       Old British line and old German trenches West of a line H.31.a.0.5 - G.36.c.6.2.

    <u>169th Infantry Brigade</u> (less 1 Bn.)

       Trenches East of above line and exclusive of the WANCOURT line.

    The Divisional Boundaries are :-

       On the North - the CAMBRAI Road
       On the South - N.3.d.6.8 - N.1.d.2.0 - M.6.b.5.5 - G.35.b.5.1.

6.   Headquarters of 167th and 168th Infantry Brigades will be about H.31. Central.

7.   ACKNOWLEDGE.

                                               B. Pakenham

Head Qrs. 56th Division.   Lieut-Colonel.
                                                General Staff.
      Issued at 1-15 p.m.

Copy No.				
1.	167th Inf. Bde.	15.	56th Div. Train.
2.	168th Inf. Bde.	16.	56th Div. M.G.O.
3.	169th Inf. Bde.	17.	56th Div. Gas Officer.
4.	3rd Division.	18.	D.A.D.O.S.
5.	14th Division.	19.	4th Aust. D.S. Colm.
6.	VIth Corps H.A.	20.	No. 2 Amm. Sub Park.
7.	VIth Corps Arty.	21.	A.D.M.S.
8.	No. 12 Squadron R.F.C.	22.	A.D.V.S.
9.	1/5th Ches. Regt.	23.	"Q"
10.	C.R.A.	24.	A.D.C.
11.	C.R.E.	25.	War Diary.
12.	A.P.M.	26.	File.
13.	193rd Div. M.G. Coy.	27.	29th Division
14.	56th Div. Signals.		

SECRET.   Copy No. 27

56th DIVISION ORDER No. 91.
----------------------------   5th May, 1917.

1. The defensive boundary of the 56th Division is to be readjusted as follows :-

   <u>Southern Boundary</u> - the COJEUL RIVER.

   <u>Northern Boundary with 3rd Division.</u> -

   Junction of HUSSAR & DRAGOON LANES -

   GRAPE Trench (inclusive to 3rd Division)

   Point O.8.a.85.90.

2. The readjustment will be made on night 6th/7th May under arrangements to be made direct between G.O.C. 168th Infantry Brigade & G.O.C. 8th Infantry Brigade (H.Q. N.5.a.86), the former assuming command on conclusion of the relief.

3. The Artillery at present covering the front to be handed over by 3rd Division will come under the tactical control of the C.R.A. 56th Division on conclusion of the relief, under arrangements to be made direct between C.R.A's concerned.

4. ACKNOWLEDGE.

                                          B Pakenham
                                          Lieut-Colonel,
                                          General Staff.

                  Issued at

Copy No. 1. 167th Infantry Bde.   15. 193rd Div. M.G.Coy.
        2. 168th Infantry Bde.   16. 56th Div. Signals.
        3. 169th Infantry Bde.   17. 56th Div. Train.
        4. 3rd Division.   18. 56th Div. M.G.Officer.
        5. 14th Division.   19. 56th Div. Gas Officer.
        6. 29th Division.   20. D.A.D.O.S.
                                       21. 4th Aust. Div. Sup. Col.
        8. VI Corps H.A.   22. No. 2 Ammn. Sub Park.
        9. VI Corps Arty.   23. A.D.M.S.
       10. No. 12 Squadron R.F.C.   24. A.D.V.S.
       11. 1/5th Cheshire Regt.   25. "Q"
       12. C.R.A.   26. A.D.U.
       13. C.R.E.   27. War Diary.
       14. A.P.M.   28. File.

War Diary

SECRET.   Copy No. 26

56th DIVISION ORDER No. 92.

9th May 1917.

Reference Trench Map 1/10,000 U.No.129.

1. 168th Infantry Brigade will carry out an attack on the evening of 11th May, 1917, at an hour to be specified later, with the object of capturing :-

   (a) TOOL TRENCH from about O.8.b.11 to CAVALRY FARM.

   (b) CAVALRY FARM and

   (c) The Trench S.E. of the Farm, which runs from about O.14.a.71 to O.14.a.93.

2. The objectives when gained will be consolidated at once and joined up with our present line, and a block will be established at the Northern end of the captured portion of TOOL TRENCH.

3. The C.R.A. will arrange direct with G.O.C. 168th Infantry Brigade for the necessary Artillery preparation and barrages, including points it is desired to shell by Heavy Artillery.

4. VI Corps Heavy Artillery is to destroy the following trenches:

   (a) TOOL TRENCH, North of O.8.b.35.34.

   (b) POLE TRENCH.

   (c) New communication trench between LANYARD TRENCH & TOOL TRENCH.

   Fire for destruction will be commenced on these trenches as soon as observation can be obtained on 10th May.

5. ACKNOWLEDGE.

B. Pakenham

Lieut-Colonel,
General Staff.

Issued at 9 p.m.

Copy No.			
1.	167th Infantry Bde.	15.	193rd Div. M.G.Coy.
2.	168th Infantry Bde.	16.	56th Div. Signals.
3.	169th Infantry Bde.	17.	56th Div. Train.
4.	3rd Division.	18.	56th Div. M.G.Officer.
5.	14th Division.	19.	~~56th Div. Gas Officer.~~
6.	29th Division.	20.	D.A.D.O.S.
7.	4th Aust. Div. Supp.Col.	21.	No. 2 Ammn. Sub Park.
8.	VI Corps H.A.	22.	A.D.M.S.
9.	VI Corps Arty.	23.	A.D.V.S.
10.	No. 12 Squadron R.F.C.	24.	"Q"
11.	1/5th Cheshire Regt.	25.	A.D.C.
12.	C.R.A.	26.	War Diary.
13.	C.R.E.	27.	File.
14.	A.P.M.		

SECRET. Copy No. 26

56th DIVISION ORDER NO. 93.

11th. May 1917.

1. 167th. Infantry Brigade (with 2 Bns. 169th. Inf. Brigade attached) will relieve 168th Inf. Brigade (plus one battalion from each of 167th and 169th Inf. Brigades) in the line between the nights 12th/13th and 14th/15th May as shown in the Relief Table overleaf, all details being settled between Brigadiers concerned.

2. 167th Brigade M.G. Coy. will during the same period relieve 168th Bde. M.G. Coy.

    The reliefs to be so arranged as to spread over at least 2 days.

3. The C.R.E. will arrange with Brigadiers concerned such R.E. or Pioneer reliefs as may be necessary.

4. The Brigadier-General Commanding 167th Inf. Brigade will assume command of the line at 10 a.m. on 14th inst.

5. Progress and completion of reliefs to be reported to Divisional H.Q.

6. Acknowledge.

B. Pakenham
Lieut-Colonel,
General Staff.

Issued at 9 p.m.

Copy No.			
1.	167th Infantry Bde.	14.	193rd Div. M.G.Coy.
2.	168th Infantry Bde.	15.	56th Div. Signals.
3.	169th Infantry Bde.	16.	" " Train.
4.	3rd Division.	17.	~~" " M.G.Officer.~~
5.	14th Division.	18.	~~" " Gas Officer.~~
6.	29th Division.	19.	D.A.D.O.S.
7.	VI Corps H.A.	20.	4th Aust. Div. Sup. Col.
8.	VI Corps Arty.	21.	No. 2 Ammn. Sub Park.
9.	No. 12 Squadron R.F.C.	22.	A.D.M.S.
10.	1/5th Cheshire Regt.	23.	A.D.V.S.
11.	C.R.A.	24.	"Q"
12.	C.R.E.	25.	A.D.C.
13.	A.P.M.	26.	War Diary.
		27.	File.

56th DIVISION - RELIEF TABLE.

Date. May.	Unit.	From.	To.	In relief of	Area on relief.
Night 12/13th.	1 Bn. 167th Inf. Bde.	Res. Bde. Area.	WANCOURT Line.	1 Bn. 169th Inf. Bde.	Support Bde. Area.
Night 13/14th.	2 Bns. 167th Inf. Bde.	WANCOURT Line.	Line.	2 Bns. 168th Inf. Bde.	Res. Bde. Area.
	2 Bns. 167th Inf. Bde.	Res. Bde. Area.	WANCOURT Line.	2 Bns. 167th Inf. Bde.	Line.
Night 14/15th	2 Bns. 167th Inf. Bde.	WANCOURT Line.	Support Bn. Areas	2 Bns. 169th Inf. Bde.	Res. Bde. Area.
	2 Bns. 169th Inf. Bde.	Support Bde. Area.	WANCOURT Line.	2 Bns. 167th Inf. Bde.	Support Bn. Areas.

SECRET.   Copy No. 25

56th DIVISION (WARNING) ORDER No. 94.

16th May 1917.

(less Artillery)
1. The 37th Division/is to relieve the 56th Division.(less Arty.)

2. The following will be the arrangements for the relief :-

19th May. 112th Infantry Brigade 37th Division - from GOUVES & MONTENESCOURT relieves 169th Infantry Brigade, sending
   1 Battalion to the HARP
   1 Battalion to trenches N.2.c & d
 * 2 Battalions to WANCOURT Line (to arrive about 9-30 p.m.)

   169th Infantry Brigade - moves to DUISANS.

   167th Infantry Brigade - 1 Battalion from WANCOURT Line moves to THE HARP, where it will remain under the orders of General Officer Commanding 167th Infantry Brigade.

* In the event of active operations taking place on the evening of 19th May, these two Battalions would probably halt in the Support Brigade Area, and the relief of the Battalion of 167th Infantry Brigade and Battalion of 169th Infantry Brigade in the WANCOURT Line would take place on the 20th by daylight, troops moving in small parties.

   111th Infantry Brigade 37th Division - BERNEVILLE to ARRAS.
   168th Infantry Brigade - ARRAS to BERNEVILLE.

20th May. 112th Infantry Brigade. - 37th Division

   2 Battalions in WANCOURT Line relieve front line Battalions 167th Infantry Brigade.
   1 Battalion in N.2.c & d relieves Support Battalion 167th Infantry Brigade.
   1 Battalion in HARP - to WANCOURT Line.

   167th Infantry Brigade - on relief proceeds to ARRAS.

   111th Infantry Brigade - 37th Division - from ARRAS; 3 Battalions to Support Bde. Area - 1 Battalion to WANCOURT Line.

21st May. Afternoon.

   63rd Infantry Brigade 37th Division - to ARRAS, etc.

   167th Infantry Brigade - to DAINVILLE, etc.

3. 112th Brigade M. G. Coy will relieve guns of 167th Brigade M. G. Coy in rear positions on 19th and in forward positions on the night 21st/22nd.

4. Reliefs of R.E., Pioneers & Field Ambulances will be arranged by the C.R.E. & A.D.M.S. respectively - R.E. Companies & Field Ambulances on relief will be billeted with their normal Brigade Groups.

P.T.O.

- 2 -

5. General Officer Commanding 37th Division will assume command of the line at 10 a.m. on 21st May.

6. Div. H.Q. will close at ARRAS at 10 a.m. 21st May and open at the same hour probably at WARLUS.

7. ACKNOWLEDGE.

B Pakenham

Lieut.-Colonel.
General Staff.

Issued at 9 p.m.

Copy No. 1. 167th Infantry Brigade.
2. 168th Infantry Brigade.
3. 169th Infantry Brigade.
4. 14th Division.
5. 29th Division.
6. VIth Corps H.A.
7. VIth Corps Arty.
8. No. 12 Squadron R.F.C.
9. 1/5th Cheshire Regt.
10. C.R.A.
11. C.R.E.
12. A.P.M.
13. 193rd Div. M.G. Coy.
14. 56th Div. Signals.
15. 56th Div. Train.
16. 56th Div. M.G. Officer.
17. 56th Div. Gas Officer.
18. D.A.D.O.S.
19. 4th Aust. Div. Supply Column.
20. No. 2 Ammunition Sub Park.
21. A.D.M.S.
22. A.D.V.S.
23. "Q".
24. A.D.C.
25. War Diary.
26. File.
27. 37th Division.

SECRET. Copy No 24

56th DIVISION ORDER No. 95.

17th May, 1917.

1. The enemy has been carrying out little or no work on any defences West of the BOIRY NOTRE DAME LINE. This line is, however, being wired, but no considerable work is being carried out on trenches.

    The enemy is working continuously on the main DROCOURT - QUEANT LINE.

    From prisoners' statements the enemy is suffering considerable losses from lack of protection against our shell fire. It is, therefore, probable that he will fall back first to the BOIRY NOTRE DAME LINE and then to the DROCOURT - QUEANT LINE as soon as these positions are fit for a protracted defence.

    This supposition is supported by statements of prisoners who state that a withdrawal is pending and that local attacks may be expected to cover this retirement.

2. (a) If the enemy retires from his present position he will be pursued

    (b) As soon as information to this effect is received 167th Infantry Brigade will at once push forward troops with the object of occupying the high ground East and S.E. of the BOIS DU VERT, and will gain touch with troops of the Divisions on its right and left.

    (c) The above line will be consolidated and covered by Strong Points East of the BOIS DU VERT and in the Northern portion of FACTORY TRENCH.

    (d) Patrols will be pushed out at once to the general line O.4.d.O.O. - O.10.Central - O.10.d.O.1. - Line of COJEUL RIVER - PONT A TROIS GUEULES to endeavour to gain touch with the enemy.

3. Until the new line is consolidated and communication assured the present front system will remain garrisoned and will form the main line of resistance.

4. The C.R.A. will arrange the necessary Artillery support and will push forward artillery as the situation demands.

5. ACKNOWLEDGE.

B Pakenham
Lieut-Colonel,
General Staff.

Issued at 2.15 p.m. by SDR to 167th Bde + CRA

Copy No. 1.	167th Infantry Bde.	14.	56th Div. Signals.
2.	168th Infantry Bde.	15.	56th Div. Train.
3.	169th Infantry Brigade.	16.	56th Div. Gas Officer.
4.	14th Division.	17.	D.A.D.O.S.
5.	29th Division.	18.	4th Aust.Div. Sup. Col.
6.	VI Corps H.A.	19.	No. 2 Ammn. Sub Park.
7.	VI Corps Arty.	20.	A.D.M.S.
8.	No. 12 Squadron R.F.C.	21.	A.D.V.S.
9.	1/5th Cheshire Regt.	22.	"Q"
10.	C.R.A.	23.	A.D.C.
11.	C.R.E.	24.	War Diary.
12.	A.P.M.	25.	File.
13.	193rd Div. M.G.Coy.		

SECRET. Copy No. 24

56th DIVISION ORDER No. 96.

17th May, 1917.

Reference Sketch Map attached.

1. The enemy is carrying out little or no work on any defences West of the BOIRY NOTRE DAME line. This is being wired but no considerable work is being carried out on trenches.

   Continuous work is being done on the DROCOURT - QUEANT LINE.

   It is probable, therefore, that the Germans will fall back to the BOIRY NOTRE DAME LINE and then to the DROCOURT - QUEANT LINE as soon as their positions are ready for a protracted defence. This is supported by prisoners statements.

2. It is of the greatest importance that the enemy should be continually harassed and forced to retire from his present position before he is ready to do so voluntarily.

3. On the evening of 19th inst. 29th Division is to capture INFANTRY HILL and the BOIS DES AUBEPINES.

4. 56th Division will co-operate with 29th Division and capture the remainder of TOOL TRENCH and those portions of HOOK TRENCH and LONG TRENCH which lie within its area.

5. Prior to Zero hour on the 19th inst. 167th Infantry Brigade will make ground North-eastwards up TOOL TRENCH with a view to capturing it as far as the point where it branches into HOOK and LONG TRENCHES (approx. O.8.b.55.45.)

6. On the 19th inst. 167th Infantry Brigade will capture :-

    (a) HOOK TRENCH. from O.8.b.55.45 to O.8.b.50.95.

    (b) LONG TRENCH from O.8.b.55.45. to O.8.b.99.95. and

    (c) Complete the capture of TOOL TRENCH if this has not already been accomplished.

7. The Dividing Line between 29th Division and 56th Division will be the communication trench which joins HILL TRENCH about O.8.a.85.92 (inclusive to 29th Division) - thence a line O.8.b.50.95 - O.8.b.99.95 - N. edge of BOIS DU VERT.

8. The objectives when gained will at once be consolidated and joined to our present front line; Strong Points will be established in LONG TRENCH, HOOK TRENCH being made the main defensive line.

9. (a) 167th Infantry Brigade will arrange to place a Machine Gun in LONG TRENCH firing N.E. to cross its fire with a Machine Gun of 29th Division firing S.E. The Brigadier-General Commanding 87th Infantry Brigade (H.Q. N.5.a. Central) will be consulted by Brigadier-General Commanding 167th Infantry Brigade as to the line of fire of this gun. 167th Infantry Brigade will also arrange to bring Machine Gun fire to bear on any counter-attack issuing from the BOIS DU VERT

    (b) Arrangements for Machine Gun barrage will be communicated later.

10. Arrangements for Artillery preparation and support will be communicated later.

/11.

11. 167th Infantry Brigade will arrange to establish visual signalling from HOOK TRENCH or TOOL TRENCH either to a Battalion H.Q. or to the Brigade O.P. whence messages can be forwarded by telephone.

12. Zero hour will be communicated later to all concerned.

13. ACKNOWLEDGE.

B. Pakenham
Lieut-Colonel,
General Staff.

Issued at 3-30 pm

Copy No. 1. 167th Infantry Brigade.
2. 168th Infantry Brigade.
3. 169th Infantry Brigade.
4. 14th Division.
5. 29th Division.
6. VI Corps H.A.
7. VI Corps Arty.
8. No. 12 Squadron R.F.C.
9. 1/5th Cheshire Regt.
10. C.R.A.
11. C.R.E.
12. A.P.M.
13. 193rd Div. M.G. Coy.
14. 56th Div. Signals.
15. 56th Div. Train.
16. 56th Div. Gas Officer.
17. D.A.D.O.S.
18. 4th Aust. Div. Supply Column.
19. No. 2 Ammn. Sub Park.
20. A.D.M.S.
21. A.D.V.S.
22. "Q"
23. A.D.C.
24. War Diary.
25. File.
26. 56th Div. M.G.O.

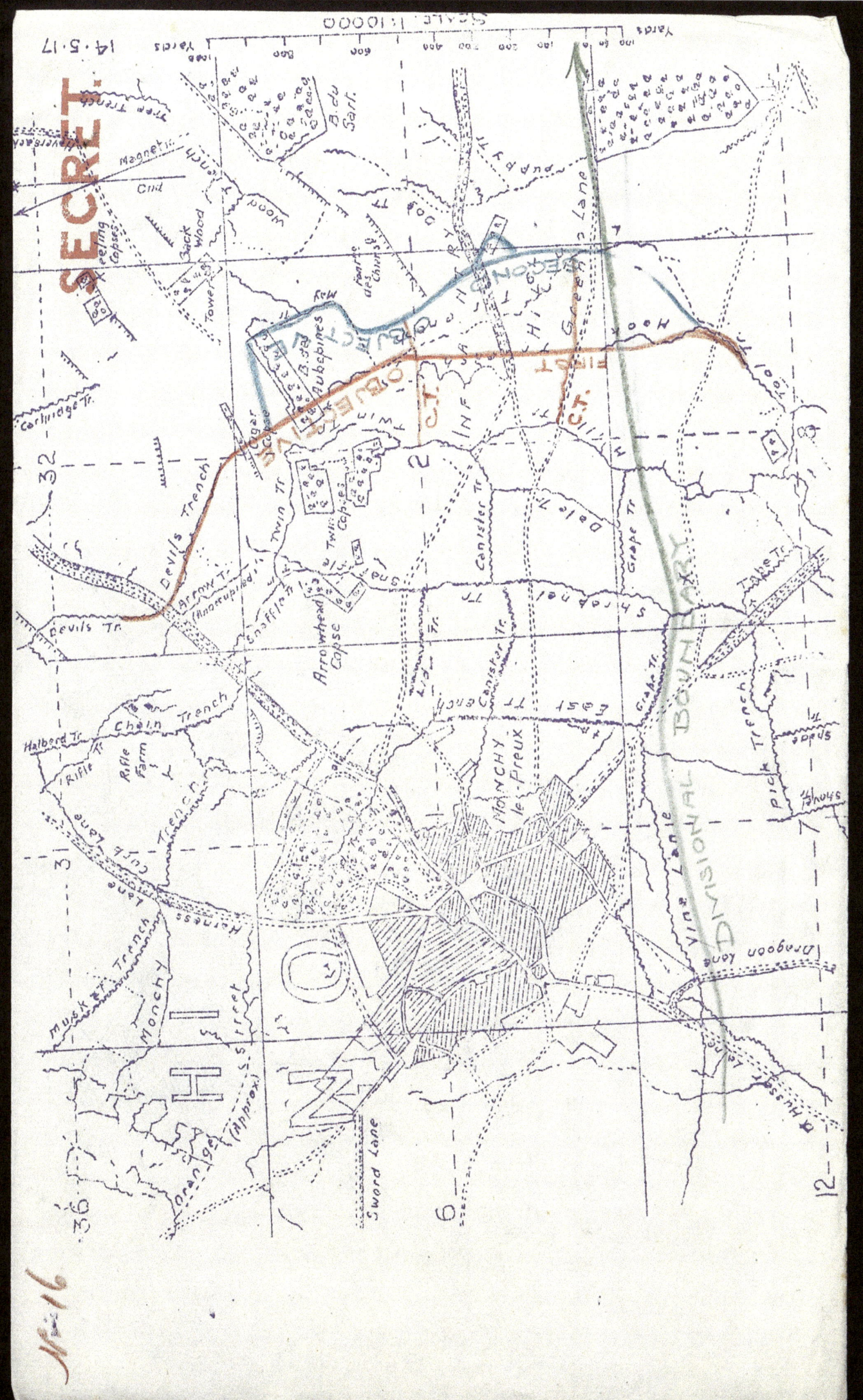

"A" Form.
MESSAGES AND SIGNALS.

Army Form C. 2121
(in pads of 100).

TO (War Diary) 167th Bde, 1st Squad RE, 29th Div, HA, 173rd CRA, V Corps Arty, 193rd MG Co, B.G.R.D

Reference Sketch Map issued with Addendum No 1 to 56th Div Order No 96 the second Objective of 56th Division should include LONG trench from its junction with TOOL trench

From: 56th Division
Time: 9.35 pm

H.D. Wallace
General Staff

SECRET.   56th Divn. No. G.3/305.
Copy No. 25

ADDENDUM NO. 1 to
56th DIVISION ORDER No. 96.
Ref. attached Sketch Map.

17th May 1917.

1. The 87th Infantry Brigade of the 29th Division will attack on the left of the 167th Infantry Brigade.

2. The objectives of the 87th & 167th Infantry Brigades are shown on the attached Sketch Map.

3. (a) The attack will take place under an intense Artillery Barrage which will open on the RED LINE at zero.

It will lift at zero plus 4 minutes and advance at the rate of 50 yards a minute to the BLUE LINE, from which it will lift at zero plus 10 minutes.

At zero the troops will leave their trenches and get as close to the Barrage as possible in order to enter the enemy's trench immediately the Barrage lifts.

(b) Instructions as to further Artillery action have been circulated by the C.R.A.

4. At zero hour, if the wind is favourable, J Special Coy. R.E. will discharge LIEVENS PROJECTORS on the BOIS DU VERT, the Sunken Road in O.3.c & North of the BOIS DU VERT.

5. At zero hour No. 1 Special Coy. R.E. is to form a smoke screen in Sq. I.32.

6. A Contact Aeroplane will be in the air after dawn on the 20th.

Troops will light Flares when called upon to do so by the Aeroplane.

7. Watches will be synchronised on the 19th at 9 a.m. and 5 p.m. by the General Staff.

8. ACKNOWLEDGE.

B Pakenham

Lieut.-Colonel.
General Staff.

DISTRIBUTION

Copy No.		No.	
1.	167th Inf. Bde.	14.	56th Div. Signals.
2.	168th Inf. Bde.	15.	56th Div. Train.
4.	14th Division.	16.	56th Div. Gas Officer.
5.	29th Division.	17.	D.A.D.O.S.
6.	VIth Corps H.A.	18.	4th Aust. Div. Supp. Col.
7.	VIth Corps Arty.	19.	No. 2 Amm. Sub Park.
8.	No. 12 Squadron, R.F.C.	20.	56th Div. M.G. Officer.
9.	1/5th Ches. Regt.	21.	A.D.M.S.
10.	C.R.A.	22.	A.D.V.S.
11.	C.R.E.	23.	"Q"
12.	A.P.M.	24.	A.D.C.
13.	193rd Div. M.G. Coy.	25.	War Diary.
3.	169th Infantry Bde.	26.	File.

SECRET.   Copy No. 25

56th DIVISION ORDER No. 97.

May 17th 1917.

1. 37th Division (less Divisional Artillery) is to relieve 56th Division (less Divisional Artillery).

2. The relief will be completed by daylight on 21st May, with the exception of that of the forward machine guns under the orders of General Officer Commanding 167th Infantry Brigade, whose relief will be carried out on the night 21st/22nd May.

3. Moves will take place in accordance with the attached March Table.

4. The relief of the front line battalions 167th Infantry Brigade will be carried out on night 20th/21st by battalions of 112th Infantry Brigade who will move into the WANCOURT LINE during the day of 20th May, and relieve the battalions of 167th Infantry Brigade & 169th Infantry Brigade located there.
Movement will be in bodies not larger than a platoon, and distances of 500 yards will be maintained between platoons.

5. All details of relief will be settled direct between Brigadiers concerned.

6. Dry weather routes are to be used as far as practicable.

500 yards between Battalions and 200 yards between Companies & Sections of transport are to be maintained on the march.

7. Reliefs of R.E. and Field Ambulances will be arranged by the C.R.E. and A.D.M.S. respectively, units marching as follows :-

R.E.   416th Field Coy. R.E. - on 20th inst.- no restrictions to BERNEVILLE.

512th Field Coy. R.E. - on 21st inst.- will be clear of ARRAS by 10 a.m. - to WARLUS.

513th Field Coy. R.E. - on 20th inst. - no restrictions - to DUISANS.

Field Ambulances will march under the orders of their respective Brigade Group Commanders.

8. 1/5th Cheshire Regiment (Pioneers) will come under the orders of C.E. VI Corps for work on roads from 21st inst., and will be finally relieved under orders to be issued later.

9. 193rd Div. M.G.Coy. will move as follows :-

Sections attached to 167th Infantry Brigade - on relief will move to WARLUS on 22nd inst. under the orders of Brigadier-General Commanding 167th Infantry Brigade.
Sections in Div. Reserve will move to WARLUS on 21st inst - in advance of 167th Infantry Brigade.

10. General Officer Commanding 37th Division will assume Command of the Line at 10 a.m. on 21st May.

/11.

11. Divisional H.Qrs. will close at ARRAS at 10 a.m. on 21st May and open at WARLUS at the same hour.

12. ACKNOWLEDGE.

B Pakenham
Lieut-Colonel,
General Staff.

Issued at

Copy No. 1 167th Infantry Brigade.
2. 168th Infantry Brigade.
3. 169th Infantry Brigade.
4. 14th Division.
5. 29th Division.
6. VI Corps H.A.
7. VIth Corps Arty.
8. No. 12 Squadron R.F.C.
9. 1/5th Cheshire Regiment.
10. C.R.A.
11. C.R.E.
12. A.P.M.
13. 193rd Div. M.G.Coy.
14. 56th Div. Signals.
15. 56th Div. Train.
16. 56th Div. Gas Officer.
17. D.A.D.O.S.
18. 4th Aust. Div. Supply Column.
19. No. 2 Ammn. Sub Park.
20. 56th Div. M.G.Officer.
21. A.D.M.S.
22. A.D.V.S.
23. "Q"
24. A.D.C.
25. War Diary.
26. File.
27. 37th Division.

MARCH TABLE TO ACCOMPANY 56th DIVISION ORDER No. 97.

Serial No.	Date May.	Unit.	From	To	Route.	Remarks.
1.	19th	112th Inf.Bde.Group.	GOUVES & MONTENESCOURT	Support Bde. Area.	DUISANS - ARRAS.	In relief of 3 Bns.169th Inf.Bde. To be clear of billets by 10 a.m.
2.	"	169th Inf.Bde. (3 Bns.)	Support Bde.Area.	DUISANS.	ARRAS	On relief not to enter DUISANS before 12.30 p.m.
3.	"	111th Inf.Bde.Group.	BERNEVILLE	ARRAS.	Road junction R.8.c. BAC DU NORD - ARRAS - DOULLENS Road.	In relief of 168th Inf.Bde. Not to enter ARRAS before noon.
4.	"	168th Inf.Bde.	ARRAS	BERNEVILLE	DAINVILLE - WARLUS	Not to enter BERNEVILLE before 2.30 p.m. To be clear of ARRAS by noon. Rear to clear BERNEVILLE by 12.30 p.m. DAINVILLE not available on and after 21st May.
5.	"	63rd Inf.Bde.Group.	SIMENCOURT.	DAINVILLE - ACHICOURT.	via BERNEVILLE, thence as in Serial No.3.	In relief of 167th Inf. Bde. & attached battalion of 169th Brigade.
6.	20th & night	112th Inf.Bde.Group.	Support Bde.Area	Line.		In relief of 112th Inf.Bde.
7.	20/21st. 20th	111th Inf.Bde.Group.	ARRAS	Support Bde.Area. (3 Bns.) WANCOURT LINE (1 Bn.)		In relief of 167th Inf.Bde. & attached Bn. of 169th Brigade.
8.	20th Night	169th Inf.Bde.(1 Bn.)	Line.	DUISANS.		On relief. No restrictions
9.	20/21st	167th Inf.Bde.	Line.	ARRAS		On relief.
10.	21st.	167th Inf.Bde.	ARRAS.	DAINVILLE	ARRAS.	
11.	21st	56th Div.H.Q.	ARRAS.	WARLUS.		Not to leave ARRAS before 10 a.m. To be clear of ARRAS by 10 a.m.

SECRET.　　　　　　　　　　　　　　　Copy No..........

56th DIVISION ORDER NO. 98.

18th May 1917.

1. Zero hour on May 19th will be 9 p.m.

2. A Corps Dropping Station will be established at N.2 Central so as to receive messages from the Contact Plane.

3. The Brigadier General Commanding 167th Infantry Brigade will detail one officer to be at this Station by daylight the 20th to report to an officer from VIth Corps Headquarters.

4. ACKNOWLEDGE.

　　　　　　　　　　　　　　　　　　　Lieut.-Colonel.
　　　　　　　　　　　　　　　　　　　General Staff.

Issued at 9 p.m.

Copy No. 1.　167th Infantry Brigade.
　　　　2.　168th Infantry Brigade.
　　　　3.　169th Infantry Brigade.
　　　　4.　14th Division.
　　　　5.　29th Division.
　　　　6.　VIth Corps H.A.
　　　　7.　VIth Corps Artillery.
　　　　8.　No. 12 Squadron, R.F.C.
　　　　9.　1/5th Cheshire Regt.
　　　10.　C.R.A.
　　　11.　C.R.E.
　　　12.　A.P.M.
　　　13.　193rd Div. M.G. Coy.
　　　14.　56th Div. M.G. Officer.
　　　15.　56th Div. Signals.
　　　16.　56th Div. Train.
　　　17.　56th Div. Gas Officer.
　　　18.　D.A.D.O.S.
　　　19.　4th Aust. Div. Supply Col.
　　　20.　No. 2 Amm. Sub Park.
　　　21.　A.D.M.S.
　　　22.　A.D.V.S.
　　　23.　"Q".
　　　24.　A.D.C.
　　　25.　War Diary.
　　　26.　File.

SECRET.   Copy No. 20

56th Division Order No. 99.
                                                           22nd May 1917.

1. Moves will take place on the 24th as per attached March Table (Appendix "A")

2. Distribution of Units on completion of move is shown in Appendix "B".

3. A distance of 250 yards between Battalions and 100 yds. between Companies and Regimental first line transport will be maintained.

4. Div. H.Q. closes at WARLUS at 12 noon on the 24th May, and re-opens at the same hour at HABARCQ CHATEAU.

5. ACKNOWLEDGE.

                                                Captain,
                                                General Staff.
Issued at 7.30 a.m.

Copy No. 1. 167th Infantry Bde.
        2. 168th Infantry Bde.
        3. 169th Infantry Bde.
        4. 1/5th Cheshire Regiment.
        5. C.R.A.
        6. C.R.E.
        7. A.P.M.
        8. 193rd Div. M.G.Coy.
        9. 56th Div. Signals.
       10. 56th Div. Train.
       11. 56th Div. Gas Officer.
       12. D.A.D.O.S.
       13. 4th Aust. Div. Sup. Column.
       14. No. 2 Ammn. Sub Park.
       15. 56th Div. M.G.Officer.
       16. A.D.M.S.
       17. A.D.V.S.
       18. "Q"
       19. A.D.C.
       20. War Diary.
       21. File.
       22. Town Major, SIMENCOURT.
       23.   "   " AGNEZ-LES-DUISANS.
       24.   "   " MONTENESCOURT.
       35.   "   " GOUVES.

APPENDIX "A"

ISSUED WITH 56th DIVISION ORDER No. 99

Date.	Unit.	From.	To.	Route.	Remarks.
May.					
24th	Div. H.Q.	WARLUS.	HABARCQ.	MONTENESCOURT.	To clear WARLUS by 11 a.m.
"	167th Bde. Group.	DAINVILLE etc.	GOUVES MONTENESCOURT.	WARLUS	(1) Not to enter MONTENESCOURT before 2.30 p.m. (2) To be clear of DAINVILLE by 2 p.m.
"	168th Bde. Group.	BERNEVILLE	SIMENCOURT	Direct.	(1) Not to enter SIMENCOURT before 11 a.m. (2) To be clear of BERNEVILLE by 12.15 p.m.
"	169th Bde. Group.	DUISANS.	AGNEZ-les-DUISANS GOUVES.	Direct.	(1) Not to enter AGNEZ-les-DUISANS before 10 a.m. (2) To be clear of DUISANS by 11.30 a.m.
"	193rd M.G.Coy.	WARLUS.	SIMENCOURT.		Under orders of B.G.U. 168th Brigade.
25th	1/5th Ches.	ARRAS.	GOUVES		No restrictions as to route or time.

APPENDIX "B"

ISSUED WITH 56th DIVISION ORDER No. 99

Area.	Troops to be accommodated.	Area Commander.	Billets allotted by
HABARCQ.	Div. H.Q. Div. R.E. H.Q. Div. Train H.Q.	Div. H.Q.	Permanent Town Major.
AGNEZ-les-DUISANS Old Internment Camp at K.17.a. Part of GOUVES.	169th Inf. Bde. 2/1st London Fld.Ambulance. 2/3rd " " " 1/5th Cheshire Regt. 513rd Field Coy. R.E. No. 4 Coy. Div. Train.	B.G.C. 169th Inf. Bde.	Town Major of AGNEZ-les-DUISANS. Permanent Town Major.
MONTENESCOURT. Part of GOUVES.	167th Inf.Bde. (less 1 Bn.) 1 Battalion 167th Inf. Bde. 416th (Edin) Fld.Coy. R.E. No. 2 Coy. Div. Train.	B.G.C. 167th Inf. Bde.	" " " " " "
SIMENCOURT.	168th Inf. Bde. Group 193rd M.G.Coy.	B.G.C. 168th Inf. Bde.	" " "

Area Commanders will arrange direct with Town Majors for the accommodation of the troops allotted to their Area.

"A" Form.
MESSAGES AND SIGNALS.

Army Form C.2121 (in pads of 100)

SECRET

TO	167 Bde	"Q"	3rd Div
	168 "	169. M.G. Coy	14th Div
	169 "	VI Corps	

Sender's Number: G.182 Day of Month: 4/5. AAA

Warning Order No 89 aaa LOB will relieve NUB and KEB in the line to night under arrangements to be made direct between Brigadiers aaa LOBVIC will take over from both PIP and NUBVIC aaa RAMVIC will remain as at present keeping right guns supporting LOB and arranging their reliefs within the Coy. as necessary aaa NUB and KEB will each place their best battalion at disposal of LOB aaa These battalions will be accommodated not further forward than the WANCOURT LINE aaa Following areas allotted for NUB and KEB aaa NUB old British and German trenches West of a line H.31.a.05 - G.36.c.60. within the Div. boundaries aaa KEB trenches East of above line within Div. boundaries including N portion of HARP and trenches in N.2.c.&d. aaa

"A" Form.
MESSAGES AND SIGNALS.

Army Form C.2121
(in pads of 100).
No. of Message ....

Prefix .... Code .... m.	Words	Charge	This message is on a/c of:	Recd. at .... m.
Office of Origin and Service Instructions.				Date ....
....	Sent		.... Service.	From ....
....	At .... m.			
....	To			
....	By		(Signature of "Franking Officer.")	By ....

TO {

| Sender's Number. | Day of Month. | In reply to Number. | A A A |

H.Q. of NUB and KEB being arranged by 'Q' about M.31 central. aaa acknowledge aaa. Added LOB NUB KEB and RAMVIC repdd 6th Corps MOSES ALICE and 'Q'

From 56th Divn.
Place
Time 11-45 am

The above may be forwarded as now corrected.
(Sgd) B Pakenham. Lt.Col.
Censor. Signature of Addressor or person authorised to telegraph in his name.
* This line should be erased if not required.

"A" Form.
MESSAGES AND SIGNALS.

Army Form C.2121
(in pads of 100).

TO: War Diary. To recipients of Order No 88
(less ADM - Div Sup Off, Train, DADOS,
HQ Divs Arty Sub Col, No 2 Am Sub Park - ADVS)

Sender's Number: G.88
Day of Month: 1/5.
AAA

Reference 56th Div. Order 88 para. 3 Line 3
insert word dotted before GREEN LINE AAA Delete
para. 12

From: 56th Divn.
Time: 2-45 PM

(Z) General Staff.

SECRET.

Copy No. 4

56th DIVISION ORDER No. 100   30th May, 1917.

1. Two Companies, 1/5th Cheshire Regiment, will relieve the Pioneer Battalion of the 61st Division (H.Q. 27, Rue Ronville, ARRAS) on 31st inst., and will come under the orders of C.E. VI Corps.

2. The two companies 1/5th Cheshires will march via GOUVES – ARNEZ-LES-DUISANS – DUISANS – ARRAS.

   A distance of 200 yards to be maintained between Coys. and between Coys. and transport. They will leave GOUVES at 2 p.m.

3. O.C. party will report to C.E. VI Corps for instructions as to work.

4. ACKNOWLEDGE.

30th May 1917.   Issued at 1.30 p.m.   Captain,
                                              General Staff.

Copies to :-
1. C.R.E.
2. 1/5th Cheshire Regt.
3. C.E. VI Corps.
4. 61st Division.
5. 37th Division.
6. 56th Div. "Q"
7. War Diary.
8. File.

War Diary

SECRET.   56th. Division No.G.3/177.

167th. Inf. Brigade.   56th. Div. Train.
168th. Inf. Brigade.   56th. Div. M.G.O.
169th. Inf. Brigade.   56th. Div. Gas Off.
                                D.A.D.O.S.
                                4th.Aus.Div.Supply Col.
                                No. 2 Ammn. Sub-Park.
                                A.D.M.S.
                                A.D.V.S.
1/5th Cheshire Rgt.   "Q"
C.R.A.   G.O.C.
C.R.E.   A.D.C.
A.P.M.   War Diary.
193rd. Div. M.G.Coy.   File.
56th. Div. Signals.

    Sub-para. d, para. 7, of 56th. Division Order No. 88 is cancelled.

    No gas shell bombardment of the enemy battery positions will take place on X/Y and Y/Z nights, but the BOIS DU VERT and BOIS DU SART will be shelled with gas shells on Y/Z night.

H.Q., 56th. Divn.   Captain,
1st. May 1917.   General Staff.

SECRET.   56th Divn. G.3/204.

167th Infantry Brigade.   A.P.M.
168th Infantry Brigade.   193rd Div. M.G.Coy.
169th Infantry Brigade.   56th Div. Signals.
~~3rd Division~~   56th Div. Train.
~~14th Division~~   56th Div. M.G.Officer
~~VI Corps H.A.~~   ~~56th Div. Gas Officer~~
~~VI Corps Arty.~~   D.A.D.O.S.
~~No. 12 Squadron R.F.C.~~   ~~4th Aust. Div. Supply Col.~~
1/5th Cheshire Regt.   ~~No. 2 Ammn. Sub Park.~~
C.R.A.   A.D.M.S.
C.R.E.   A.D.V.S.
                                 "Q"
                                 G.O.C.
                                 A.D.C.
                                 War Diary.
                                 File.

Z Day is 3rd May, 1917.

Zero hour is 3.45 a.m.

ACKNOWLEDGE.

Head Qrs. 56th Divn.   [signature]
2nd May, 1917.   Lieut-Colonel,
                                                General Staff.

SECRET.   56th Divn. G.9/35.

167th Infantry Bde.	56th Div. Train.
168th Infantry Bde.	56th Div. M.G.Officer.
169th Infantry Brigade.	56th Div. Gas Officer.
3rd Division.	D.A.D.O.S.
14th Division.	4th Aust. Div. Sup. Column.
VI Corps H.A.	No. 2 Ammn. Sub Park.
VI Corps Arty.	A.D.M.S.
No.12 Squad. R.F.C.	A.D.V.S.
1/5th Ches. Regt.	"Q"
C.R.A.	G.O.C.
C.R.E.	A.D.C.
A.P.M.	War Diary.
193rd Div. M.G.Coy.	File.
56th Div. Signals.	

SIGNAL COMMUNICATIONS DURING FORTHCOMING OPERATIONS.

Motor Cyclists will be stationed at the following points for the forthcoming Operations :-

(1) Point on the road approximately N.15.b.2.3. - Four Motor Cyclists.
These will be available for the Brigades D.R.L.S. and telegrams, should other means of communication fail, and for specials.

(2) H.31 central. Three Motor Cyclists.

(3) Divisional Headquarters, ARRAS - Eight Motor Cyclists.

Runners from the Brigade concerned will act as connecting link with No. 1 Motor Cyclist Post.

VISUAL.

Divisional Visual Stations will be established as follows for use in case other means of communication fail :-

No. 1 Station - approximately N.1.b.4.8. connected by telephone to Divisional Headquarters.

No. 2 Station will be a re-transmitting station situated approximately N.9.a.5.7.

No. 3 Station will be situated approximately N.10.c.6.1.

No. 2 Station will not work forward unless in case of necessity, but will accept "DD" Messages from No. 3 Station during the operations.
These Stations will be established on the 1st May.

The main lines of communication will be by telegraph and telephone.
There will be a direct telegraphic laddered line to each Brigade, a direct telephone pair to each Brigade, and a laddered pair for communication between the two Brigades. The Left Brigade will be connected by telephone to the Brigade on its Left, and the Right Brigade will be connected by telephone to the Brigade on its Right.

/WIRELESS.

- 2 -

WIRELESS.

The Wireless Station is established at N.16.a.0.9. and is working to Corps directing set.
Messages should be sent in Code.
The Code in use will be the Playfair System; the keyword will be changed at 6 p.m. every evening as follows :-

6 p.m.	1st May	to 6 p.m.	2nd May		DURHAM.
"	2nd "	" "	3rd "		WHISKEY.
"	3rd "	" "	4th "		ORANGE.
"	4th "	" "	5th "		SCOTCHMAN.
"	5th "	" "	6th "		ENGLAND.
"	6th "	" "	7th "		PARLIAMENT.

The second Wireless Set is placed at the disposal of the 169th Infantry Brigade Commander, and when this is sent forward it requires a carrying party of 4 men, and an Officer from the Battalion concerned to supervise its erection and for encoding and decoding messages.

B Pakenham

Head Qrs. 56th Divn.
1st May, 1917.

Lieut-Colonel,
General Staff.

SECRET.   *War Diary Copy*   56th Division No.G.3/164.

167th Infantry Brigade.
168th Infantry Brigade.
169th Infantry Brigade.
1/5th Cheshire Regiment.
C.R.A.
C.R.E.
193rd Div. M.G.Coy.
56th Div. Signals.
56th Div. M.G.Officer.
"Q"
War Diary.
File.

----

1. The G.O.C. Division, in issuing the attached instructions of the VI Corps, wishes to emphasise the following points :-

   (a) Para. 3. Mopping Up Parties - He does not consider that special parties are necessary for this purpose as there can be no deep dugouts from which the enemy can emerge, but trenches must not be over run, they must be properly cleaned up by the attacking troops.

   (b) Para. 4. Particular attention is to be paid to this and supports and reserves used as indicated.

   (c) Para. 5. This is most important and sufficient care has not been taken on previous occasions to see that this is carried out. The Red Line must be consolidated at once and held against all counter-attacks. It is hoped to push up Divisional Machine Guns on the South Side of the COJEUL which will materially assist by enfilade fire in repelling counter-attacks. Strong patrols pushed forward down the slopes and dug in will help to break up any counter-attack.

   (d) Para. 6. This is not possible under present conditions but lines can be laid up GORDON TRENCH and full use made of visual signalling.

   (e) Para. 8. This will only be possible if full and precise information of the situation on our front is sent back quickly to Divisional Headquarters. The importance of this must be impressed on all ranks.

   (f) Para. 12. The importance of lighting flares when called for by contact aeroplanes is very great and platoon and company Commanders must see that this is done on a prearranged plan. The promiscuous lighting of flares is useless and only leads to false information.

   (g) Forward dumps in our present front line of Stokes Mortar and M.G. ammunition and wire requires attention. It is not possible to carry up any quantity of these during the operations and a little forethought makes all the difference.

B. Pakenham

Head Qrs. 56th Divn.
1st May, 1917.

Lieut-Colonel,
General Staff.

SECRET.

VI Corps No. G.X.1/H/140.

56th Division.

The following instructions issued by the Corps Commander are forwarded for information:-

1. The enemy is holding the front opposite the VI Corps with about 8 regiments disposed in depth. His troops are fairly fresh and up to the present have not shown any great loss of moral. His trenches are very incomplete and he has only a few improvised dugouts, consequently it is hoped that continuous artillery fire may reduce his numbers and moral before the attack takes place. The enemy's defences consist of no regular system but of disconnected trenches. These trenches appear to be well sited and difficult to observe. The enemy is also employing a large number of machine guns which are sited in banks, trenches and shell holes with the object of enfilading our advance. The enemy has considerably increased his artillery on the Corps front and has now some 200 guns in action in VI Corps Counter-Battery Area.

2. The attack of the VI Corps is complicated owing to the left being so far refused, but the Corps Commander does not consider that this in itself adversely affects the chances of the success of the main attack.

If the XVII Corps decide to attack ROEUX from the West as on previous occasions the 12th Division will also attack Eastwards along the valley of the SCARPE. If, on the other hand, XVII Corps decide not to attack ROEUX but to capture the HAUSA WOOD RIDGE from the North, then the 12th Division will maintain a defensive position to the West of HARNESS LANE and attack in a North-easterly direction with their right on KEELING COPSE, forming a defensive flank roughly on the line HAVERSACK TRENCH, SHELL TRENCH, NEW TRENCH.

The attacks of the 56th and 3rd Divisions will be due East and will be continued without a pause until the RED Line is captured.

3. The Corps Commander wishes to impress on Divisional Commanders the necessity for having parties detailed for "mopping up" in all trenches which it is possible to locate previous to the attack. Instances have occurred since the first positions were taken on the 9th April of the leading waves passing over trenches held by Germans who ultimately were able to stop the forward movement of supports and to cut off the waves which had already passed.

4. It is possible that during the attack certain points in the enemy's line may hold out. These points must not be allowed to delay the rate of our advance and must be dealt with by supports moving round and attacking them in rear. Troops that have been checked are best assisted by reserves being pushed in behind the parts of the line where the attack has been successful so that the portions of the enemy's position that are still holding out may be turned.

5. On reaching the Red Line immediate steps must be taken to consolidate the position as from past experience the enemy is certain to counter-attack violently within a

/very

very short time.   Patrols must be pushed out to secure points of vantage and to cover the consolidation of the Red Line. Machine Guns should also be pushed up rapidly to places from which counter-attacks can be met.

6. Since leaving the old trench systems it has been impossible to bury cable so as to ensure good communications, but on good communications depend very largely our successes. The Corps Commander wishes Divisional Commanders to take all possible steps to ensure communications. Each Division should have at least one line buried up to their present front line or to some point from which observation can be obtained over their front by the 2nd May.   If this is not possible in the time it should be buried in the most exposed places. Full use must be made of power buzzers and visual signalling. Trench wireless sets should only be used in an emergency as they tend to jam aeroplane signals to the Artillery. The Corps Wireless Officer will make out a scheme for keeping communication by means of wireless, and this will be communicated as soon as possible to Divisions.

7. It is extremely important to prevent any leakage of information, consequently no mention of any attack will be made on any telephone or telegraph instrument, except Fullerphone, within 5000 yards of the front line unless in cypher, and then only when it is impracticable to send any other way. Fullerphones should be used and if more are required application should be made to Corps Headquarters. Hastily laid metallic circuits are not safe and consume a considerable amount of cable. They should therefore not be used except by orders of G.O.C. Division.

8. In the event of the enemy becoming demoralised through our successes and the failures of his counter-attacks, it is possible that an opportunity may occur for a fresh Division to be passed through the three attacking Divisions on the evening of Z Day. The objective of this Division would be the capture and consolidation of the GREEN LINE. During the advance of this Division there is to be no rifle fire of any kind, so that all those who open fire may be recognised as enemies. Whether the reserve Division is ordered to advance or not must depend on circumstances, but so that a Division may be ready the following arrangements are being made.

29th Division will arrive at ARRAS on the evening of Z. minus one day and on the morning of Z. Day. It will be billetted in ARRAS and will during Z. Day move out to a preliminary position of readiness about the BROWN LINE. As far as can be foreseen at present this Division should be prepared to advance with all three Brigades in line, Brigades distributed in depth.

The Right Brigade will probably be ordered to move straight along the CAMBRAI Road as far as the ST. ROHART FACTORY, where it would cross the COJEUL River and occupy the ground from REMY to the COJEUL River.

The Centre Brigade would move directly to BOIRY NOTRE DAME and occupy the high ground to the East and North East of that village.

The Left Brigade moving to the North of MONCHY would be required to capture the slopes of the hill to the North of GIG-SAW WOOD, looking down on the village of HAMBLAIN-LES-PRES.

The route to be taken by the Left and Centre Brigades depends on whether the enemy still holds the villages

/of

- 3 -

PELMES and ROEUX. If he does, both Brigades will have to keep on the high ground of the MONCHY spur. If on the other hand the whole valley of the SCARPE has been captured, then the Left Brigade will move along the PELVES Road and thence on the high ground by QUARRY WOOD.

9. In the event of the 29th Division being ordered forward each Brigade will be supported by one Divisional Artillery as shown below :-

<u>Right Brigade.</u>   29th Divisional Artillery.

<u>Centre Brigade.</u> 17th Divisional Artillery.

<u>Left Brigade.</u>   33rd Divisional Artillery.

15th Division will remain in its present billets but ready to move at an hour's notice in case of necessity. Further instructions as to the use of the 29th Division will be issued later.

10. To enable the 29th Division to concentrate in ARRAS the 3rd, 12th and 56th Divisions will arrange for their reserve Brigades to be clear of ARRAS by 8 p.m. on Y. Day.

11. During operations Divisions will render situation reports every hour to Corps Headquarters. Important information will be sent at any time irrespective of the hour of report.

12. Aeroplanes working with the Infantry of the VI Corps will be marked with one black band under both lower 'planes. Streamers will be attached to each plane immediately behind the black band.

13. The Corps Dropping Ground for aeroplane messages will be established at N.2 central.

14. Detachments of Lovat Scouts for purposes of observation have been attached to Corps Heavy Artillery and to Divisional Artillery.

15. An officer from Corps Headquarters will visit each Divisional Headquarters and Corps Heavy Artillery Headquarters between the hours of 9 a.m. and 11 a.m. and between 5 p.m. and 8 p.m. on X. and Y. Days with the object of synchronizing watches. Watches of the Divisional General Staff and R.A. will be checked at these times.

16. The Corps Forward Cage for the collection of prisoners is situated at H.27.d. Central.

17. At present no Tanks are available for these operations.

18. The Corps Machine Gun Officer is preparing a scheme by which it is suggested to cover the whole front of the attack with machine gun fire. He will submit these proposals to Divisional Commanders who, if they concur, will carry out the scheme through their Divisional Machine Gun Officers.

19. In the event of the 29th Division being able to operate as mentioned in para. 8, the Corps Mounted Troops will be placed at the disposal of the G.O.C. 29th Division.

VI Corps.   (Sgd.) LOCH,
30th April 1917.   B.G. G.S.

SECRET. 56th Divn. G.3/262.

167th Infantry Brigade.
168th Infantry Brigade.
169th Infantry Brigade
1/5th Cheshire Regt.
C.R.A.
C.R.E.
193rd Div. M.G.Coy.

56th Div. Signals.
A.D.M.S.
A.D.C.
"Q"

   On May 11th at 7.30 p.m. the XVII Corps are attacking the CHEMICAL WORKS, ROEUX CEMETERY, and the buildings North of the DOUAI Railway.

2. On May 12th at 6.30 a.m. the attack will be continued with the object of capturing and consolidating the Line ROEUX CEMETERY, CORONA, CUPID, CHARLIE & WISH Trenches.

3. On May 12th at 6 p.m. the 3rd & 12th Divisions will capture DEVILS TRENCH.

4. On May 17th the 29th Division will take INFANTRY HILL.

5. ACKNOWLEDGE.

Head Qrs. 56th Divn.
11th May, 1917.

B Pakenham
Lieut-Colonel,
General Staff.

AA/III

56th Divn. Tactical Progress
Reports.
(whilst in VI Corps)

(Two copies of each to be kept in here — one
office file — one War Diary)

WAR DIARY COPIES.

SECRET.

56th Division Tactical Progress Report No. 21
from 5 p.m. 19th May to 5 p.m. 20th May 1917.

On receipt of current copy of Tactical Progress Report in the trenches, previous copy to be burnt.

PART I OPERATIONS.
Attack. In conjunction with the Division on our left, an attack was made last night with the object of securing HOOK & LONG Trench and part of TOOL Trench occupied by enemy. Our troops entered TOOL TRENCH but were heavily bombed from both flanks, and were forced to retire to our original line.
Artillery. Fired as usual on enemy trenches and movement. About 500 men in parties of 50 were engaged in O.29.c. with very satisfactory results. About 60 men were fired on near BOW Trench and several casualties caused.
Patrols. A patrol reconnoitred the ground in front of LANYARD TRENCH. Enemy sent up frequent Very Lights.

PART II INTELLIGENCE.
Hostile Artillery. Our front system was heavily bombarded early this morning. N.18.c. & d. and O.13.c. were shelled throughout the afternoon by 4.2's and 77 mm. The CAMBRAI RD. was heavily shelled with 5.9's and 77 mm. at 8.45 a.m.
Hostile M.Gs. During the night a M.G. was firing from O.14.b.5.1. and another from Northern end of LANYARD TRENCH.
Movement. Considerable movement was seen in LANYARD TRENCH, which appears to be strongly held. A party of about 50 of the enemy was seen to leave the building in the vicinity of ROHART FACTORY. Movement was seen in SPUR and POLE TRENCHES and in P.1.a.
General. Signalling with a Green Lamp was seen last night about 11.50 p.m. from the ridge by ROHART FACTORY.
The light German Field Gun discovered in front of CAVALRY TR. about O.14.c.1.6. has now been brought into our lines

Head Qrs. 56th Divn.
20th May, 1917.

H. J. Malleson
Lieutenant,
for Captain,
General Staff.

SECRET.

56th DIVISIONAL TACTICAL PROGRESS REPORT No. 20
from 5 p.m. 18th May to 5 p.m. 19th May 1917.

On receipt of current copy of Tactical Progress Report in
the trenches, previous copy to be burnt.

PART I OPERATIONS.
Artillery   Fairly active during the past 24 hours.

An enemy battery firing at O.29.c.1.2. was engaged successfully by one of our batteries, which obtained a direct hit on one gun. Casualties were also caused.

Patrols. At 9.20 p.m. an attempt was made to rush the enemy block at O.8.b.2.2. The trench here was found to be strongly held and our party was forced to withdraw, bringing their wounded with them.

A patrol from our Right Company left our lines to reconnoitre LANYARD TRENCH at its junction with the ARRAS-CAMBRAI Road. Work was heard in progress in the trench and Very Lights were fired from it. No snipers were met with outside the trench.

Another patrol discovered the presence of a hostile post near the cross roads at O.8.d.10.15.

Other patrols have nothing to report.

Machine Guns. 1,250 rounds were fired into BOIS DU VERT last night.

L.T.Ms. During the past 24 hours 460 rounds have been fired.

PART II INTELLIGENCE.
Hostile Artillery has been below normal during the last 24 hours Intermittent shelling has been carried out on RAKE TRENCH, GORDON ALLEY, PICK, TAPE and TOOL TRENCHES. MONCHY and GUEMAPPE were shelled at intervals throughout the day by 4.2's and 5.9's. One of our batteries in N.17 was heavily shelled by 5.9's and 4.2's with balloon observation during the afternoon.

At 2.30 p.m. the enemy put down a barrage on our front line between MONCHY and the COJEUL RIVER which lasted for 2 minutes.

An enemy battery was seen active at V.2.a.3.7.

Enemy transport. A large amount of transport has been massed during the day at J.29.c. and K.19.b. The majority of this transport consisted of wagons with a number of horses grazing.

An engine and seven trucks were also seen on light railway J.29.c.

Enemy Working Parties. The enemy appeared to be endeavouring to consolidate a line of shell-holes in front of LANYARD TRENCH about 250 yards in front of our Right Company.

Hostile Aircraft Very active yesterday evening. Three enemy squadrons of 8 'planes patrolled our front line between 6 p.m. and 8.30 p.m. Two 'planes were brought down, one believed to be ours and one the enemy's.

Balloons were seen from O.11.d.0.3. on true bearings :-
99° 105° 112° 119° 30' and from 9.19.a.9.1.
on true bearings 128° 30' 119° and 53°.

Enemy Movement. Movement has been seen during the day at the following :- Road in I.26.c. & d.
O.8.a. & b.
Road in I.36.c. & d.
J.29.c. (two motor lorries moving Northwards)
P.20.b.

Considerable amount of movement was seen South and East of BOIRY NOTRE DAME - it was dealt with by Field Guns.

There has been continuous movement all day in the back areas, especially on the DROCOURT LINE in V.1.b. & d. and V.7.b. One of our batteries claim 12 casualties caused among men moving in the open near VIS-EN-ARTOIS

General. A light German Field Gun bearing date 1917 has been discovered situated in front of CAVALRY TRENCH about O.14.c.1.6. Dead Germans were lying near the Gun and an effort will be made to-night to bring the gun into CAVALRY TRENCH.

P.T.O.

- 2 -

<u>General</u> (Continued)   At the commencement of the bombing attack the enemy put up a red light and two yellow lights, but no immediate result was observed.

At 10.30 a.m. four aeroplanes were seen to descend behind copse at J.22.d.5.0.

Head Qrs. 56th Divn.
19th May, 1917.

Maitland
Captain
for General Staff.

SECRET.

**56th DIVISIONAL TACTICAL PROGRESS REPORT No.19
from 5 p.m. 17th May to 5 p.m. 18th May 1917.**

On receipt of current copy of Tactical Progress Report
in the trenches, previous copy to be burnt.

PART I OPERATIONS.

Artillery. We fired on back areas during the night and as usual during the day.

Patrols. An Officers' patrol left FARM TRENCH after dusk reaching a point about 200 yards from LANYARD TRENCH. They then patrolled parallel to it in a Southerly direction. Sounds of a pick being used were heard and a M.G. was seen to be firing from the Northern end of the Trench.

Another patrol went out about 200 yards from TOOL TRENCH but found no trace of the enemy in front of LANYARD TRENCH. An Officers' Patrol reconnoitred TOOL TRENCH North of the block, and found that it was held by 6 or 8 posts of about 4 men each.

Sniping. Our snipers have been active to-day, and 15 hits are claimed.

L.T.Ms. TOOL TRENCH North of the block was again bombarded.

PART II INTELLIGENCE.

Hostile Artillery. - Below normal to-day.
Last night our Posts in front of CAVALRY FARM received about 150 shells of various calibres. From 8.35 a.m. to 9.50 a.m. the trenches in O.19.d. and the Railway Cutting in O.24.b. were fairly heavily shelled with 5.9's and 77 mm. The WANCOURT-GUEMAPPE Road was shelled at intervals during the night and morning, and the CAMBRAI Road during the morning with shrapnel.

Hostile Machine Guns. A M.G. fired at intervals from about O.14.b.6.0. either from LANYARD TRENCH or a shell hole in front of it.

Movement. Considerable movement was seen this morning on the SAILLY BOIRY NOTRE DAME Road.

Transport was seen in J.29. - on the track North of CIGARETTE COPSE and on the track in O.6.a. A good deal of movement of men was noticed on Mound about 800 yards S.E. of CORNER COPSE. About 200 horses were seen grazing in K.19.b. A hostile battery was seen firing on a true bearing 63° 30' from N.24.b.6.0. The tripod erected at Southern of BOIS DU SART has disappeared.

General. At 9.30 p.m. last night three red lights apparently in front of BOIS DU VERT were sent up and floated in the air for two minutes. This was repeated again five minutes later. Lights were also sent up from the south end of FACTORY TR.

New work.- The following work was carried out by us during the night 17/18th :-
Excavation commenced for two Company Headquarters in each sub-section - average depth reached 7 ft. - KNIFE TRENCH continued Northwards from O.8.a.8.2. towards O.8.a.8.5. - average depth 3 ft. and width 2.ft. 6" - commencement made on connecting posts in Left Sub-section, from Right Post O.8.c.9.1. a trench 3' 6" was dug to post O.8.c.8.4. This trench is not continuous, short gaps being left in places - from O.8.c.8.4. trench continued Northwards for 70 yards - average depth 3' 6" - C.T. O.8.a.8.1. to O.8.d.1.8. cleared to an average depth of 4' 6" - C.T. O.8.c.25.05 to O.7.d.7.2. widened and deepened to 4 ft. throughout.

Head Qrs. 56th Divn.
18th May, 1917.

H. F. Malleson
Lieutenant,
for Captain,
General Staff.

SECRET.

56th DIVISIONAL TACTICAL PROGRESS REPORT No.19
from 5 p.m. 17th May to 5 p.m. 18th May 1917.

On receipt of current copy of Tactical Progress Report in the trenches, previous copy to be burnt.

PART I OPERATIONS.

Artillery. We fired on back areas during the night and as usual during the day.

Patrols. An Officers' patrol left FARM TRENCH after dusk reaching a point about 200 yards from LANYARD TRENCH. They then patrolled parallel to it in a Southerly direction. Sounds of a pick being used were heard and a M.G. was seen to be firing from the Northern end of the Trench.

Another patrol went out about 200 yards from TOOL TRENCH but found no trace of the enemy in front of LANYARD TRENCH. An Officers' Patrol reconnoitred TOOL TRENCH North of the block, and found that it was held by 6 or 8 posts of about 4 men each.

Sniping. Our snipers have been active to-day, and 15 hits are claimed.

L.T.Ms. TOOL TRENCH North of the block was again bombarded.

PART II INTELLIGENCE.

Hostile Artillery. - Below normal to-day. Last night our Posts in front of CAVALRY FARM received about 150 shells of various calibres. From 8.35 a.m. to 9.50 a.m. the trenches in O.19.d. and the Railway Cutting in O.24.b. were fairly heavily shelled with 5.9's and 77 mm. The WANCOURT-GUEMAPPE Road was shelled at intervals during the night and morning, and the CAMBRAI Road during the morning with shrapnel.

Hostile Machine Guns. A M.G. fired at intervals from about O.14.b.6.0. either from LANYARD TRENCH or a shell hole in front of it.

Movement. Considerable movement was seen this morning on the SAILLY BOIRY NOTRE DAME Road.

Transport was seen in J.29. - on the track North of CIGARETTE COPSE and on the track in O.6.a. A good deal of movement of men was noticed on Mound about 800 yards S.E. of CORNER COPSE. About 200 horses were seen grazing in K.19.b. A hostile battery was seen firing on a true bearing 63° 30' from N.24.b.6.0. The tripod erected at Southern of BOIS DU SART has disappeared.

General. At 9.30 p.m. last night three red lights apparently in front of BOIS DU VERT were sent up and floated in the air for two minutes. This was repeated again five minutes later. Lights were also sent up from the south end of FACTORY TR.

New work. - The following work was carried out by us during the night 17/18th :-

Excavation commenced for two Company Headquarters in each sub-section - average depth reached 7 ft. - KNIFE TRENCH continued Northwards from O.8.a.8.2. towards O.8.a..8.5. - average depth 3 ft. and width 2.ft. 6" - commencement made on connecting posts in Left Sub-section, from Right Post O.8.c.9.1. a trench 3' 6" was dug to post O.8.c.8.4. This trench is not continuous, short gaps being left in places - from O.8.c.8.4. trench continued Northwards for 70 yards - average depth 3' 6" - C.T. O.8.a.8.1. to O.8.d.1.8. cleared to an average depth of 4' 6" - C.T. O.8.c.25.05 to O.7.d.7.2. widened and deepened to 4 ft. throughout.

Head Qrs. 56th Divn.
18th May, 1917.

H. J. Malleson
Lieutenant,
for Captain,
General Staff.

SECRET.

56th DIVISIONAL TACTICAL PROGRESS REPORT No.19
from 5 p.m. 17th May to 5 p.m. 18th May 1917.

On receipt of current copy of Tactical Progress Report
in the trenches, previous copy to be burnt.

PART I OPERATIONS.

Artillery. We fired on back areas during the night and as usual during the day.

Patrols. An Officers' patrol left FARM TRENCH after dusk reaching a point about 200 yards from LANYARD TRENCH. They then patrolled parallel to it in a Southerly direction. Sounds of a pick being used were heard and a M.G. was seen to be firing from the Northern end of the Trench.

Another patrol went out about 200 yards from TOOL TRENCH but found no trace of the enemy in front of LANYARD TRENCH. An Officers' Patrol reconnoitred TOOL TRENCH North of the block, and found that it was held by 6 or 8 posts of about 4 men each.

Sniping. Our snipers have been active to-day, and 15 hits are claimed.

L.T.Ms. TOOL TRENCH North of the block was again bombarded.

PART II INTELLIGENCE.

Hostile Artillery. - Below normal to-day.
Last night our Posts in front of CAVALRY FARM received about 150 shells of various calibres. From 8.35 a.m. to 9.50 a.m. the trenches in O.19.d. and the Railway Cutting in O.24.b. were fairly heavily shelled with 5.9's and 77 mm. The WANCOURT -GUEMAPPE Road was shelled at intervals during the night and morning, and the CAMBRAI Road during the morning with shrapnel.

Hostile Machine Guns. A M.G. fired at intervals from about O.14.b.6.0. either from LANYARD TRENCH or a shell hole in front of it.

Movement. Considerable movement was seen this morning on the SAILLY BOIRY NOTRE DAME Road.

Transport was seen in J.29. - on the track North of CIGARETTE COPSE and on the track in O.6.a. A good deal of movement of men was noticed on Mound about 800 yards S.E. of CORNER COPSE. About 200 horses were seen grazing in K.19.b. A hostile battery was seen firing on a true bearing 63° 30' from N.24.b. 6.0. The tripod erected at Southern of BOIS DU SART has disappeared.

General. At 9.30 p.m. last night three red lights apparently in front of BOIS DU VERT were sent up and floated in the air for two minutes. This was repeated again five minutes later. Lights were also sent up from the south end of FACTORY TR.

New work.- The following work was carried out by us during the night 17/18th :-

Excavation commenced for two Company Headquarters in each sub-section - average depth reached 7 ft. - KNIFE TRENCH continued Northwards from O.8.a.8.2. towards O.8.a..8.5. - average depth 3 ft. and width 2.ft. 6" - commencement made on connecting posts in Left Sub-section, from Right Post O.8.c.9.1. a trench 3' 6" was dug to post O.8.c.8.4. This trench is not continuous, short gaps being left in places - from O.8.c.8.4. trench continued Northwards for 70 yards - average depth 3' 6" - C.T. O.8.a.8.1. to O.8.d.1.8. cleared to an average depth of 4' 6" - C.T. O.8.c.25.05 to O.7.d.7.2. widened and deepened to 4 ft. throughout.

Head Qrs. 56th Divn.
18th May, 1917.

H. I. Malleson
Lieutenant,
for Captain,
General Staff.

SECRET.

56th DIVISIONAL TACTICAL PROGRESS REPORT No.18
from 5 p.m. 16th May to 5 p.m. 17th May 1917

On receipt of current copy of Tactical Progress Report
in the trenches, previous copy to be burnt.

PART I OPERATIONS.

Artillery. Fired on St.ROHART FACTORY and back areas during the night and as usual during the day. At 4.45 p.m. we carried out a shoot on LANYARD TRENCH.

Patrols. An Officers' patrol went out at 2 a.m. to a distance of 200 yards in front of our right Bn. No sign of the enemy was found.

TOOL TRENCH north of the block and LANYARD TRENCH were reconnoitred, both were found to be strongly held by M.Gs. with a screen of snipers in front.

Trench Mortars. TOOL TRENCH North of the block has been bombarded at irregular intervals. When fire was opened red parachute lights were fired from enemy's line, and a barrage of light shells was immediately put down.

PART II INTELLIGENCE.

Hostile Artillery. Hostile Artillery fire was below normal during the last 24 hours. Our front and support trenches and GORDON ALLEY received attention at intervals throughout the day and night, mostly by shells of heavy calibre. WANCOURT, GUEMAPPE and N.17.c. and d. were intermittently shelled with 5.9's and 4.2's from 11 a.m. to 1 p.m.

Hostile Sniping and Trench Mortars. Snipers were very active from North of block in TOOL TRENCH. A light T.M. is reported to have fired from enemy portion of TOOL TRENCH against our block. Rifle grenades also fell in HILL TRENCH.

Movement. Considerable movement was seen in the early morning in SPUR TRENCH. From 8.45 to 9 a.m. work was seen in progress in LANYARD TRENCH, at O.9.c.3.2. Three six horse vehicles were seen moving in a North-westerly direction in O.6.c. Small parties were seen on road in I.36.c. At 4 p.m. lamp signalling was seen in OCEAN WORK at O.29.b. and d.

General. Men exposing themselves S. of the ARRAS-CAMBRAI Road drew no fire.

New work. The following work was done by us during the night 16th/17th :- C.T. 400 yards long dug from SPADE to KNIFE Trenches O.8.b.25.05 to O.7.d.9.2. to O.7.d.7.2. - average depth 3 ft. - average width 2' 6" Sites for Company Headquarters dug-outs reconnoitred.

The following work has been done to rear defences during week ending 6 a.m. 16.5.17 :- WANCOURT - FEUCHY LINE. A two bay H.W. entanglement has been nearly completed in front of this line from the ARRAS-CAMBRAI to the TILLOY - WANCOURT Road. The new entanglement has been strengthened by old German wire and fire bays have been prepared at suitable intervals. Wire has been extended from Strong Point at N.18.b.0.9. to join up the Strong Point at N.18.c.6.8. which has been deepened and wired. An apron fence has been erected Southwards to the Eastern end of the pond at N.18.c.75.15 from N.18.c.6.8.

H.F. Malleson

Lieutenant,
for Captain,
General Staff.

May 17th 1917.

SECRET.

56th DIVISIONAL TACTICAL PROGRESS REPORT No. 17.
from 5 p.m. 15th May to 5 p.m. 16th May 1917

On receipt of current copy of Tactical Progress Report
in the trenches, previous copy to be burnt.

PART I OPERATIONS.

Artillery. Our artillery shelled LANYARD TRENCH and back areas during the night.

Patrols. Patrols went out from Northern end of SADDLE TR. and got within a few yards of TOOL TRENCH North of the block. Movement was seen and enemy snipers were active from shell holes.

Patrols were also sent out from our right flank and reconnoitred the ground in front of our position. No definite information could be obtained owing to continuous shelling of our front line and NO MAN'S Land by the enemy.

Trench Mortars and snipers. Our T.Ms. bombarded TOOL TRENCH North of the block at irregular intervals with good effect.- our snipers claim three hits to day.

PART II INTELLIGENCE.

Hostile Artillery. Fairly active during the last 24 hours. During the night N.18.a. & C./8 wards shelled with 5.9's and 4.2's. Noticeable attention was paid to GORDON ALLEY, SADDLE LANE and TAPE TRENCH. At 7.45 a.m. the CAMBRAI ROAD in O.7., N.11 & 12. were shelled with 8" Howitzers, and the roads at N.16.d. at intervals with 5.9's. GUEMAPPE, CAVALRY FARM, Copse in O.a Central and KNIFE TRENCH received attention from 5.9's and 4.2'sz

Movement. Little movement was seen to day owing to bad visibility.

A German was seen to enter a dugout about O.9.c.9.8. in the road bank. The dugout was shelled and three direct hits on the entrance claimed. Five Germans left the dugout of whom three became casualties.

New Work. The following work has been carried out by us during the last 24 hours :-

The three Southern Posts in TOOL TRENCH have been joined up forming a good trench - C.T. between CAVALRY TRENCH and TOOL TRENCH cleared, deepened and widened - C.T. from O.8.a. 8.1. to O.8.d.1.8. improved in many places but not yet completed - KNIFE TRENCH improved for 80 yards S.E. from O.8.a.8.1. - TAPE TRENCH cleared and improved - 100 yards wire one bay deep put out along TAPE TRENCH from O.8.a.3.3. towards O.8.a.5.2. - 6 ft. pickets put out along C.T. running South of COPSE O.8.a. central between KNIFE TR. and TOOL TR.

H. F. Malleson

Head Qrs. 56th Divn.
16th May, 1917.

Lieutenant,
for Captain,
General Staff.

SECRET.

56th DIVISIONAL TACTICAL PROGRESS REPORT No. 16
from 5 p.m. 14th May to 5 p.m. 15th May 1917.

On receipt of current copy of Tactical Progress Report
in the trenches, previous copy to be burnt.

PART I OPERATIONS.

Patrols.
A patrol left CAVALRY TRENCH at O.14.c.0.4. and proceeded along light railway track as far as O.14.d.10.45 where it was fired on by a sniper, who appeared to be about O.14.b.4.1. Very Lights were being sent up from LANYARD TRENCH. Other patrols went out about 200 yds. in front of our posts and encountered none of the enemy. TOOL TRENCH was reconnoitred at 10.30 p.m. N. of the block - the trench was found to be occupied but no movement could be seen.

Patrols from our left flank found a screen of snipers in shell holes about 100 - 150 yards in front of our posts.

Artillery. - Our artillery fired as usual on enemy trenches and back areas. A concentrated burst of fire was directed on LANYARD TRENCH this afternoon. An enemy battery was observed in action at O.29.c.20.35 about 6.20 p.m. and was engaged with good results. One direct hit was obtained and stretcher bearers were seen to be very busy afterwards.

PART II INTELLIGENCE.

Hostile Artillery. Enemy artillery has been active at intervals. N.18.a. & c. were shelled for 20 minute periods during the evening and at 3.30 a.m. The WANCOURT Roads also received attention at the same time. SADDLE, PICK and TAPE TRENCHES were shelled with 5.9's and 8" during the day. CAVALRY FARM and our front line trenches were heavily shelled during the night and in the afternoon. GUEMAPPE and MONCHY received attention at 1.30 p.m. Heavy bursts of fire throughout the day on O.13. and N.17., 18., 22 and 23.

Snipers. Active from shell holes in front of TOOL TRENCH throughout the night, and during the day from BOIS DU VERT.

Movement. - Very little movement seen. At 6.20 p.m. 30 men were seen in twos and threes moving S.E. up the slope between O.6.d.87.75 and P.1.a.2.4. in fatigue dress

Work. - New digging visible at O.16.c.9.2. and along 60 contour in O.16.d. Trenches at O.16.c.8.1. appear to have been improved.

General. - Enemy put two rounds of 77 mm into LANYARD TRENCH at 10 a.m. and red lights breaking into two were sent up.

New work. - The following work was done during the night 14/15th :-
Forward dumps with wiring material established at O.8.a.2.4. and O.8.a.8.1, with the purpose of wiring the line TAPE TRENCH to TOOL TRENCH immediately South of Copse O.8. Central - Knife Rests for blocking main ARRAS-CAMBRAI Road carried to CAVALRY TRENCH - C.T. O.14.a.4.9. to O.14.a.7.7. improved and C.T. O.8.c.4.5. to O.8.c.8.0. completed.

H.F. Malleson

Head Qrs. 56th Divn.
15th May, 1917.

Lieutenant,
for Captain,
General Staff.

SECRET.

56th DIVISIONAL TACTICAL PROGRESS REPORT NO. 15
from 5 p.m. 13th May to 5 p.m. 14th May 1917.

On receipt of current copy of Tactical Progress Report in the trenches, previous copy to be burnt.

PART I OPERATIONS.

Artillery. Our artillery fired as usual on enemy trenches and movement and searched Back Areas.

Patrols. A Patrol left FARM Trench at 2-30 a.m. and proceeded in the direction of LANYARD Trench. No wire could be seen. Voices could be heard plainly.

Sniping. Our snipers claimed 4 hits to-day, firing from O.8.b.2.2.

Machine Guns. On further investigation it is found that 6 machine guns were captured in TOOL Trench on the evening of the 11th and not 3 as at first reported. Of these, two are the ordinary model and four are water-cooled guns, with M.G. actions, shortened barrels, butt attachment and mounted on a tripod.

PART II INTELLIGENCE.

Hostile Artillery. SADDLE Trench received attention with 5.9's and 4.2 shells during the night and early this morning. Apparently in answer to the Chinese bombardment carried out by the Divisions on our left this afternoon the enemy put down a heavy barrage on our front and support trenches N. and S. of the ARRAS - CAMBRAI Road. Intermittent shelling of S.W. corner of WANCOURT from 2-30 p.m. to 4 p.m. Flashes of a battery of 4.2's were observed at approximately J.31.c.90.75. Flashes from a hostile battery were also seen at 3 a.m. on a true bearing of 94° from N.17.c.5.2.

Enemy Movement. Considerable movement of men, horses and limbers during the day in P.2.b and along road in O.5.d. Movement was seen and fired on along the road S. and S.E. of BOIRY in O.9.d. Movement was heard last night in shell-holes and rifle-pits in front of TOOL Trench.

Work Report. The following work has been done by us during the last 24 hours :-
Loop cut round block in GORDON ALLEY - block established 4 bays deep and wire entanglement put across SUNKEN ROAD O.8.c.9.3.

H. F. Malleson

H.Q. 56th Division.
14th May 1917.

Lieutenant,
for Captain,
General Staff.

P.T.O.

ANNEXE TO 56th DIVISIONAL TACTICAL PROGRESS REPORT No.15.

Prisoners.- Two men belonging to the 5th Grenadier Regiment, 36th Division deserted and gave themselves up in our front line about O.8.c.84. shortly before dawn to-day.
    They belong to the 6th Coy. 2nd Battalion and were Company Machine Gunners.

Relief. - The 2nd Battalion relieved the 3rd Battalion in the front line on night 12/13th. The 3rd Battalion went back to rest in ECOURT ST.QUENTIN, and the 1st Battalion is in support in the Wood W. of ETERPIGNY - P.13.a. Prisoners state that the 1st Battalion lost severely as some of their dead were still being buried yesterday.

Order of Battle.- Remains as before :-
        175th I.R.
        128th I.R.
        5th Grenadier Regt.
Method of Holding Line.
    The left of the 5th Grenadier Regiment rests on the ARRAS - CAMBRAI Road. Two Companies are in front line, LANYARD TRENCH, viz: 6th Coy against the road with the 7th Coy. on its right. The 5th Coy. is 150 yards behind and the 8th 150 yards behind again. Coy. strength averages 110.

Machine Guns. - Prisoners state that their own Company Machine Gun position is in LANYARD TRENCH, 25 yards South of the ARRAS - CAMBRAI ROAD.
    A Machine Gun belonging to the Regimental Machine Gun Company with its crew was destroyed by a shell the day before yesterday. A second one shared the same fate yesterday; both were approximately 200 - 300 yards N. of ST.ROHART FACTORY. The FACTORY itself is said to be unoccupied owing to continuous shelling.

Intentions. - A rumour is said to be current that a withdrawal to the DROCOURT QUEANT LINE will take place about the 20th inst.

Moral. - Appears to be poor. Prisoners state that they gave themselves up because they were tired of the War after nearly three years of fighting, and that they consider Germany is fast losing, an opinion which is rapidly spreading in the Army and at home. Many others would willingly give themselves up, but are afraid of getting shot on approaching the British Lines.

SECRET.

56th DIVISIONAL TACTICAL PROGRESS REPORT No. 14
from 5 p.m. 12th May to 5 p.m. 13th May 1917.

On receipt of current copy of Tactical Progress Report in the trenches, previous copy to be burnt.

PART I OPERATIONS.

Artillery. Our artillery fired as usual on enemy trenches and movement.

Lewis Guns. Positions have been improved.

Snipers. Those posted in TOOL TRENCH reported 13 hits.

Stokes Mortars. Between 5 and 5.30 p.m. several rounds were fired, causing S.O.S. to be sent up by enemy.

PART II INTELLIGENCE.

Hostile Artillery. Battery positions in O.17.a. and O.18.a. have been shelled at intervals during the last 24 hours with 8" and 5.9's. GORDON ALLEY, RAKE and SHRAPNEL TRENCHES and the CAMBRAI Road in O.7.c. received most attention to-day, and a few 5.9's fell in MONCHY, GUEMAPPE and WANCOURT.

Movement. About 4 a.m. small parties of the enemy were observed from our extreme left flank moving in a S.E. direction about 400 yards away. Fire was opened and about 20 casualties caused. A party of 30 Germans were seen approaching BOIRY NOTRE DAME at 8 a.m.

A party of 20 of the enemy was observed last night about 7 p.m. to enter shell holes 200 to 300 yards in front of our posts.

Aircraft. Very active between 5 and 7 a.m. A bluish coloured fast type of 'plane resembling the NIEUPORT was seen.

Eight balloons were seen in the air during the day.

General. New work appears to have been done about O.14.d.2.8.

At 7.25 p.m. explosions were observed near VIS-EN-ARTOIS and BOIRY NOTRE DAME.

New Work. The following work was done by us during the last 24 hours :-

Strong Point at O.8.a.3.7. improved and deepened - 100 yards of wire erected in O.8.a. from E. to W. on Northern side of C.T. running from SADDLE TRENCH to PICK TRENCH - three C.T's from old front line to TOOL TRENCH deepened to between 4 and 5 feet for the most part - advanced posts strengthened and wiring commenced along whole front.

H. G. Malleson

Head Qrs. 56th Divn.
13th May, 1917.

Lieutenant,
for Captain,
General Staff.

SECRET.

56th DIVISIONAL TACTICAL PROGRESS REPORT No. 13
from 5 p.m. 11th May to 5 p.m. 12th May 1917.

On receipt of current copy of Tactical Progress Report in the trenches, previous copy to be burnt.

PART I OPERATIONS.

Attack. At 8.30 p.m. two Battalions attacked TOOL TRENCH, CAVALRY FARM and trenches between O.14.a.95.45 and O.14.a.6.0. The attack was in the nature of a surprise, the assaulting battalions actually gaining objectives before enemy was able to put down an effective barrage.

Immediately the troops left their trenches the enemy fired double RED Very Lights from direction of SPUR TRENCH and INFANTRY HILL. As soon as the objectives were gained Lewis Gun Position were established and Strong Posts formed

Practically no opposition was encountered in the trenches as many of the enemy attempted to run away and a large number were accounted for by our Lewis Guns.

Touch was obtained early between the Battalions and on the left flank a bombing block was established. In the early morning a Stokes Mortar Battery was of much assistance at this point firing 250 rounds in bursts of 10 deliberate. During the night the positions were consolidated and three C.T's cut back to CAVALRY TRENCH. Many dead were found in TOOL TRENCH as the result of our artillery fire.

Lewis Guns. These were placed in positions well forward and fired on retreating enemy with good results.

At 3 a.m. a German Officer and orderly approached our position; Finding themselves close to us they attempted to run away but were fired on, the officer being killed and the man wounded.

Artillery. Our artillery during the day fired on enemy movement and trenches and on the following N.F. targets :-
O.18.b.8.6.   O.5.a.06.05.
O.30.b.0.3.   O.30.b.2.7.

PART II INTELLIGENCE.

Hostile artillery. Yesterday evening within two minutes of our troops advancing a barrage was put down more particularly heavy on CAVALRY and RAKE TRENCHES and lasted for about an hour.

During the day hostile fire has been below normal. O.14.c. & d. O.19.c. & d. shelled during the morning. TOOL TRENCH from O.8.b.5.4. to O.2.d.4.0. by Field Guns all day Special attention was paid to GUEMAPPE and CAVALRY TRENCH N. of ARRAS - CAMBRAI Road   Intermittent firing on our batteries in N.17 and N.18 throughout the night. During the latter part of the afternoon an 8" Howitzer fired rounds on our batteries in N.18.a. It appeared to have a balloon spotting for it, and fired a round each time our batteries opened fire.

Hostile M.Gs. and Snipers.   M.G. fire met during the advance, on the left, but snipers less active than usual.

Movement. Observed and fired on at O.9.a.0.6. O.15.b.5.5.

FACTORY TRENCH in O.15.b. appears to be very strongly held and considerable movement in and about the trench was fired at. Three enemy ammunition wagons were observed in O.6.a. They disappeared from view behind Copse in O.6.a.0.6. at 12.45. Pack horses were observed in the same place at 1 p.m. and were fired on. A working party at O.9.d.1.1. was engaged. A small party of the enemy was seen approaching TOOL TRENCH early this morning. Lewis Guns opened and the party dispersed.

/General

- 2 -

<u>General.</u>   Three enemy M.Gs. were captured, one being placed in position for our own use.
   A German was seen coming out of an O.P. in Copse at I.36.d.6.0.
   Golden rain appears to be the enemy's signal for barrage fire.
   A large fire was observed between 11 p.m. and 11.30 p.m. from N.16.b.5.8. on a true bearing of 74 degrees.

<u>New work.</u> The following has been carried out by us during the last 24 hours :-
   Three C.T's started between outposts front line and TOOL TR.
      (1) approximately S.E. from O.8.a.8.1.   (2) approximately O.8.c.5.6. to O.8.c.7.4.   (3) approximately O.14.a.4.9. to O.14.a.7.6.   Average depth 3 ft. but the two Northern ones are very shallow at their Western ends.

H. J. Malleson

Head Qrs. 56th Divn.
12th May, 1917.

Lieutenant,
for Captain,
General Staff.

SECRET.

ANNEXE TO 56th DIVISIONAL TACTICAL PROGRESS REPORT NO. 13.

Prisoners. - The following unwounded prisoners were captured by us :-

<u>36th Division.</u>
128 I.R.		1 N.C.O.	9 men.
5 Gren. Regt.		1 "	
		2 N.C.Os.	9 men.

The 36th Division was in the line in front of ST. QUENTIN and was relieved on 8th/9th April when it went into rest for a month.

The 5th Gren. Regt. relieved the 41st I.R. - 221st Divn. on the night of May 7th. The 128th I.R. went into the line on May 9th. Prisoners state that the 221st Division suffered severely while it was in the line.

<u>Order of Battle.</u>   North to South.
 175 I.R.
 128 "
  5 Gren. Regt. left flank 200 yards N. of Cavalry Fm.

<u>Method of Holding Line.</u>
 128th I.R. had 3 Coys. in the line, the 4th was due to reinforce owing to the 3 Coys. having suffered severely, but it is uncertain whether it actually did.
 5th Gren. Regt. had two Coys in front line and two in Support in the QUARRY by ST. ROHART FACTORY.
 Each Regiment had one Battalion in support and one in reserve.
 No information could be obtained about the 175th I.R.
 Coy. strength 100 - 130 men.
 CAVALRY FARM and TOOL TRENCH 200 yards N. of ARRAS - CAMBRAI Road were not held owing to continuous shell fire.

<u>Moral.</u> Stated to be bad owing to our continuous bombardment and the lack of proper trenches. Our fire prevents the regular supply of food and makes it impossible to bring hot meals up to the front line.
 The N.C.O. 5th Gren. Regt. states that the men in his platoon ran back when our barrage started in spite of his orders to stand fast. He saw several hit on their way so decided to stay where he was. He was very pleased to be caught.

<u>Intentions.</u> Nothing is known of any intended voluntary withdrawal; though no definite orders have been published it is an understood thing that the ground is to be hotly contested and our advance delayed as much as possible.

<u>Lights.</u>   Prisoner thinks -
   GREEN is for barrage fire.
   YELLOW to lengthen range.
 The N.C.O. 128th I.R. stated that an attack had been expected on the evening of the 10th but that they were quite taken by surprise when it actually came.
 The following is taken from the German Wireless Press:-
 <u>Army Group Crown Prince Rupprecht.</u>
 After the heaviest artillery preparation the English attacked yesterday evening on both sides of the ARRAS-LENS ARRAS-DOUAI and ARRAS-CAMBRAI Roads in thick masses in places. In most places they were repulsed by our troops but when they succeeded in entering our positions they were thrown back with loss by our counter-attacks. Fighting continues at ROEUX Station.

SECRET.

56th DIVISION TACTICAL PROGRESS REPORT No.12.
from 5 p.m. 10th May to 5 p.m. 11th May 1917.

On receipt of current copy of Tactical Progress Report
in the trenches, previous copy to be burnt.

PART I OPERATIONS.
   Artillery. Our artillery fired according to programme and on enemy trenches and movement.
   Aeroplanes. Great activity during the day over enemy's lines.

PART II INTELLIGENCE.
   Hostile artillery has been very active especially against our battery positions in N.17 and 18 during the last 24 hours
   At 8.5 p.m. in reply to salvoes from our 18-pdrs. KNIFE, STRING, SPADE, BRIDLE and SADDLE TRENCHES received great attention. During the day the enemy appeared to be throwing a quantity of shells about aimlessly. GORDON ALLEY was shelled intermittently throughout the day, and STRING TRENCH during the afternoon.
   From 2 p.m. to 2.30 p.m. MONCHY and FEUCHY CHAPEL were shelled with 4.2's and 5.9's.
   Movement. A certain amount of movement was seen in TOO Tr. during the morning. A considerable amount of transport was seen about 3 p.m. on road in O.5.d. and O.6.c. At about 4.30 p.m. movement of transport S.E. from BOIRY was reported, and considerable movement of troops and transport observed travelling Westwards between ESTREES and TORTEQUENNE
   Hostile Aircraft. More active than usual. 'Planes flying over our lines between 7 a.m. and 9.50 a.m. were driven off by our A.A. Guns. Balloons were up and down at intervals during the day.
   General At 3.40 p.m. a fire apparently of ammunition was seen in P.32.a. A dump is reported to have been blown up in CHERISY. During relief last night enemy fired green rockets which burst into two stars. A short bombardment of our lines followed. At 10 a.m. the enemy put a number of 5.9's on his side of TOOL TRENCH. Golden rain rockets were constantly being sent up all along TOOL TRENCH. Germans were seen running from shell holes in front of LANYARD in advance of our creeping barrage

   New work. The following work has been carried out by us during the last 24 hours:- Strong Point at O.8.a.15.40. completed to a depth of 3' 6" - two C.T's from KNIFE TRENCH to CAVALRY TRENCH deepened to 4' approximately, O.14.a.9.3. (1) O.14.a.3.9 to O.14.a.0.9 (2) O.8.c.2.1. to O.8.c.4.0. - trench connecting posts 1, 2 and 3 west of Copse at O.8. central deepened to 4' - parts of KNIFE TR. deepened.

Head Qrs. 56th Divn.
11th May, 1917.

H. F. Malleson
Lieutenant,
for Captain,
General Staff.

SECRET.

56th DIVISION TACTICAL PROGRESS REPORT NO. 11
from 5 p.m. 9th May to 5 p.m. 10th May 1917.

On receipt of Tactical Progress Report in the trenches previous copy to be burnt.

PART I OPERATIONS.

Patrols. Patrols examined CAVALRY FARM at 11 p.m. and 1 a.m. and found it and the trench S.E. of it unoccupied. TOOL Trench between O.8.d.1.9 and O.8.c.70.35 was reconnoitred. A sap was discovered at O.8.c.70.35 held by a M.G. and 5 men, who opened fire.

Artillery. Two successful shoots were carried out by 4.5" Hows to-day on TOOL Trench. Much damage was done and many casualties observed. One German was thrown about 50 feet into the air. A few more hurriedly left the trench for a dug-out in rear of it, where they are now buried. Many of the enemy evacuated the trench and were shelled by our 18 pounders. Some of the casualties caused crawled into shell-holes, others remained where they fell. TOOL Tr. was reported full of troops.

STOKES MORTARS. At 12-45 p.m. Stokes Mortars bombarded TOOL Trench with excellent effect, causing many casualties. The enemy left the trench and scattered towards BOIS DU VERT and to dug-outs at about O.8.d.5.8.

PART II INTELLIGENCE.

Hostile Artillery Fairly quiet during the last 24 hours. Our battery positions in N.17 and N.18 were persistently shelled with 5.9's during the day. A few gas shells fell in O.18.a at 5-45 a.m. Our trenches North of CAVALRY FARM received a few 4.2's and 77 mm: O.14.c.6.5 and O.14.c.70.65 were shelled by 4.2" Hows. during the morning. Early in the afternoon our Front and Support trenches in O.13 and the O.P. in GORDON ALLEY received a good deal of notice. Direction of heavy gun appears to be REMY, VIS EN ARTOIS and BOIRY. A new 5.9 gun, which enfilades the ARRAS - CAMBRAI Road, is reported and has been active throughout the day.

Machine Guns. Reported at following places - INFANTRY HILL, ST. ROHART FACTORY, and at O.8.c.70.35.

Movement. Considerable amount of movement reported in O.9.a. A stretcher party was seen at 7 p.m. moving from O.14.d.5.4 to O.15.c.6.5. Some men without equipment left trench about O.9.a.4.5 at 11-45 a.m. and disappeared in direction of BOIRY NOTRE DAME. Five men seen at O.8.c.9.5. Much movement near Mound about P.1.a, true bearing about 63° 15' from N.24.b.80.15.

New Work. Two thick belts of wire have been reported running E. to W. to O.16.c.9.1. New earth visible on parapet of LANYARD Trench at O.14.b.65.70.

General. An enemy S.A.A. dump about O.8.d.1.1 was blown up by 1 of our 18-pounder batteries. At 4-5 p.m. flashes of a gun could be seen approximately at J.26.b.5.3.

New Work. The following work has been carried out by us - Strong Post O.8.@.2.7 completed to depth 4' 6" - Strong Post started at O.8.a.3.3 only 6" deep - New C.T. from O.8.a.1.5 to O.8.a.7.3, deepened to 4' 6" - JUNCTION Trench from North end of KNIFE Trench to SADDLE LANE deepened to 4' 6" - Continuation of KNIFE Trench to North of SADDLE LANE connected to posts 1, 2, and 3 and back to SADDLE Trench. Average depth 2' 6" - Two new C.T's started between CAVALRY and KNIFE Trenches - C.T. between CAVALRY Trench and North end of new Support Line deepened to 4' 6" - Front line trenches improved and deepened.

H.Q. 56th Division.
10th May 1917.

H. F. Malleson
Lieutenant.
for Captain,
General Staff.

SECRET.

**56th DIVISION TACTICAL PROGRESS REPORT No. 10
from 5 p.m. 9th May to 6 p.m. 10th May 1917.**

On receipt of Tactical Progress Report in the trenches
previous copy to be burnt.

PART I OPERATIONS.
  Patrols. A patrol examined CAVALRY FARM at 1 a.m. and found it unoccupied. Trench S.E. of the FARM also appeared to be unoccupied. Very Lights were sent up from LANYARD TRENCH South of the ARRAS - CAMBRAI ROAD and from TOOL TRENCH North of the Road. Patrols located a Post in TOOL TRENCH between O.8.c.8.2. and O.8.c.8.5. and report wire in front of TOOL TRENCH between O.8.d.1.9. and O.8.b.1.2. but none South of this.
  Aeroplanes. Our aircraft has been active drawing considerable hostile M.G. fire.
  Artillery. Our artillery fired as usual on enemy trenches, Strong Points and movement.

PART II INTELLIGENCE.
  Hostile Artillery. Rather below normal during the last 24 hours.
  At 11.17 a.m. GORDON ALLEY was heavily shelled from direction of O.10.d. Battery positions in N.17 and N.18 were very heavily shelled by 4.2's and 5.9's from 11 a.m. to 12.15 p.m. and again at 3.30 p.m. from the direction of O.19.d. or O.6.c. About 400 rounds are reported to have fallen on these positions during the morning.
  At 12.45 p.m. enemy put down a heavy barrage of field guns and 5.9's on our reserve line from CAMBRAI Road to WANCOURT TOWER. It was heaviest on the left and lasted till 12.55 p.m.
  FEUCHY CORNER and N.12.d. were intermittently shelled by 5.9's from 12 noon to 2.30 from direction of I.29. occasional rounds fell in GUEMAPPE. CAVALRY FARM was shelled intermittently with 77 mm.
  Hostile M.Gs. Active during hours of "Stand To" evening and morning. A considerable amount of fire was from INFANTRY HILL where there is a large mound which appears to be a M.G. emplacement.

  Sniping. Usual sniping from TOOL TRENCH.
  Movement. Men seen carrying dug-out frames in LANYARD TRENCH. TOOL TRENCH is reported strongly held. A few Germans were seen walking up STIRRUP LANE and were shelled. Three men laying wires along road S.E. from BOIRY through O.5.d. A party of men seen entering wood in O.11.c. Individual men wearing soft caps with red band seen in trench O.9.b.5.5. The track between SPUR TRENCH and TOOL TRENCH is used by individual men proceeding to TOOL TRENCH. A considerable amount of movement has been observed during the day. Observers report no trace of enemy West of LANYARD TRENCH South of ARRAS - CAMBRAI ROAD
  Hostile Aircraft. Hostile aeroplanes were in sight during the shelling of our Battery positions this morning, but no zone call was picked up. One hostile balloon was seen at 3.30 p.m. on a true bearing 85 degre from N.24.b.7.3.
  General. The Y shaped portion of TOOL TRENCH in O.8.c. appears to be a Strong Point. At 2.15 p.m. four or five golden rain rockets were sent up from SPUR TRENCH - no apparent action followed.

H.F. Malleson

Head Qrs. 56th Divn.
9th May, 1917.

Lieutenant,
for Captain,
General Staff.

SECRET

**56th DIVISION TACTICAL PROGRESS REPORT No. 9
from 5 p.m. 7th May to 5 p.m. 8th May 1917.**

On receipt of current copy of Tactical Progress Report
in the trenches, previous copy to be burnt.

PART I OPERATIONS.
    Patrols. A patrol reconnoitred TOOL TRENCH between O.8.c.8.1. and O.8.c.7.4. at 2.45 a.m. and found it strongly held. There appears to be a Strong Point at O.8.c.7.4.
    The Copse in O.8. central was examined and found to be unoccupied A fixed rifle apparently in TOOL TRENCH fires through the centre of the Copse.
    CAVALRY FARM was found to be unoccupied this morning.
    Aeroplanes.- Our aircraft was very active between 5 and 8 p.m. A considerable amount of M.G. fire was directed at them.
    One of our 'planes was attacked by hostile craft but succeeded in driving the enemy Eastwards.

PART II INTELLIGENCE.
    Hostile Artillery. Very quiet last night and to-day. All guns firing seemed to be shooting at long range. Our Trench System and Communications received attention during the night. N.17.a. & c. were shelled with 4.2's and 5.9's yesterday afternoon till 8 p.m. A few 77 mm. shells fell in CAVALRY TRENCH about 2.30 p.m.
    From 10 a.m. till noon an 11" Howitzer fired four shells into GUEMAPPE at half hour intervals.
    At 6 p.m. to-night our batteries in N.17.a. and N.18.a. report that they are being heavily shelled by 5.9's at long range from direction of 80° true bearing from 18.a. central. O.13.a.9.7. is also being shelled. This lasted till about 6.50 p.m.
    Hostile Snipers. Slight activity from the direction of TOOL Trench.
    Explosions. Two enemy dumps blew up near BOIRY NOTRE DAME. The first at 6.30 p.m. and the second at 7.25 p.m. Ten explosions were heard this morning a long way behind VIS EN ARTOIS.
    Movement. Little movement could be seen to-day owing to bad visibility. A certain amount seen in and about SPUR TRENCH at 3 p.m.
    General. Several golden rain lights were fired from TOOL TRENCH while enemy's guns were firing about 7 p.m. A considerable number of his shells were falling short.

H. F. Malleson, Lieut.
for Capt.
General Staff.

Head Qrs. 56th Divn.
8th May, 1917.

SECRET.

56th DIVISION TACTICAL PROGRESS REPORT No. 8
from 5 p.m. 6th May to 5 p.m. 7th May 1917

On receipt of current copy of Tactical Progress Report
in the trenches, previous copy to be burnt.

PART I OPERATIONS.

through O.14.c. & d.

Patrols. 3 went out from CAVALRY TRENCH, proceeded about 700 yards S.E. of the Trench, but met no enemy; they reported CAVALRY FARM still being shelled by the enemy.

Artillery. Enemy movement and trenches were fired on during the day. Howitzer Batteries bombarded ROHART FACTORY, FACTORY TRENCH and LANYARD TRENCH.

Lewis Guns. Fire was directed on various points where movement had been noted during the day and in reply to M.G. fire. Bursts on ROHART FACTORY and between TOOL and LANYARD TRENCHES.

Aeroplanes. Active during the day at low altitude.

PART II INTELLIGENCE.

Hostile Artillery. Quiet. Intermittent fire directed on N.17.a, & c. with 4.2's and 5.9's during the day, and N.11.b. & d. with 5.9's during afternoon. Battery positions in N.18.a. during the night and Town of ARRAS during early hours of the morning. A few gas shells fired on ARRAS - CAMBRAI Road. Enemy guns reported firing from REMY WOOD, BOIS DU SART JIG-SAW WOOD and BOIRY NOTRE DAME.

Machine Guns. Active during the night from Copse in O.14.d. Central and INFANTRY HILL.

Snipers. All enfilade. One located in a tree in Copse O.2.d.9.5.

Movement. Little movement was observed during the day. Enemy observed in trench about O.14.b.61.50. apparently used for observation. Germans seen to walk one by one from SPUR Trench to TOOL Trench at intervals during the day. Observed repairing wire from about O.8.d.1.1. to TOOL TRENCH. Runners seen going to Chalk Pit in O.15.c.2.8. from over the Crest. Individuals were seen moving about in LANYARD and POLE TRENCHES.

Aircraft. Active during the day at great altitudes. Hostile balloons were observed from N.18.a.3.1. at true bearing as follows :-

    101 degrees - descended between 12.30 and 1.30 p.m.
    106   ")
    109.30 ") Up for short periods at a time
    117.30 ") throughout the day.

Work. The following work was carried out by us on night 6/7th inst.- 370 yards of fire trench were widened and deepened to 4' 6" from approximately O.13.b.8.5. to O.13.d.7.7. Fire-steps left in eight bays. 56 yards of fire trench were dug 3 ft. deep running S.W. from above. 30 yds. of fire trench were dug 2 ft. deep running S. from end of KNIFE TR. at

Head Qrs. 56th Divn. O.8.c.5.5.
7th May, 1917.

H. F. Malleson.
Lieut.
for Captain,
General Staff.

SECRET.

56th DIVISION TACTICAL PROGRESS REPORT No. 7.
from 5 p.m. 5th May 1917 to 5 p.m. 6th May 1917.

On receipt of current copy of Tactical Progress Report in the trenches, previous copy to be burnt.

PART I OPERATIONS.

PATROLS. A patrol tried to enter CAVALRY FARM during daylight, but was unable to approach owing to heavy M.G. fire from INFANTRY HILL and TOOL TRENCH. A second patrol was successful and found the farm unoccupied by the enemy, but was forced to withdraw owing to severe hostile shelling. The enemy shells the farm intermittently.

A patrol reconnoitred TOOL Tr. in O.8.c. and O.14.a at midnight and found it strongly held.

ARTILLERY. Our artillery fired in answer to S.O.S. signal at about 9-30 p.m. last night and as usual during the day. Seven direct hits were obtained on a suspected M.G. emplacement in TOOL Tr. about O.8.c.7.3. The emplacement which took the form of a mound disappeared and twenty Germans were observed to run away over the open from this spot. Two stretcher cases were seen to leave later.

LEWIS GUNS. Several hostile parties near ST. ROHART'S FACTORY were dispersed by M.G. fire.

PART II INTELLIGENCE.

About 10-15 p.m. in answer to a succession of green lights the enemy opened a heavy barrage. Our artillery immediately replied; fire decreased at 11-30 p.m.

The right of front was heavily shelled at dawn to-day. During the day hostile artillery has been rather below normal. N.17.a was shelled by 5.9 Hows. all the morning. GUEMAPPE and the Railway in N.24.a and b were shelled with 5.9's and 4.2's. KNIFE Tr., CAVALRY Tr., and BULLET Tr., also N.17.d and N.18.d were intermittently shelled during the day. Fire on our trenches was much more accurate to-day than formerly.

MACHINE GUNS. Quiet. Fire reported from BOIS du VERT, INFANTRY HILL and during the night from TOOL Tr.

HOSTILE SNIPERS. Active.

ENEMY MOVEMENT. Parties in LANYARD Tr. were engaged by our artillery. Stretcher bearers were seen working backwards and forwards at O.21.b.5.9 and also on CAMBRAI ROAD at entrance to VIS EN ARTOIS. Hostile working parties seen in TOOL Tr. and ST. ROHART'S FACTORY. Transport seen on road from BOIRY moving S.E. through O.5.d. Three Germans left SPUR Tr. and entered TOOL Tr. about O.14.a.80.85. Four Germans entered TOOL Tr. at the same spot from SUNKEN Road at O.9.c.35.60: our artillery opened fire on TOOL Tr.

HOSTILE AIRCRAFT. Less active. The following call was intercepted from a German 'plane -
Ta. Ta. Ta.   GUT GUT GUT.

GENERAL.

There appears to be a trench and some wire South West of COPSE in O.16.c.85.10. O.P's suspected at O.9.a.7.3 and O.9.a.7.5.

H.Q. 56th Division.
6th May 1917.

for Captain.
General Staff.

SECRET.

56th DIVISION TACTICAL PROGRESS REPORT No.6
from 5 p.m. 4th May 1917 to 5 p.m. 5th May 1917.

On receipt of current copy of Tactical Progress Report
in the trenches, previous copy to be burnt.

Part 8 INTELLIGENCE.

Patrols. Patrol left CAVALRY TRENCH to reconnoitre CAVALRY FARM. It was found to be unoccupied, but heavy M.G. fire was experienced from the direction of TOOL TRENCH. Two patrols left CAVALRY TRENCH to reconnoitre TOOL TRENCH, but had to return owing to M.G. fire and snipers.

Artillery. Our artillery fired on enemy trenches and movement. Several Germans were shelled out of LANYARD TRENCH near CAMBRAI ROAD, and several casualties inflicted.

PART II INTELLIGENCE.

Hostile Artillery has been quiet during the last 24 hours. During the night the valleys were sprinked with gas shells. From 7.20 to 7.25 a.m. our front line was shelled from O.8.b.2.2. to O.8.b.9.2. Golden rain was sent up and range was increased. MONCHY and N.24.b. & d. were shelled at intervals during the day.

Machine Guns. Active during the night from the direction of O.2.d. & ST. ROHART FACTORY.

Movement. Considerable movement was seen during the day in FACTORY TRENCH, LANYARD TRENCH, SUNKEN ROAD O.9. Central. During the morning enemy were seen walking in twos and threes from SPUR to TOOL TRENCH; also between FACTORY TRENCH and QUARRY. A stretcher party was seen about 10.50 a.m. led by a man carrying a red cross flag moving from ST. ROHART FACTORY towards LANYARD TRENCH. Another stretcher bearer party was seen moving towards FACTORY TRENCH from O.15.a.5.0. At 11 a.m. 30 Germans were shelled in O.15.c.9.8, five casualties were caused.

Aircraft. Hostile aeroplanes crossed our lines on several occasions during the morning. A hostile balloon was located from N.24.b.8O.15. at 51° true bearing. It was on the ground.

Head Qrs. 56th Divn.
5th May, 1917.

Captain,
General Staff.

SECRET.

**56th DIVISIONAL TACTICAL PROGRESS REPORT No. 5.
from 5 p.m. 3rd May to 5 p.m. 4th May 1917.**

On receipt of current copy of Tactical Progress Report
in the trenches, previous copy to be burnt.

PART I OPERATIONS.
   Artillery. Much movement has been seen and engaged by our artillery, and enemy trenches have been shelled as usual.
   Prisoners. Early this morning a wounded officer and 15 men of the 41st I.R. were captured in CAVALRY FARM. This party was fired at from TOOL TRENCH on its way over to our lines and one German hit.

PART II INTELLIGENCE.
   Hostile Artillery. During the night gas shells were fired into WANCOURT MARLIERE N.17 and N.23. During the day STRING TRENCH N.12., N.18.c. & d. N.24.a. & b., O.7 c. & d. were all shelled intermittently.
   Between 3 and 4 p.m. hostile artillery was active against GUEMAPPE MARLIERE and the CAMBRAI Road in N.11 & 12., but on the whole hostile artillery was not nearly as active as usual.
   Sniping. There has been a certain amount of sniping N. of CAVALRY FARM.
   Movement. There has been considerable enemy movement reported during the last 24 hours. A large number of stretcher cases were seen being taken through O.29.d. and 25.c. Enemy also busy with stretchers around VIS EN ARTOIS. Wounded were being carried away from TOOL TRENCH. Considerable movement near ROHART FACTORY was successfully engaged by our artillery.
   Throughout the day there was movement in small parties along the road in O.9.b. and about LANYARD and FACTORY Trenches
   General. A probable O.P. was located in O.15.b.25.90. Two pigeons were released from about O.15.c.2.8. When VIS EN ARTOIS was shelled by heavies this afternoon a large number of Germans were seen to run out of the Village to the WOOD in O.21.b. and d.
   Aircraft. At 4.20 p.m. two enemy planes over MONCHY appeared to be directing a shoot by hostile heavies on N.11.b.

John D. Crosthwaite Capt.

Head Qrs. 56th Divn.
4th May, 1917.

General Staff.

SECRET.

56th DIVISIONAL TACTICAL PROGRESS REPORT No.4
from 5. 0 p.m. 1st May to 5. 0 p.m. 2nd May 1917.

On receipt of current copy of Divisional Tactical Progress Report in the trenches, previous copy to be burnt.

PART I OPERATIONS.
    Artillery. Our artillery fired on German trenches and movement Visibility good.
    Patrols. At 1 a.m. 1 Officer 1 Sgt. and 2 men patrolled CAVALRY TRENCH going in a North-easterly direction. The enemy were not encountered.

PART II INTELLIGENCE.
    Hostile Artillery. The enemy artillery active during the day, the following points being shelled intermittently:-
        LES FOSSES FARM from 8 a.m. to 12.45 p.m.
        STRING TR " 12.15 p.m. to 3 p.m.
    O.25.d.2.8.
        WANCOURT - Battery in O.12.a.
    8" Armour piercing shell fired from the direction of BOIS DU VERT fell on LES FOSSES FARM. The shells burst 14 secs. after the report of the gun was heard in N.11.b.
    Movement. Men were seen passing along TOOL TRENCH at intervals during the day.
    A working party in FACTORY TRENCH O.15.b. was dispersed by our artillery. Men seen later during the day in this vicinity displayed considerable nervousness and at 9.55 a.m. four men were seen carrying a stretcher in Southerly direction behind FACTORY TRENCH.
    Movement was also seen at the following points :-
        BOIS DU VERT
        QUARRY at N.15.c.2.7.
        Cross roads O.8.d.1.1.
        Ruined building O.16.d.5.0.
        Railway O.15.a.3.2. to PIT TRENCH.
    General. Enemy appeared to be nervous during the night, constantly firing Very Lights.
    Strong Point is reported at O.15.c.40.75.
    Six enemy balloons were up early this morning.

Head Qrs. 56th Divn.
2nd May, 1917.

                Captain,
                Intelligence, General Staff.

SECRET.

**56th DIVISION TACTICAL PROGRESS REPORT No. 3
from 5 p.m. 30th April to 5 p.m. 1st May, 1917.**

On receipt of current copy of Divisional Tactical
Progress Report, previous copy to be burnt.

PART I OPERATIONS.
   Artillery.   Active all the day.   Enemy trenches were shelled and registration carried out.   From 12.50 to 1 p.m. our Howitzers shelled VIS EN ARTOIS, and also carried out a shoot with gas shells.   From 4 a.m. to 4.8 a.m. our practice barrage was put down as ordered by Corps.
   Machine Guns.   During the practice barrage this morning M.Gs. co-operated along their barrage lines.
   Sniping.   Our snipers fired on movement about CAVALRY FARM and on CAMBRAI Road, but no hits can be claimed definitely.

PART II INTELLIGENCE.
   Hostile Artillery.   Slightly above normal - 5.9's and 4.2's were active against N.12. N.11 and N.13.a.   From 4.10 to 4.45 a.m. a fairly heavy barrage was put down in N.18.a. At 3 p.m. WANCOURT and N.17.a. were heavily shelled by Field Guns. Between 2 and 2.30 p.m. front line area was heavily shelled with 4.2's and 5.9's.   In reply to our practice barrage this morning hostile barrage called for by Red Flares was put down behind our front line, and hostile M.Gs. traversed our front line trenches at the same time, most of the shooting appeared to be high.
   Patrols.   Small patrols were dispersed at dawn and dusk by L.G. fire.
   Movement.   Movement was seen near strong point O.8.b.15.10. Two men were seen crawling along trench at O.14.a.8.1.   At 3 pm. smoke was seen in trench at O.14.a.85.30 and earth was thrown over the parapet here.   Men were seen to enter LANYARD TRENCH singly and in two's during the day.   Slight movement was seen E. and immediately W. of BOIS DU VERT.
   Aircraft.   Hostile aeroplanes over our lines at 5.30 a.m. 10.30 a.m. and 4.30 p.m. and were seen to drop white lights.
   At 7.45 p.m. enemy balloon was seen on the ground probably about J.31.d.3.5.

Head Qrs. 56th Divn.
1st May, 1917.

Captain,
Intelligence, General Staff.

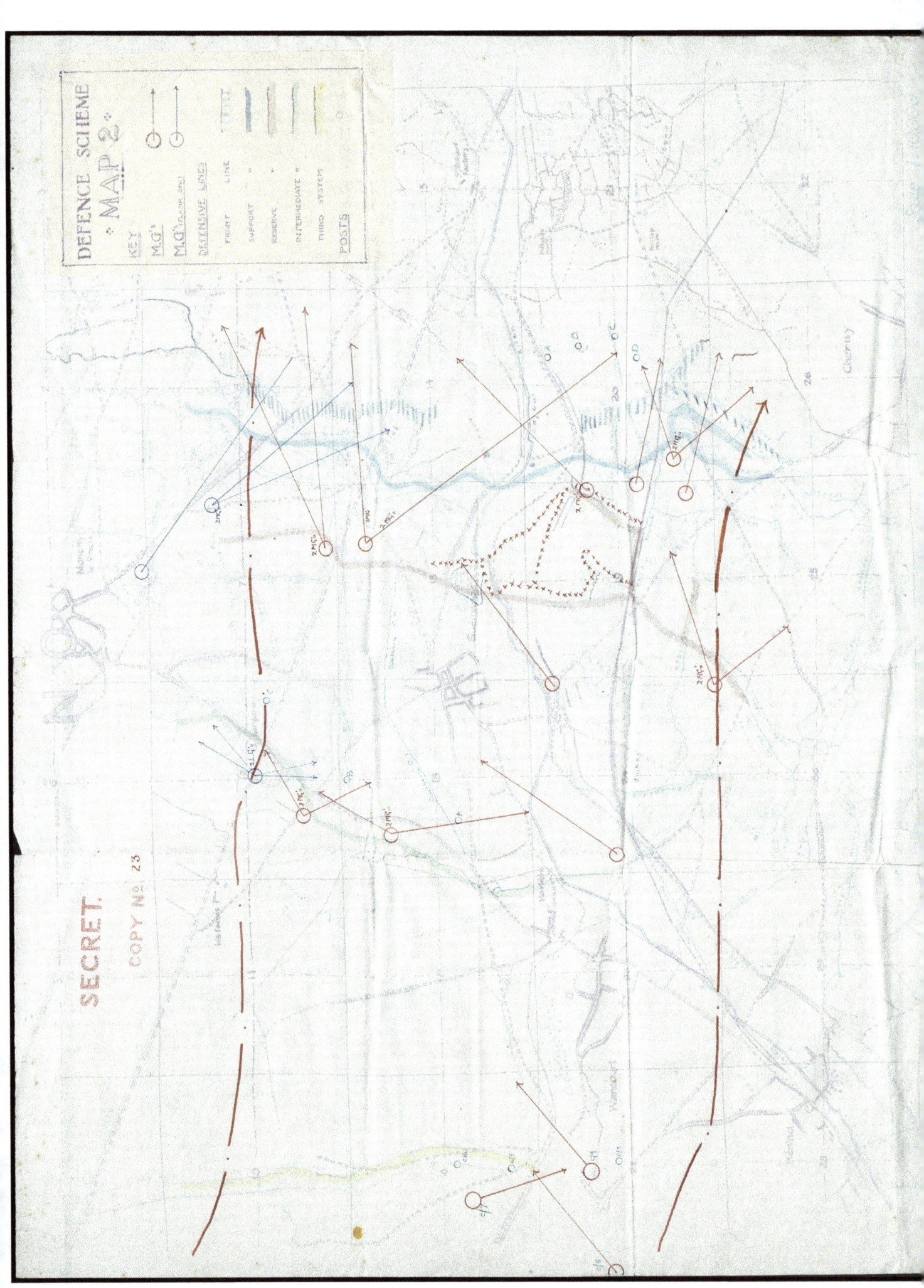

GLOSSARY.

Abbaye, Abb⁰	Abbey
Abreuvoir, Ab⁰	Watering place
Abri de douanes	Customs-shelter
Aciérie	Steel works
Aiguilles	Points (Ry.)
Allée	Alley, Narrow road
Ancien - ne, Ancⁿ	Old
Aqueduc	Aqueduct
Arbre	Tree
,, éventail	,, fan-shaped
,, décharné	,, bare
,, fourchu	,, forked
,, isolé	,, isolated
,, penché	,, leaning
Arbrisseau	Small tree
Arc	Arch
Ardoisière, Ard⁰	Slate quarry
Arrêt	Halt
Asile	Asylum
,, d' aliénés	Lunatic asylum
,, de charité	
,, des pauvres	
,, de refuge	Asylum
Auberge, Aub⁰	Inn
Aune	Alder-tree
Bac	Ferry
,, à taille	
Bains	Baths
Place aux bains	Bathing place
Balise	Boom, Beacon
Banc de sable	Sand-bank
,, ,, vase	Mud-bank
Baraque	Hut
Barrage	Dam
Barrière	Gate, Stile
(Machine à) Bascule	Weigh-bridge
Bassin	Dock, Pond
,, d'échouage	Tidal dock
Bassin de radoub	Dry dock
Bateau phare	Light-ship
Blanchisserie	Laundry
B.M. (borne militaire)	Mile stone
B⁰ décime (kilométrique)	
Boulangerie	
Fab⁰ de boulons	Bolt Factory
Boue	Buoy
Brasserie, Brass⁰	Brewery
Briqueterie, Briq⁰	Brickfield
Brise-lames	Breakwater
Bureau de poste	Post office
,, de douane	Custom house
Butte	Butt, Mound
Cabane	Hut
Cabaret, Cab⁰	Inn
Câble sous-marin	Submarine cable
Calvaire, Calv⁰	Calvary
Canal de dessèchement	Drainage canal
Canal d'irrigation	Irrigation canal
Fab⁰ de caoutchouc	Rubber factory
Carrière, Carr⁰	Quarry
,, de gravier	Gravel-pit
Caserne	Barracks
Champ de courses	Race course
,, manœuvres	Drill-ground
,, tir	Rifle range
Chantier	Building yard
,,	Ship yard
Chantier de construction	Slip-way
Chapelle, Ch⁰⁰	Chapel
Charbonnage	Colliery
Château d'eau	Water tower
Chaussée	Causeway
Chemin de fer	Railway
Cheminée, Ch⁰⁰	Chimney
Chêne	Oak tree
Cimetière, Cim⁰⁰	Cemetery
Clocher	Belfry
Clouterie	Nail factory
Colombier	Dove-cot
Corne	
Cour des marchandises	
Couvent	Convent
Crassier	
Croix	Cross
Darse	
Démoli - e	
Détruit - e, Dét⁰	
Déversoir	
Digue	
Distillerie, Dist⁰⁰	
Douane	
Bureau de douane	
Entrepôt de douane	
Dynamitière, Dynam⁰⁰	
Dynamiterie	
Écluse	
Échauette, Ech⁰⁰	
École	
Écurie	
Église	
Écrailleric	
Embarcadère, Emb⁰⁰	
Estaminet, Estam⁰	
Étang	
Fabrique, Fab⁰	
Fab⁰ de produits chimiques	
Fab⁰ de faïence	
Faïencerie	
Ferme, F⁰⁰	
Filature, Fil⁰⁰	
Fonderie, Fond⁰⁰	
Fontaine, Font⁰⁰	
Forêt	
Forme de radoub	
Forge	
Fosse	
Four	
,, à chaux	

Remblai	Embankment
Remise des Machines	Engine-shed
aux	
Réservoir, Rés⁰	Reservoir
Route cavalière	Bridle road
Rubanerie	Ribbon Factory
Ruine	
Ruines	Ruin
En ruine	
Ruiné - e	
Sablière	Sand-pit
Schlemmerie, Schlem⁰⁰	
Sapin	Fir tree
Saule	Willow tree
Saunerie	Salt-works
Scierie, Sc⁰	Saw-mill
Sondage	Boring
Source	Spring
Sucrerie, Suc⁰	Sugar factory
Tannerie	Tannery
Tir à la cible	Rifle range
Tissage	Weaving mill
Tôlerie	Rolling mill
Tombeau	Tomb
Tour	Tower
Tourbière	Peat-bog, Peat-bed
Tourelle	Small tower
Tuilerie	Tile works
Usine à gaz	Gas works
,, électrique	Electricity works
,, métallurgique	Metal works
,, à agglomérés	Briquette factory
Verrerie, Verr⁰⁰	Glass works
Viaduc	Viaduct
Vivier	Fish Pond
Voie de chargement	
,, déchargement	
,, d'évitement	Siding
,, formation	
,, manœuvre	
Zinguerie	Zinc works

SECRET.

ADDENDUM No. 2 to
56th DIVISION ORDER No. 96.

56th Divn. No. G. 3/315.
Copy No. 25

17th May 1917.

Ref. attached Sketch Map.

1. The Divisional Machine Gun Officer will arrange as follows with the Brigadier-General Commanding 167th Infantry Brigade for the co-operation of 167th Bde. M.G.Coy. and its attached guns of 193rd Div. M.G.Coy. in the Machine Gun barrage scheme of 29th Division :-

   (a) 4 guns (only 2 firing at a time) from a position about N.12.b.94. to form a barrage East of the Northern portion of the BOIS DU VERT.

   (b) 2 guns - from positions S. of the COJEUL RIVER, to form a barrage E. & S.E. of the Southern portion of the BOIS DU VERT.

2. The Sketch Map attached shows the barrage lines. Details will be communicated by the Divisional M.G.Officer.

3. The guns allotted for this barrage should be laid on these lines throughout the attack, during the night 19th/20th inst. and until no longer required by Brigadier-General Commanding 167th Infantry Brigade.

4. The above arrangements are additional to those ordered in para. 9 (a) 56th Division Order No. 96.

5. ACKNOWLEDGE.

John D. Crosthwaite Capt
for Lieut-Colonel,
General Staff.

Issued at

Copy No.			
1.	167th Infantry Bde.	14.	56th Div. Signals.
2.	188th Infantry Bde.	15.	56th Div. Train.
3.	169th Infantry Bde.	16.	56th Div. Gas Officer.
4.	14th Division.	17.	D.A.D.O.S.
5.	29th Division.	18.	4th Aust.Div.S.Col.
6.	VI Corps H.A.	19.	No.2 Amm.Sub Park.
7.	VI Corps Arty.	20.	56th Div.M.G.Officer.
8.	No. 12 Squadron R.F.C.	21.	A.D.M.S.
9.	1/5th Cheshire Regt.	22.	A.D.V.S.
10.	C.R.A.	23.	"Q"
11.	C.R.E.	24.	A.D.C.
12.	A.P.M.	25.	War Diary.
13.	193rd Div. M.G.Coy.	26.	File.

LOCATION TABLE.

MAY	1	2	3	4	5	6	7	8	9	10	11	12	13	14	15
Div. H.Q.	ARRAS	15 Rue de la Paix													
167th Inf. Bde. H.Q.	LEFT				H.31 (Cntrl)	G.30.c								LINE	
1st Ldn. Rgt.	Reserve	R	R	Reserve										L	L
3rd. " "	Reserve	Support	L	Line	G 36			L. Support	C	C			R. Reserve	R	R
7th. M.X.	Support	L		Reserve								L. Reserve		R. Reserve	Support
8th. " "	Line	Reserve		Support				L. Support						L. Reserve	
168th Inf. Bde. H.Q.		H.31 Cntrl			Line										ARRAS
4th Ldn. Rgt.	ARRAS	HARP	N.9.a.		R	R	R	R. Support	R.	R.	R. Support	R	R	G.30.c	G 36
12th " "		O.G.L.	HARP		R. Support	R	R	L.	L.	L.	L. Support	L	L	G 36	G 36
13th " "		O.G.L.	HARP		L. Support	L	L	C.	Reserve	Reserve					
14th " "		HARP	N.3.C.		L	L	L.							G 36	
169th Inf. Bde. H.Q.	RIGHT			Reserve	H.31 (Cntrl)										
2nd Ldn. Rgt.	Support	L.	L.	Reserve	HARP										
5th Ldn. Rgt.	L.	R.	R.	Line	HARP										
9th " "	R.				N.2.c.&.d.										
13th " "		Support			Reserve			Reserve	L. Support	L. Support	R. Reserve	R. Reserve	N.2.c.&.d	R. Reserve	
		Reserve													
Div. Arty. 280 F.Bde.	Detached to VII Corps.														
281 "															
Pioneers															

LOCATION TABLE.

MAY	16	17	18	19	20	21	22	23	24	25	26	27	28	29	30	31
Div. H.Q.	ARRAS	15, Rue de la Paix				WARLUS			HABARCQ							
167th Inf. Bde. H.Q.	LINE					DAINVILLE			MONTENESCOURT							
1st Ldn. Rgt.	L	SUPPORT	R			DAINVILLE			GOUVES							
3rd " "	R	L. RESERVE	L			DAINVILLE			MONTENESCOURT							
7th Mx. "	SUPPORT	R	R	R	R	ARRAS										
8th " "	L. RESERVE	L	L	L	L	ARRAS										
168th Inf. Bde. H.Q.	ARRAS			BERNEVILLE					SIMENCOURT							
4th Ldn. Rgt.	ARRAS			BERNEVILLE					SIMENCOURT							
12th " "																
13th " "																
14th " "																
169th Inf. Bde. H.Q.	Habarcq			DUISANS					AGNEZ-lez-DUISANS							
2nd Ldn. Rgt.	HABP			DUISANS												
5th Ldn. Rgt.	HABP			DUISANS	DUISANS				AGNEZ-les-DUISANS							
9th " "	R. RESERVE															
13th " "	M2GR			DUISANS												
Div. Arty. H.Q. 280 Bde. 281 Bde.	DETACHED TO VII CORPS.															
Pioneers 2 coys. 2 coys.	LINE ARRAS					ARRAS (DETACHED TO VI CORPS)			GOUVES							

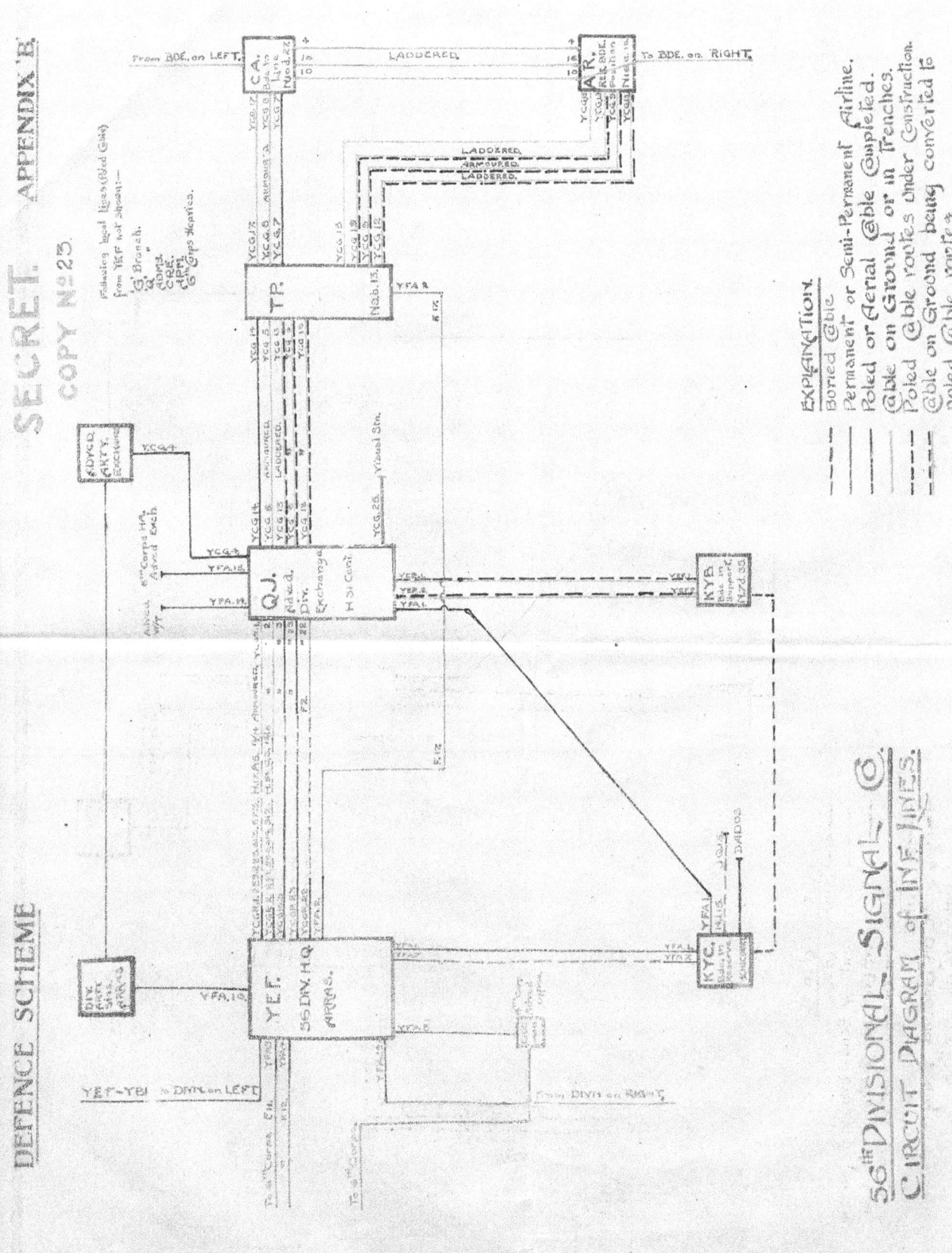

App VI

Miscellaneous

"C" Form
MESSAGES AND SIGNALS.

| Prefix | Code | Words 17 | Received From By | Sent, or sent out At To By | Office Stamp |

Handed in at ... Office 11.45 m. Received 11.57 m.

TO 56 D.W.

*Sender's Number	Day of Month	In reply to Number	AAA
G 730	12		

Following telegram Third Army begins aaa I congratulate you and your troops on the complete success of the various attacks made yesterday and this morning aaa These successes are very satisfactory not only in themselves but as showing that the enemy is beginning to weaken under the repeated heavy blows inflicted on him during all the hard fighting of the past five weeks aaa From CHIEF Ends

FROM Sixth Corps
PLACE & TIME 11.30 pm

"C" Form (Duplicate).
MESSAGES AND SIGNALS.

Army Form C. 2123.

AM RR 27

Handed in at .... Office ......m. Received ......m.

TO 5th Div'n

Sender's Number: A 726
Day of Month: 12

Corps Commander congratulates you and your Division on your success yesterday which he feels convinced you will maintain

FROM Sixth Corps
PLACE & TIME 10.30 pm

CONFIDENTIAL.

J6/17

WAR DIARY
of
GENERAL STAFF BRANCH
56th DIVISION

From 1st June 1917 to 30th June 1917.

(6202) W 11186/M1151 350,000 12/16 McA. & W., Ltd. (Est. 781) Forms/W 3091/3. Army Form W. 3091.

Cover for Documents.

Nature of Enclosures.

Notes, or Letters written.

Army Form C. 2118.

WAR DIARY
or
INTELLIGENCE SUMMARY.
(Erase heading not required.)

Instructions regarding War Diaries and Intelligence Summaries are contained in F.S. Regs. Part II. and the Staff Manual respectively. Title pages will be prepared in manuscript.

Place	Date	Hour	Summary of Events and Information	Remarks and references to Appendices
HABARCQ	June 1st.		Training. Capt. L.A.Newnham, Bde-Major, 169th Brigade went to N.Z.Division as G.S.O.2.	
	2nd.		168th Brigade Sports. Lt.Col. B.Pakenham, G.S.O.1, returned from leave.	
	3rd		Capt. Carden Roe joined 169th Brigade as Bde-Major from 29th Division.	
	4th		1st day of 167th Brigade Horse Show.	
	5th		2nd day of Horse Show. VI Corps O.O.received for relief of 61st Division in the line.	
	6th	9 pm	O.O. No.101 issued for relief.	APPENDIX I.
	7th	6 am	VI Corps O.O. for attack by 3rd Division received.	
		9 pm	O.O.No.102 issued with orders for co-operation in this attack.	APPENDIX I.
	8th 9th) 10th) 11th)		16th London Regiment moved up to reserve area. Relief was carried out without incident as detailed in O.O.101, and the command of the Sector passed to 56th Division at 10 a.m.	
ARRAS.	11th	10 am	G.O.C. 56th Division took over Command of the CAMBRAI ROAD Sector. O.O.: No.102 issued for move of 2 Bns. 168th Brigade from ARRAS to BEAURAINS CAMP. A quiet day in the Line.	APPENDIX I
	12th		A prisoner was captured by 1/16th London Regiment (Q.W.R.) on the right sub-section at dawn. Enemy artillery was active on both areas during the evening. Z day for 3rd Division attack issued.	APPENDIX I.
	13th		Zero hour for attack by 3rd Division issued. Quiet day.	APPENDIX I
	14th	7.20 am.	3rd Division attacked and took HOOK & LONG Trenches without difficulty owing to the complete surprise, capturing 175 prisoners. 56th Divn. assisted with M.G.Barrage, L.T.M. and rifle fire. Our trenches on the left were heavily shelled in connection with this operation.	

Army Form C. 2118.

WAR DIARY
or
INTELLIGENCE SUMMARY.
(Erase heading not required.)

Instructions regarding War Diaries and Intelligence Summaries are contained in F. S. Regs., Part II. and the Staff Manual respectively. Title pages will be prepared in manuscript.

Place	Date	Hour	Summary of Events and Information	Remarks and references to Appendices
	June 14th	p.m. 5.30	Hostile counter-attack was repulsed, our M.G's. and artillery co-operating. First warning of the enemy's assembly was given by the 16th London Regiment (Q.W.R.) enabling effective fire to be brought to bear immediately. 2nd London Regiment claim many casualties amongst enemy retiring near BOIS DU VERT after this attack. O.O. No. 104 for action in case of enemy withdrawal issued.	APPENDIX1.
	15th		Patrols were active to our front along the whole sector. Quiet day.	
	16th	a.m. 2-30	Enemy counter-attacked 3rd Div. line again and succeeded in driving in two advanced posts, but the whole line was maintained. The left of our line received heavy shelling during this, and our M.G's, L.G's and artillery replied vigorously. Many casualties are again claimed amongst the enemy retiring after their attack. There was heavy shelling of the trenches and back areas throughout the morning and especially on 2nd line trenches in the afternoon.	
	17th		Posts were established in isolated lengths of trenches in O.26.b. Positions for four posts in O.20.b and d were sited and routes to them laid out. Our patrols were active over the whole front. Back areas received considerable attention from hostile artillery in the morning. VI Corps Defence Scheme was received. O.O. No. 105 for relief of 169th Infantry Bde. by 168th Infantry Bde. issued.	Appendix
	18th	1 a.m.	The posts in O.20.b and d were taped and the whole front covered by them wired during the night. Two attempts were made to dislodge the enemy from a short length of trench at O.26.b.3.7 without success. A hostile attack on the posts established the night before in O.26.b was repulsed. Heavy hostile counter-attack developed against the Division on our left. Our troops opened an S.O.S. lines and swept the front attacked with L.G. The line on our immediate left was held and such enemy as had penetrated our lines were disposed of by 11 a.m. A quiet day on the divisional front. 12th Divisional Artillery came under the orders of 3rd Division at noon.	
	19th		During the night the posts in O.20.b and d were dug and garrisoned before the morning. The day was very quiet.	
	20th		Work was continued on posts without interference from the enemy. WANCOURT was heavily shelled with gas shells during the night. Except for some shelling of back areas, a quiet day.	

Army Form C. 2118.

WAR DIARY
or
INTELLIGENCE SUMMARY.
(Erase heading not required.)

Instructions regarding War Diaries and Intelligence Summaries are contained in F.S. Regs., Part II. and the Staff Manual respectively. Title pages will be prepared in manuscript.

Place	Date	Hour	Summary of Events and Information	Remarks and references to Appendices
	June 21st		Communication trenches were commenced joining back the posts in O.20.b and d to APE trench. A quiet day. 40th Bde. R.F.A., 3rd Divisional Artillery was transferred to left Division during the night.	
	22nd		A prisoner of the 458th I.R. was captured in O.20.d and several others of his party killed. He died before he could be interrogated. WANCOURT ridge was heavily shelled during the day. Divisional Defence Scheme was issued.	Appendix IV
	23rd		A prisoner of the 458th I.R. was captured in O.20.d during the night. A quiet day. 42nd Bde. R.F.A., 3rd Divisional Artillery withdrew from action during the night.	
	24th		A trench from the junction of SPOOR - JACKDAW trenches was dug between our front line, and the posts in O.20.b and d. Enemy T.M's were busy during the night, and hostile H.A. was active on back areas, especially along the CAMBRAI Road.	
	25th		A quiet day. Work was continued on the new trench. VI Corps O.O. for the relief of the 56th Division by flank Divisions received.	
	26th		Hostile artillery was fairly active during the period.	
		p.m. 9.0	O.O. No. 106 for 12th Division to take over portion of Divisional area on the left issued.	Appendix I
	27th		Hostile artillery was active against the WANCOURT ridge. A considerable number of H.V. guns were firing. The relief of the 61st Divisional Artillery by 9th Divisional Artillery was completed during the night.	
	28th	a.m. 2.0	The enemy attacked our posts in O.26.b. The attack on the N. post was repulsed, but the garrison of the S. post was forced to withdraw. The post was immediately re-occupied, but one of our men was found to be missing. A quiet day.	
	29th	noon	Nothing to report in the line. C.R.A. 9th Divisional Artillery took over command of Artillery covering the Division from C.R.A., 56th Division.	

Army Form C. 2118.

WAR DIARY
or
INTELLIGENCE SUMMARY.

(*Erase heading not required.*)

Instructions regarding War Diaries and Intelligence Summaries are contained in F. S. Regs., Part II. and the Staff Manual respectively. Title pages will be prepared in manuscript.

Place	Date	Hour	Summary of Events and Information	Remarks and references to Appendices
	June 29th		56th Div. O.O. No. 107 issued with orders for relief of the Division in the line.	Appendix I
	30th		A quiet day.	

[signature]

Captain,
General Staff.
56th Division.

SECRET.

56th Divn. G.3/355.

56th DIVISION.

Narrative of operations from 28th April to 21st May 1917.

MOVES.

27th April. On 27th April 167th Infantry Brigade relieved the Reserve Brigade of 15th Division.

On the night 28th/29th it relieved the two leading Brigades of the 15th Division, 169th Infantry Brigade taking its place in Support, while 168th Infantry Brigade had moved into ARRAS in Reserve during the day.

29th April. The command of the line was taken over by 56th Division at 10 a.m. on 29th and on the same night, 169th Infantry Brigade took over from 167th Infantry Brigade the right section of the line, the dividing line being the ARRAS - CAMBRAI Road.

30th April. 56th Division Order No. 88 was issued on the 30th for the attack on 3rd May.

2nd May. On the evening of the 2nd May 168th Infantry Brigade was moved up out of ARRAS, two battalions being in or about THE HARP and two in the old German line East of ARRAS. The 169th and 167th Infantry Brigades also concentrated that night for the attack on the next morning, their final dispositions being :-

On the right -- 169th Infantry Brigade.
    Right front Battalion - 5th London Regiment.
    Left   "   "   - 2nd   "   "
    Support   - 9th   "   "
    Reserve   - 16th "   "

On the left -- 167th Infantry Brigade.
    Right front battalion - 1st London Regiment.
    Left   "   "   - 7th Middlesex Regt.
    Support   - 3rd London Regiment.
    Reserve   - 8th Middlesex Regt.

A sketch map is attached showing the assembly areas, dividing lines between Brigades and the objective.

OPERATIONS OF 3rd MAY.

3rd May. Zero hour was 3.45 a.m., it being then dark, and no reports were received for a considerable time.

169th Infantry Brigade.

At 5.15 a.m. a F.O.O. reported that our men could be seen digging in in front of ST.ROHART FACTORY and that 14th Division on the right appeared to have reached its objective.

At 7 a.m. the Brigade reported that the 2nd London Regiment had two platoons and four Machine Guns in the trench S.E. of CAVALRY FARM, but that the enemy appeared to be holding TOOL Trench.

/The

The 2nd London Regiment was also holding a portion of LANYARD Trench, and more of the same Battalion, together with 5th London Regiment were in Trench N.15.a.0.5. to the CAMBRAI Road. The 5th London Regiment was also holding a Trench close to the PIT near ST.ROHART FACTORY.

No further news was received until 10.45 a.m. when 169th Infantry Brigade reported that bombers of the 9th London Regiment had rushed CAVALRY FARM after a bombardment by Stokes Mortars - they had bombed the dug-outs and taken 22 prisoners, and were proceeding to bomb up TOOL Trench, to aid in which 4.5" Howitzers were turned on the trench in front of them.

At 10.50 a.m. 3rd Division asked for our guns to lift off TOOL Trench as they had troops in it who were going to bomb Southwards and at 11.35 a.m. they reported that they held that trench at the Northern end to East of the COPSE in O.8 Central

At 3.50 p.m., however, it was confirmed that the enemy was holding the whole of TOOL Trench, and that the 3rd Division was in touch with 7th Middlesex Regiment in our original line. Meanwhile at 11.50 a.m. the 14th Division on our right reported that both their attacking Brigades were being heavily counter-attacked and had been driven back, and at 12.30 p.m. it reported that it was in its original line. About the same time 169th Infantry Brigade reported that it had no troops North of the ARRAS-CAMBRAI Road, but that it still held the trench immediately West of the PIT in O.15.c.

The situation, therefore, was that while the troops on the right and left were back on their original line, 169th Brigade held a narrow wedge of ground at the bottom of a valley and projecting about 1,000 yards forward, and very open to attack from the high ground on either flank. This wedge, however, was occupied until after dark when the enemy bombarded the whole front very heavily, and at 11.15 p.m. it was reported that the 2nd and 5th London Regiments had been driven in.

The General Officer Commanding 169th Infantry Brigade was, therefore, ordered to hold our original front line and to re-organise, and he issued the necessary orders to carry this out. Before these orders reached the 2nd and 5th London Regiments, however, they had organised a fresh advance and pushed out and re-occupied all the ground they had won during the day except CAVALRY FARM, where the Germans appeared to be holding the line of the CAMBRAI Road as a T - head to the South end of TOOL Trench.

This prevented all communication with the troops who were forward, except along the bottom of the valley, and the troops were therefore withdrawn an hour before sunrise, in accordance with the previous orders. During this period an officer and 15 Germans came out and surrendered in the neighbourhood of CAVALRY FARM.

187th Infantry Brigade.

At 5.54 a.m. it was reported that the 7th Middlesex Regiment had met with heavy Machine Gun and Rifle fire and failed to reach TOOL Trench.

/At

At 6.40 a.m. a wounded officer of 1st London Regiment reported that his Battalion had made two attacks but was each time driven back by Machine Gun fire, and that it was back in its original trenches.

The 168th Infantry Brigade was ordered at 7.10 a.m. to move two Battalions up to the WANCOURT LINE and two Battalions to THE HARP in view of the uncertainty as to the situation on the front of the 167th Infantry Brigade and the fact that the casualties were reported to be heavy.

At 8.55 a.m. it was reported that the Reserve Bn. (8th Middlesex Regiment) was prevented from moving up by a heavy hostile barrage.

During the morning it was reported that numbers of Germans could be seen reinforcing TOOL Trench along STIRRUP LANE, and these were dealt with by field and heavy artillery.

At one time (10.25 a.m.) it was thought that the enemy was retiring from the BOIS DU VERT as a large number were seen moving S.E. from there, and, with a view to taking advantage of any opportunity, the Reserve Battalion was kept in readiness; but there was no sign of any weakening of the enemy on our immediate front. There was no further incident of note on the front of this Brigade - it was pinned to its original ground by M.G. and Artillery fire and had many of its troops lying out in shell holes about 80 yards from TOOL TRENCH.

Some small parties did undoubtedly pass over TOOL Trench and reached LANYARD Trench, but they were completely cut off and were never able to gain touch with the 169th Infantry Brigade on the right.

General Notes.

(a) There is an unanimous opinion that Zero hour was too early.

In the dark, signals to advance cannot be seen, nor can whistle signals be heard owing to the bombardment. Consequently Officers could only pass the order to advance down the extended line, and, as each man advanced as he received the order, the waves became zig-zag in shape with the officers at the forward points.

(b) In one instance a tape was laid out in front of our front line. This was found a great help in correcting the alignment and in assisting the direction, there being no landmarks visible.

(c) The barrage was very good, but the pace (100 yards in 3 minutes) too slow considering the dry state of the ground.

There is a natural inclination among assaulting troops to reach their objective as quickly as possible, and so the rear waves push on while the leading wave is kept back by the barrage. This tends to dangerous thickening of the line and to premature mixing of units.

For the first part of the advance, at any rate, a pace of 100 yards in 2 minutes would be better on dry soil: the barrage could lessen its rate of advance later

/as

as the Infantry get less fresh.

(d) Mopping up is still of great importance. CAVALRY FARM was not properly mopped up, two separate parties of prisoners being captured in the vicinity long after the leading wave had passed beyond it.

It is thought that TOOL Trench also had Machine Guns in it which came up after the leading wave passed, but there is little doubt that the bombardment had made the trench unrecognisable as such, and the darkness was against proper "Mopping Up".

(e) A good many Germans were found killed by the bombardment and many more were disposed off by the bayonet and rifle fire by 169th Infantry Brigade, of which all ranks were satisfied that they had inflicted heavier losses than they had themselves sustained.

(f) The PIT contained several M.Gs. and at least one Light Trench Mortar. Two M.Gs. were found blown up by 4.5" Howitzers which had made excellent practice here.

(g) No hostile M.Gs. or Infantry were met with along the COJEUL RIVER, along which a flanking platoon had been sent especially to deal with such a situation.

(h) S.E. of CAVALRY FARM the CAMBRAI Road is embanked 7 ft. or 8 ft., but it is swept by fire from the direction of ST.ROHART FACTORY, and troops who formed a defensive flank along it suffered severely from enfilade fire.

(i) The enemy was found to be occupying shell-holes in front of his trenches as well as the trenches themselves.

4th - 10th May.

During this period 168th Infantry Brigade took over the line from 167th and 169th Infantry Brigades, the relief being complete on the morning of 5th May.

One Battalion of 167th Infantry Brigade and one from 169th Infantry Brigade remained attached to 168th Infantry Brigade.

The Divisional front was re-adjusted in accordance with orders from VI Corps, the 168th Infantry Brigade taking over from 3rd Division additional frontage as far North as O.8.a.8.8.; this was completed by 5 a.m. 7th May.

Our patrols endeavoured on several occasions to enter TOOL Trench, but on each occasion found it held by the enemy in some strength.

Much work was done in deepening trenches, improving and constructing communication trenches and wiring.

On 9th May, 56th Division Order No. 92 was issued for an attack to be made on TOOL Trench on the evening of 11th inst.

During the whole of this period the German Artillery was active.

11th May. — Operations of 11th May.

The attack by 168th Infantry Brigade on TOOL Trench was carried out at 8.30 p.m.

/For

For two days previously, the trench was systematically kept under steady enfilade fire from 4.5" howitzers in N.23 which had been specially placed there for this purpose.

A steady destructive fire was kept up and great precautions were taken to prevent the enemy suspecting that an attack was intended.

A practice barrage of 18 prs. on TOOL Trench on the evening of the 10th drew a heavy hostile barrage rather quickly, and it was, therefore, decided that the steady bombardment of the objective should continue up to the last possible moment, and that there should be nothing in the nature of a barrage opening at Zero hour.

The attack was carried out by the 4th London Regt. on the right, and by the 14th London Regt. (London Scottish) on the left, the dividing line being an E. and W. line between Squares O.8 and O.14.

The exact objectives were :-

(1) Trench S.E. of CAVALRY FARM, O.14.a.7.1. to O.14.a.9.3.

(2) CAVALRY FARM.

(3) TOOL Trench from the ARRAS-CAMBRAI Road O.14.a.6.5. to about O.8.b.2.2.

Except for CAVALRY FARM, the objectives were practically out of sight behind a spur which ran between the two lines.

The assault was a complete surprise to the enemy.

On the right the 4th London Regt. had very little opposition and it appeared that this part of the objective was not held in any strength.

On the left there were some casualties in the Left Company of the London Scottish from machine gun fire from a N.E. direction, but the actual occupants of the trench made little resistance.

Six machine guns were captured (one of these by a gun team of 168th M.G. Coy., which at once turned the gun on the enemy).

A party of about 50 Germans broke and fled, but were caught by Lewis gun, machine gun and rifle fire in the open, and practically annihilated.

A considerable number of German dead were found in the trench, and 11 unwounded prisoners taken.

As soon as the trench was captured a block was formed at the North end by filling it in for about 40 yards, and the position was consolidated, while the portion of the trench north of the objective was kept under steady fire by artillery and Stokes Mortars, and a slow sweeping barrage placed in front to prevent counter-attack, either by bombing from the north or over the open ground from the east.

The trench was also thinned out by withdrawing to our original line after dark troops in excess of the numbers required for the garrison.

The principal lessons of this small operation appear to be :-

    (a)   The efficacy and demoralising effect of a steady observed enfilade bombardment by howitzers.

    (b)   The advantage to be gained by frequently altering the hour of an attack, the enemy having become accustomed to attacks at dawn.

    (c)   The advisability of occasionally doing without an 18 pr. creeping barrage opening at Zero. In this case the enemy barrage came down on our front line some 3 or 4 minutes after our assaulting troops had left it. Although 6 m.g's. were captured in the trench, some were taken unmounted and none were used effectively.

    (d)   The limiting of one's objective when the enemy is plentifully supplied with artillery.

12th - 17th May   During the nights of 11th-12th May, three communication trenches were dug connecting our old front line with TOOL Trench and the latter was strengthened.

167th Inf. Brigade (with 1 Bn. 169th Inf. Bde. attached) relieved 168th Inf. Brigade (with 1 Bn. each of 167th and 169th Inf. Brigades attached) between the nights 12th-13th and 14th-15th May.

Considerable work was carried out repairing and deepening trenches, and active patrolling was carried out.

18th May   At 9.20 p.m. 18th May, 167th Inf. Brigade carried out a bombing attack on the northern portion of TOOL Trench with a view to capturing it as far north as O.8.b.55.50.

This attack was carried out by 8th Middlesex Rgt., who attempted a surprise attack. They started by successfully passing the block (where the trench had been filled in for 40 yards at the northernmost point previously captured), and made good another 30 yards; but they came up against very strong opposition and were unable to progress, and having fought for an hour and suffered some 10 to 15 casualties, they withdrew, bombers covering the party while the wounded were removed.

As the element of surprise had gone, no further attempt was made.

As a reconnaissance on the night 17th/18th showed that the trench appeared to be only held by about 6 posts of 4 men each, and as this attack came up at once against strong resistance and enemy were seen both in front of and behind TOOL Trench, it appears likely that the Germans were also contemplating a surprise attack, which was frustrated by ours.

/The

- 7 -

The Officer in command of the party is satisfied that the enemy had many casualties as the trench was full of Germans and cries were heard when our rifle grenades fell among them.

19th May At 9 p.m. 19th May, an attack was carried out by 167th Infantry Brigade on :-

(1) TOOL Trench from our block about O.8.b.2.2. to its junction with HOOK Trench and LONG Trench about O.8.b.55.45.

(2) HOOK trench from junction with TOOL Trench to about O.8.b.50.95.

(3) LONG Trench from junction with TOOL Trench to O.8.b.99.95.

The 29th Division on our left was to capture the continuation of (2) and (3) on INFANTRY HILL, the BOIS DES AUBEPINES and DEVILS TRENCH. The attack was made under an 18-pdr. barrage which, opening at Zero and remaining on TOOL and HOOK Trenches till Zero plus 5 minutes crept forward at the rate of 100 yards in 2 minutes till it reached a line just West of the BOIS DU VERT.

Behind the 18-pdr. barrage other batteries swept ground from which Machine Gun fire was likely. The B.G.C. entrusted the carrying out of the attack to the 8th Middlesex Regiment, and placed at the disposal of the Officer Commanding that Battalion two Companies of 1st London Regiment for the purpose of holding our original line in the event of the attack being successful.

Owing to the late hour and the dust from the barrage, observation of the attack was not obtained and for a long time no reports were received as there was a failure to establish visual signalling and all telephone lines in advance of Battalion H.Q. were cut.

At 1.25 a.m. Brigadier-General Commanding 167th Infantry Brigade reported that he had received a message timed 1 a.m. from O.C. 8th Middlesex Regiment that the attack had failed and that our troops were back in their own trenches. He also believed from reports received that the attack of 29th Division on our left had also failed.

From reports subsequently received our troops reached the first objective in the centre, but not on the flanks and were subjected to heavy bombing attacks. All the Officers became casualties and our men were finally forced to withdraw after sustaining casualties of about 40% of the attacking force.

At 5.30 a.m. the 29th Division confirmed this and reported that their line was then the same as before the attack.

19th - 20th May. On the 19th May, 112th and 111th Brigades of 37th Divn. relieved 169th and 168th Infantry Brigades respectively.

On the early morning of 20th and on the night 20th/21st

/May

May 112th Brigade relieved 167th Brigade in the line, the 111th moving up to the Support Area.

The command of the line was handed over at 10 a.m. on 21st inst.

General.

During the time the Division was in the line the following casualties were sustained. -

Period.	Killed. O.	Killed. O.R.	Wounded. O.	Wounded. O.R.	Missing O.	Missing O.R.	Total. O.	Total. O.R.
29th April - 2nd May.	-	35	5	130	-	6	5	171
3rd May.	9	115	18	683	10	192	37	990
4th May - 10th May.	7	85	11	285	2	16	20	386
11th May - 12th May.	5	41	4	136	-	14	9	191
13th May - 18th May.	3	54	1	141	-	10	4	205
19th May.	1	3	1	36	1	15	3	54.
20th May.	-	2	1	11	-	-	1	13
21st May.	-	6	-	6	-	-	-	12
TOTALS.	25	341	41	1428	13	253	79	2022

22nd May, 1917.

C. Hull Major-General,
Commanding 56th Division.

Distribution
167 }
168 } Bdes
169 }
CRA
CRE
'Q'
1 per Battalion.
1/5 Cheshires.

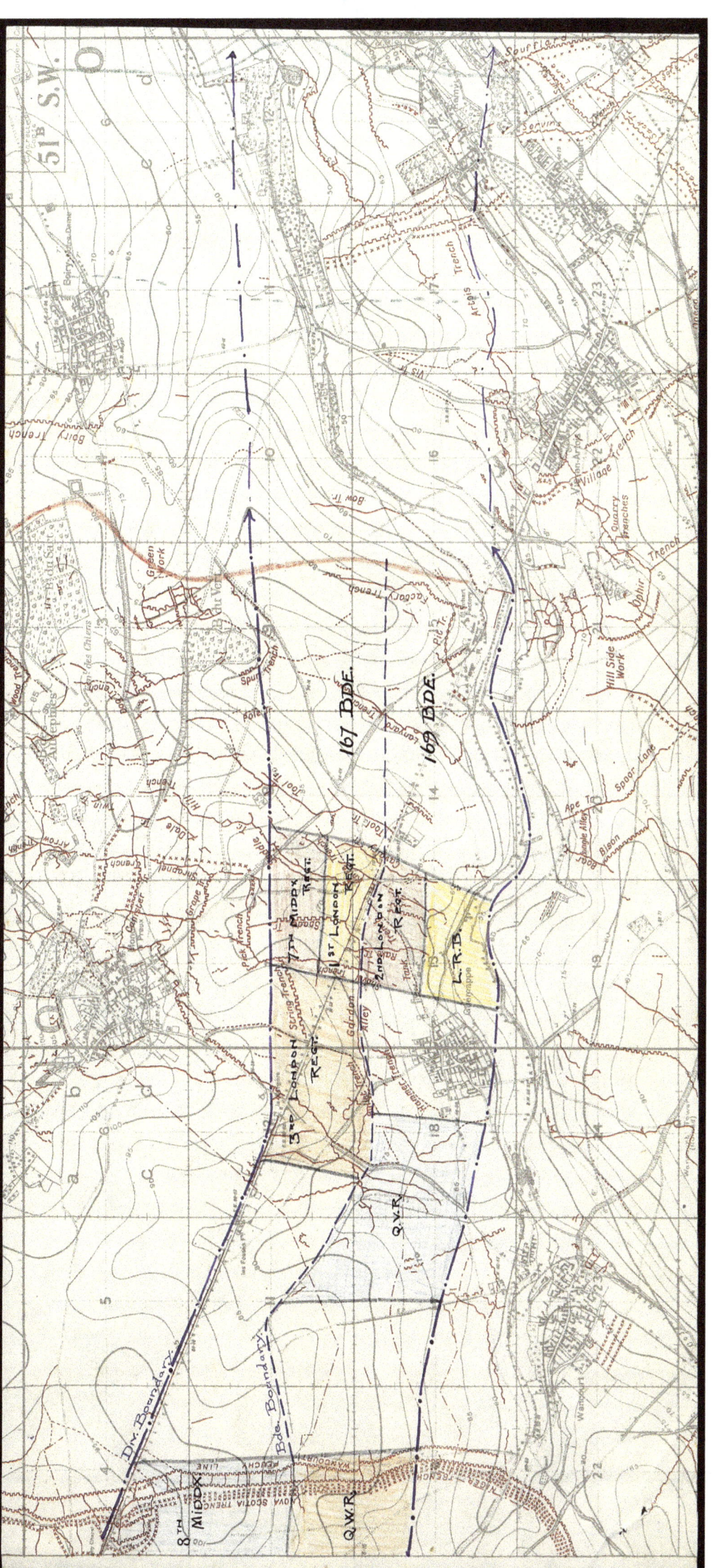

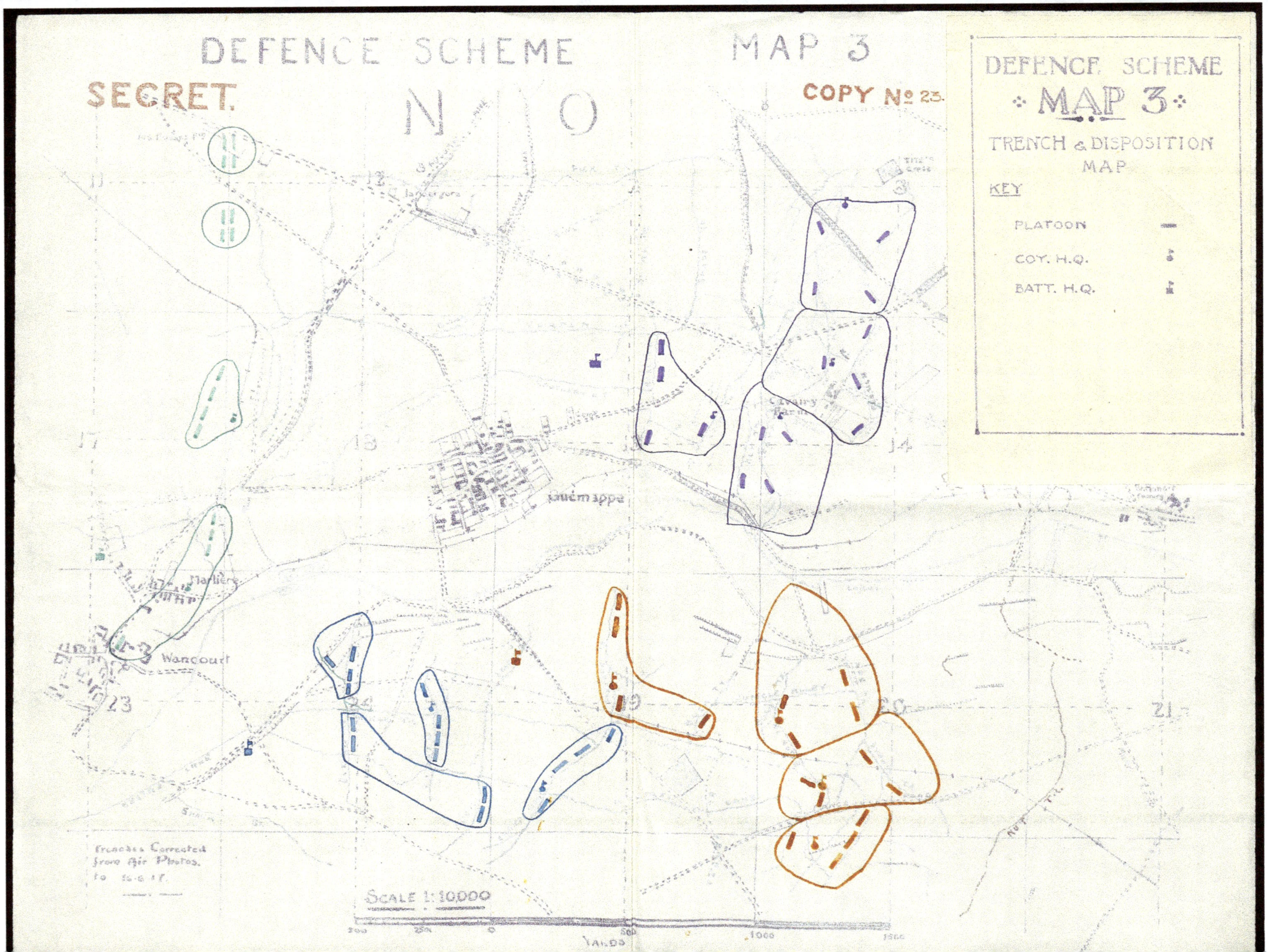
DEFENCE SCHEME MAP 3
SECRET.
COPY No 23.
N
O
DEFENCE SCHEME
MAP 3
TRENCH & DISPOSITION MAP
KEY
PLATOON
COY. H.Q.
BATT. H.Q.
Guémappe
Wancourt
Marlière
Cavalry Farm
13
14
15
17
18
19
20
21
23
24
Trenches Corrected from Air Photos. to 16.6.17.
SCALE 1:10,000
YARDS
0
500
1000
1500

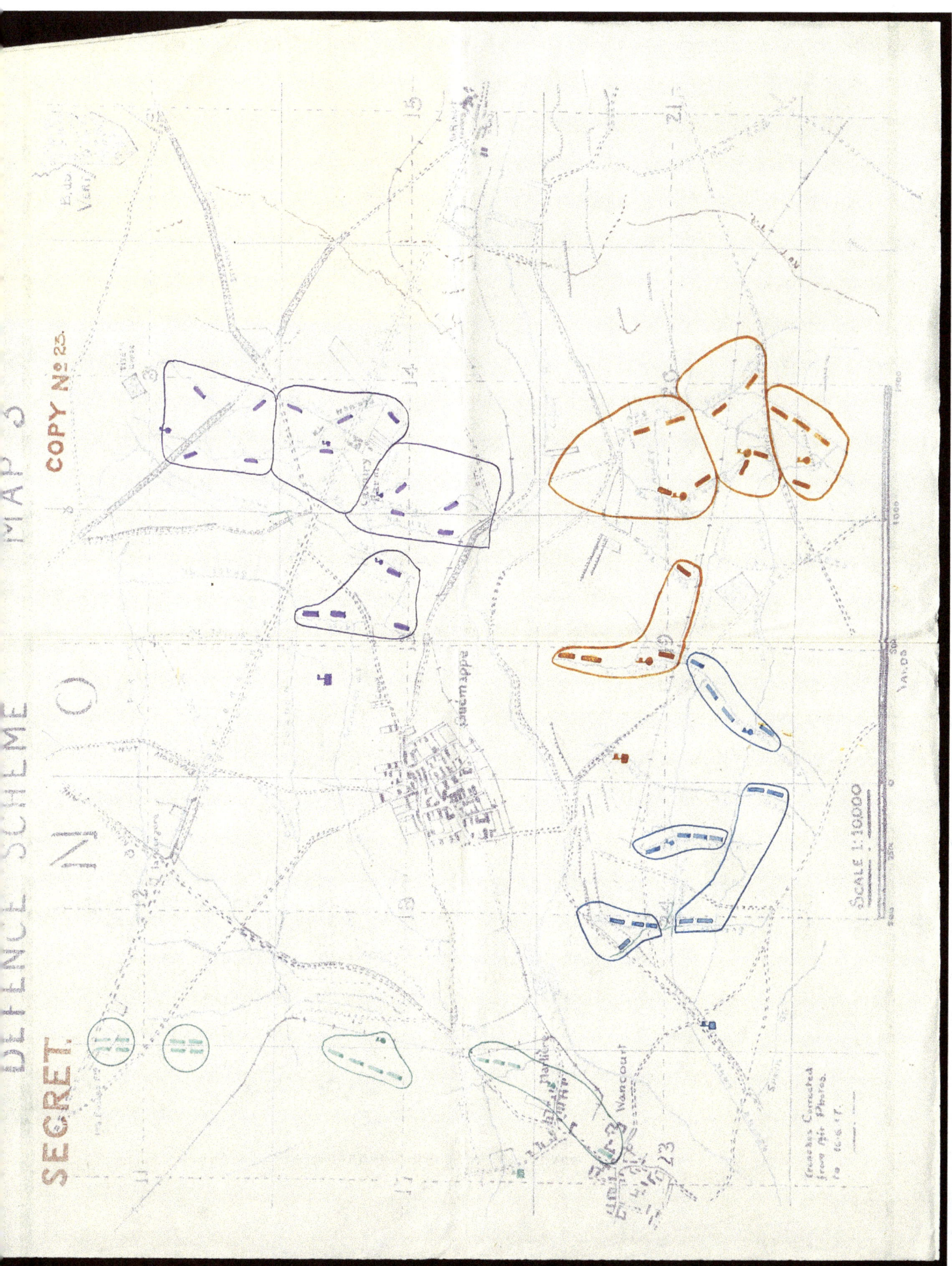

SECRET.   Copy No. 23

DEFENCE   SCHEME
for the
CAMBRAI   ROAD   or   RIGHT
DIVISIONAL SECTOR of the
VI CORPS FRONT.

ISSUED
by   *B Pakenham*
56th DIVISION   Lieut-Colonel,
JUNE 22nd, 1917,   General Staff.
   To

Copy No. 1. G.O.C.   13. "Q"
        2. VI Corps   14. 1/5th Cheshire Regt.
        3. 3rd Division.   15. Div. M.G.Officer.
        4. 12th Division.   16. Div. T.M.Officer.
        5. 18th Division.   17. 56th Div. Train.
        6. 50th Division.   18. 4th Aust.Div.S.Col
        7. G.S.O.I.   19. A.D.M.S.
        8. 167th Inf. Bde.   20. A.P.M.
        9. 168th Inf. Bde.   21. Div. Gas Officer.
       10. 169th Inf. Bde.   22. O.C. Depot Bn.
       11. C.R.A.   23. War Diary.
       12. C.R.E.   24. File.

****

1. GENERAL DESCRIPTION OF DIVISIONAL FRONT.
2. BOUNDARIES.
3. NEIGHBOURING TROOPS.
4. LINES OF DEFENCE.
5. DISTRIBUTION OF TROOPS.
6. ACTION IN CASE OF ATTACK.
7. ANTI GAS MEASURES.
8. ARTILLERY SUPPORT.
9. MACHINE GUN SUPPORT.
10. INFANTRY COMMUNICATIONS.
11. ARTILLERY COMMUNICATIONS.
12. LIAISON WITH ARTILLERY.
13. MEDICAL ARRANGEMENTS IN DIVISIONAL AREA.
14. ADMINISTRATIVE DIVISION OF DIVISIONAL AREA.
15. LIGHT TRAMWAYS.
16. LIST OF DUMPS.

1. GENERAL DESCRIPTION OF THE DIVISIONAL FRONT.

The CAMBRAI ROAD or the Right Divisional Sector of VI Corps has a frontage of 2700 yards, and lies astride of the COJEUL RIVER.

The Southern part of the line is situated on a high spur, which runs forward from WANCOURT TOWER parallel to and on the right bank of the COJEUL RIVER. This spur gives observation over the whole of the portion of the Corps front between the River and INFANTRY HILL, and its possession by us is, therefore, of the utmost importance.

The line on the left bank of the COJEUL runs up a spur towards INFANTRY HILL; the Copse at O.8 central is a point of great importance on this spur, as it overlooks the front line Southwards to the River. This copse is in the Left Divisional Sector. About 400 yards East of our front line is the BOIS DU VERT, which has a commanding view over the greater part of our system.

II & III. BOUNDARIES & NEIGHBOURING TROOPS.

The Divisional Boundary and positions of Headquarters of neighbouring Troops are found on Map No. 1.

IV. LINES OF DEFENCE.

The following Lines of Defence exist within the Divisional Boundaries :-

1. The Front Line System.
2. The Intermediate Line.
3. The old German Third Line, called the Third System.

The front line system is divided into :-

Front   - Marked in dotted Blue Lines.
Support   -   "   "   Blue.
Reserve Lines   "   "   Red.

/The

The Reserve Line South of the River has been strengthened by the inclusion of BUCK Trench into that system.

"T" heads are being constructed off KESTREL & SHIKAR LANES to :-

(a) Cover the dead ground between GANNET & EGRET.

(b) Enfilade a hostile advance between BUCK & EGRET.

The Northern face of the Bastion thus formed is being wired.

The Reserve Line South of the River is a Line of the utmost importance, and, being of great natural strength, presents a formidable obstacle to a frontal attack and enfilades a hostile advance North of the River.

The Intermediate Line. - (Marked in Green on Map) is sited on the reverse slopes and runs from LA BERGERE in front of MARLIERE, then across the River along SHIKAR to and along BUZZARD Trench.

In front of this line are 2 posts :-

A.   N.18.c.6.8.

B.   N.18.b.0.9.

Posts A. & B. will hold one Platoon each.

The Third System.

In rear of the Intermediate Line is the Third System, (marked in Yellow on Map). This consists of the WANCOURT LINE, which runs through N.10 Central and N.16. Central. There are 3 strong points - C3 (N.22.b.1.1.) holds 1 Platoon, C5 (N.16.d.05.30.) and C6 (N.16.d.1.8.) are capable of holding 2 Sections each.

There are also three M.G.Posts :-

C4   N.22.b.0.4.

C7   N.16.a.8.7.

C8   N.21.b.8.2.

M.Gs. are ear-marked to occupy these Posts in case of attack.

V. DISTRIBUTION OF TROOPS.

   The distribution of troops in the Divisional Area is shewn on Map No. 1.

   The distribution of the forward Brigade (down to Platoons) is shewn on Map No. 3.

VI. ACTION IN CASE OF ATTACK.

   (a) In event of a local attack against part or whole of the Divisional front, the enemy will, if he penetrates the Line, be immediately ejected by a counter-attack.

   (b) No ground which can be held will be voluntarily evacuated. Should the enemy succeed in capturing a portion of the line, the remainder of the line will hold on, blocking the flanks towards the enemy and manning the defences in rear so as to form a 'pocket' in which he can be held up pending a counter-attack.

   (c) In event of a general attack on the Corps or Army front, the Reserve Line will form the main line of defence; from this line a prepared counter-attack can be launched in order to drive the enemy out of any portion captured by him.

   (d) With regard to (a & b) the Brigade Defence Schemes will legislate for immediate counter-attack and the units ear-marked for this duty will reconnoitre thoroughly the ground over which they may have to counter-attack.

   (e) With regard to (c) the Reserve Line is in process of being strengthened.

   The Line South of the River is of utmost importance, as it presents a formidable barrier to a hostile attack on it, and enfilades an enemy advance against our Trench System North of the River.

   (f) The Reserve Line, therefore, must not be lost

/and

and will be sufficiently garrisoned to deny it to the enemy.

(g) The garrison for this line is two Battalions, viz:-
1 North and 1 South of the River.

(h) Should these Battalions be taken for counter-attack, their place will be taken by the 2 Reserve Battalions.

(i) Battalion Commanders will make out Defence Schemes for their Sub-Sectors, and each Company Commander will have a plan ready for the immediate ejection of the enemy, should he, by means of a raid or attack, obtain a footing in the Company front.

VII. ANTI-GAS MEASURES.

A list of STROMBOS HORNS and other appliances for giving warning of Gas Attacks from front to rear is given in Appendix "A"

The following is the chain of communication :-

(a) By telephone & Strombos Horn from the Coy. to Flank Coys. & Battalion H.Q.

(b) From Battalion H.Q. to Brigade H.Q. and Flank Bns.

(c) From Brigade H.Q. to the Division and to flank Brigades.

The Division will warn the Corps, Divisional Troops and Flank Divisions and the Town Commandant, ARRAS.

The Town Commandant, ARRAS, is responsible for the Alarm being given in the City by the ringing of the bells at the Church of LES ARDENTS.

It must be clearly understood that the B.G.C. Brigade in the line will not send back the Gas Alarm until the report of gas is substantiated.

VIII. ARTILLERY SUPPORT.

The Divisional front is covered by :-

(a) The Corps Heavy Artillery.

(b) Field Artillery commanded by the C.R.A. 56th Division.

/Details

Details are not issued as to number of guns, as both heavy and field are continually changing at present.

IX. **MACHINE GUN SUPPORT.** has been arranged under Corps and Divisional arrangements, and Machine Guns employed (see Map No.2) have been sited to give the maximum stopping effect.

These Machine Gun Positions will not be altered without the sanction of the G.O.C. Division.

X & XI. **INFANTRY AND ARTILLERY COMMUNICATIONS.** - See Map No. 1 & Appendix "B".

The permanent Scheme of Communications in the Divisional Area - details of all lines from the Division to the 3 Brigades

    (i) Under construction.
    (ii) Completed.

are with reference to Appendix "B" dealt with below :-

1. **Permanent Cable Routes.**

    (i) The construction of a permanent poled cable route to each Brigade is being carried out.

    (ii) A poled cable route to the old Right Brigade Headquarters (N.16.a.1.8.) is also under construction in readiness for the Brigade in Support if it moves up.

    (iii) Poled Cable Routes are shown on the attached diagram as follows :-

        (a) Poled Cable Routes completed - Lines shown in RED.

        (b) Cable Routes under construction - Lines shown in DOTTED RED.

2. **Permanent Routes.**

    (i) A permanent route has been constructed, galvanised iron wire, from ARRAS to approximately N.8.d. central.

- 8 -

    (ii) It contains 8 pairs.

    (iii) One pair of these is allotted by Corps for the Brigade in Line.

    (iv) A further pair has been called for to be brought into use on a forward move of the Brigade in Support.

3. <u>Armoured Cable Routes.</u>

Two armoured cable routes from Advanced Exchange at TILLOY (H.31 central) passing through the Test Station at AIRY CORNER (N.9.a.8.6.) and thence on to the Brigade in Line, and to the Brigade Headquarters in Support (when they move up) are in good working order.

4. <u>Laddered Lines.</u>

    (i) Laddered Lines from the Advanced Exchange at TILLOY, passing through the Test Station at AIRY CORNER are being converted into Poled Cable Routes.

    (ii) The two laddered routes running forward from this Test Point to the Brigade in Line (and the proposed position of Headquarters for the Brigade in Support, N.16.a.1.8.) will also be converted to Poled Cable Routes.

5. <u>Buried Routes.</u>

Buried Routes out of ARRAS are shown in purple dotted lines on diagram.

Their maintenance is a very difficult matter, Faults are caused by the damp, as the cables run through the sewers.

Portions of the routes which show considerable loss are being replaced by poled cable.

/XII.

XII. <u>LIAISON WITH ARTILLERY.</u>

In addition to all units being wired up to their Supporting Artillery - Liaison Officers are detached from the Artillery on the following scale :-

<u>Heavy Artillery.</u>

1 Officer for each Battalion in the Line.

<u>Field Artillery.</u>

1 Officer at Brigade Headquarters.

1 Officer with each Battalion in the Line.

XIII. <u>MEDICAL ARRANGEMENTS IN DIVISIONAL AREA.</u>

<u>Regimental Aid Posts.</u>

Are situated at :-

(1) O.19.a.0.2.   (3) N.24.c.1.6.
(2) N.18.d.3.8.   (4) N.17.d.1.3.

<u>Advanced Dressing Station.</u>

In MARLIERE CAVES at N.17.d.1.3. is capable of accommodating at least 100 lying cases.

<u>Advanced Dressing Posts.</u>

Situated :-

(1) At Gunpits near LES FOSSES FARM at N.11.a.7.6.

(2) In Sunken Road near HENINEL at N.22.d.8.3.

<u>Ambulance Cars.</u>

Stand at :-

(a) N.4.d. central.
(b) N.16.c. central.

and by signal move to <u>CAR TERMINI</u> at :-

N.11.a.9.9. and N.16.d.4.0.

<u>An Additional Dressing Post.</u>

Is situated in Prinz Rupprecht Strasse, TILLOY-Lez-MOFFLAINES at H.31.c.6.5. for (Reserve Brigade) casualties in back areas. At this post also, all Motor Ambulance Cars not actually on the road are parked.

<u>Divisional Main Dressing Station.</u>

Is at Hospital St. Jean and Convent St. Sacrament, ARRAS, about 50 cases in each building and capable

/of

of being kept underground during shelling.

Routes of Evacuation.

Wounded are conveyed to Regimental Aid Posts by hand carriage, and thence by hand carriage and wheeled stretchers, via : an an Advanced Dressing Post or Station to Car Termini. From these termini they are taken by cars to Divisional Main Dressing Station.

2 Red Cross trucks are available on the tramway for evacuation from the A.D.S. in MARLIERE CAVES to Car Termini at N.16.d.4.0.

XIV. ADMINISTRATIVE AREAS.

For purposes of Area discipline and administration the Divisional Area is sub-divided into the following Brigade Areas :-

Forward Brigade Area.

Eastern Boundary -	Front Line Trenches.
Western Boundary -	FEUCHY CHAPEL-NEUVILLE VITASSE Road (exclusive)

Support Brigade Area.

Eastern Boundary -	FEUCHY CHAPEL - NEUVILLE VITASSE Road (inclusive) and to include Advanced Divisional Ammunition Dump at and around Cross Roads N.8.d.
Western Boundary -	Road from TILLOY to North end of BEAURAINS (exclusive - thence round Eastern Outskirts of BEAURAINS - BEAURAINS-MERCATEL Rd.

Reserve Brigade Area.

Eastern Boundary. -	BEAURAINS and BEAURAINS - TILLOY Road (inclusive)
Western Boundary. -	Railway running through G.32, G.31 and R.6.a.

XV. LIGHT TRAMWAYS.

Existing Tramways and proposed extensions are shown on Map No. 1 in Green and Black, respectively.

XVI. DUMPS.

A list of R.E. Dumps is shown below :-
RITZ DUMP   -   G.29.o.5.9.
WANCOURT ROAD DUMP -   N.8.a.5.7.
MARLIERE DUMP   -   N.23.b.35.80.

APPENDIX "A"

LOCATION OF STROMBOS HORNS.

Forward Brigade.	N.10.d.4.6.
H.Q., Right Battn.	O.19.a.2.5.
Support "	N.24.c.1.8.
" Left Battn.	O.13.a.8.6.
Support "	N.17.d.2.3.
Support Brigade.	H.31.d. Central.

H.Q. Battns.

    (a) N.1.b.
    (b) N.1.a.
    (c) G.36.b. (DEVIL'S WOOD)
    (d) N.2.a. (BOIS DES BOEUFS).

Reserve Brigade.   G.33.c.1.5.

H.Q. Battns.

    (a) ACHICOURT   M.2.a.6.8.
    (b) ACHICOURT   G.32.d.8.4.
    (c) ARRAS   SCHRAMM, East Block.
    (d) ARRAS   SCHRAMM, West Block.

Div. H.Q. - H.21.c.6.4.

1 in Reserve at Div. Gas School,
                  70, Rue d'Amiens, ARRAS.

****

56th Division Tactical
Progress Reports.

WAR DIARY COPIES.

Papers for GSO I

War Diary

56th DIVISIONAL TACTICAL PROGRESS REPORT No.1
from 12 noon 11th June to 12 noon 12th June, 1917.

Not to be taken in front of Bn. H.Qrs.

PART I OPERATIONS.
  Patrols. The following reports were received from patrols last night :- Work was heard in NUT Trench.
         Shell holes 170 yds. East of TOOL Trench were occupied. A bomb was thrown into one, in which voices were heard, M.G. fire was then opened on the patrol from the direction of LANYARD TR.
         A line of shell-holes were found to be connected up at about O.14.b.0.7. - these were not occupied.
         LANYARD TR. was occupied.
  Artillery. Our artillery carried out a shoot according to programme.
  T.Ms. Our L.T.Ms. ranged on the line of shell-holes in O.8.d.

PART II INTELLIGENCE.
  Identifications. A prisoner was captured near SPOOR LANE early this morning. He belonged to 3rd Bn. 458th I.R. 236th Divn.
  Hostile Artillery. Fairly quiet during the night. A few 5.9's from the direction of BOIRY fell in N.23.b. at 2.15 a.m. Between 6 a.m. and 9 a.m. about 40 4.2's were fired on N.22.d. Our front and support trenches between O.2.d. and the CAMBRAI Rd. received heavy bursts of fire from a 77 mm. gun at 7.40 a.m. and again at 8 a.m. N.15.b. and N.16.a. were shelled at intervals with section salvoes by 4.2's and 5.9's from the direction of BOIRY. A hostile 'plane is believed to have been registering the battery. From 7 a.m. to 9.30 a.m. ARRAS and ACHICOURT were shelled with H.V. Heavy Gun. At 9.30 a.m. the aeroplane which appeared to be observing for this shoot was brought down near ARRAS.
  Hostile M.Gs. Two independent sources report an enemy M.G. at O.14.b.7.1.
  Hostile Aircraft. Very active yesterday evening and early this morning.
         Our L.G. fire is reported to have driven several planes off.
  Hostile Patrols. An enemy patrol approached SPOOR Lane along the Railway track shortly before daylight. The patrol was fired on and when it got light a man was seen crawling in the grass about 100 yards from our trenches. A Sergeant went out and brought him in.
  Hostile Movement. 1.30 p.m. Considerable movement about large mound J.31.d.4.3. also on road from BOIRY in O.12.a. 5.30 p.m. A horsed limber was seen by the bank at P.1.b.4.7. 5.30 a.m. Men were seen leaving FACTORY and LANYARD Trenches disappearing over the ridge.

12th June, 1917.

Captain,
for General Staff.

P.T.O.

PRELIMINARY EXAMINATION OF MAN BELONGING TO
3rd Bn. 458th Infantry Regt. 236th Div.

<u>Method of Capture</u>. Prisoner stated that he was sent out on patrol as leader with four other men, starting about 11 p.m. they lost their way and came under British and German shell fire. Prisoner lost his men and thinks they all became casualties. He eventually was caught near APE Tr. at about 3 a.m.

<u>Line held</u>. 236th Divn. holds The SENSEE CHERISY front They relieved 18th Res. Divn. 8 days ago.

<u>Method of holding line</u>. Prisoner states that his Regiment has 3rd Bn. in front line holding line of shell holes and 2nd Bn. in support, but could not give its position. The 1st Bn. is in reserve in the neighbourhood of VIS-EN-ARTOIS distributed in quarries outside the Village.

<u>Machine Guns</u>. No light M.G. have been issued so far.

<u>Food</u>. Good, but nothing hot can be brought up owing to shell fire

<u>Intentions</u>. Nothing is known of any intended withdrawal. Patrol had orders to find out British Order of Battle. All papers likely to be of use to us were taken off them. An attack by the British is expected owing to the continual bombardment, and all ranks in the front line have orders to keep strictest vigilance night and day.

<u>Reliability</u>. Prisoner is not very reliable and is unwilling to give any information.

****

War Diary

56th DIVISIONAL TACTICAL PROGRESS REPORT No. 2.
from 12 noon 12th June to 12 noon 13th June 1917.

On receipt of current copy of Tactical Progress Report in
the trenches, previous copy to be burnt.

PART I, OPERATIONS.

Artillery. Our artillery fired as per programme on enemy trenches and movement.
The suspected O.P. at O.22.a.1.3 was registered.
Patrols. Patrols report LANYARD Tr. occupied on both sides of the CAMBRAI Road. A machine gun was firing from where the trench crosses the CAMBRAI Road, and another from its southern extremity. Some wire was found at O.14.b.75.60.
A patrol at about O.20.d.3.3 drew rifle fire from its front.
Trench Mortars. Stokes Mortars fired 30 rounds registration.

PART II, INTELLIGENCE.

Hostile Artillery has been somewhat active chiefly on back areas. During the evening the COJEUL Valley was somewhat heavily shelled, while the CAMBRAI Road and RAKE and SPADE Trenches received some fire. N.15.b. was shelled with 4.2's and 5.9's in section salvoes throughout the afternoon, from the direction of BOIRY, and at 3.30 p.m., about 30 - 8" were fired on the same target from the direction of VIS-EN-ARTOIS. N.18.c. was also shelled with 5.9's, as were O.19.a. and O.19.c.
N.17.d. and N.18.c. were heavily shelled with 4.2's in the evening, and between 7 and 9 am, receiving about 200 shells in each period.
At 9 p.m., about 20 rounds 8" fell in N.24.a.
Hostile Trench Mortars. A light T.M. fired on junction of SADDLE Lane with front line from about O.14.b.8.5.
Movement. Work was seen in progress at O.21.d.7.7, and later a party of Germans leaving the North corner of TRIANGLE WOOD were dispersed by our artillery fire.
Movement was seen in small parties near CORNER COPSE and Mound in J.31.d., and in O.6.b.
Men were seen in a house at O.23.a.9.8., also in the trench system about O.29.central.
During the morning there was some work and movement in the trenches in O.21.d. No signs of occupation were observed in the line of shell holes in O.8.d. throughout the period.
New work. There is a new short trench O.9.c.4.8. Consertina wire has been put out in the southern part of BOIS DU VERT.

John D. Crosthwaite
Captain.
General Staff.

Headquarters, 56th Div.,
13th June 1917.

War Diary

SECRET.

**56th DIVISIONAL TACTICAL PROGRESS REPORT No. 3
from 12 noon 13th June to 12 noon 14th June 1917.**

On receipt of current copy of Tactical Progress Report
previous copy to be burnt.

PART I OPERATIONS.
  Artillery. Our artillery fired on back areas and tracks
throughout the night and in support of the 3rd Div. Attack
this morning.
  Patrols. The North bank of the COJEUL was patrolled in
O.14.d. but touch was not obtained with the enemy.
The small semicircular trench in O.20.b. was examined.
There were no signs of recent occupation but a corpse and
two British spades were found in the trench. There is a
path running towards the enemy's lines from this trench.
Two men of a strong fighting patrol got through the enemy
wire about 100 yards South of MANGE LANE - 8 Germans
climbed out of the trench and opened fire. The wire
was too thick to allow of our patrol rushing this party.
  Trench Mortars. 100 rounds were fired on the shell-holes
in O.8.d. in support of the attack on our left.

PART II INTELLIGENCE.
  Hostile Artillery. Hostile artillery was very quiet
during the afternoon, and although active this morning
obtained very few hits on our trenches. O.14.b. O.1.
O.2. and O.8.b. all received attention during the day.
N.23.c. was heavily shelled this morning and WANCOURT
received some attention.
  Trench Mortars. Granatenwerfer fired on APE Trench during
the night from direction of ST. ROHART FACTORY.
  Movement. Considerable movement in O.21.b. and d. Men
were seen to enter the ruined house at O.22.a.8.9. on
several occasions. There was considerable movement of
small parties on the roads in rear. This morning
between 5 and 6.45 several stretcher parties were seen
between O.27.c. and VIS-EN-ARTOIS.
  Aircraft. Hostile aircraft were active yesterday evening
and this morning flying low over our lines - they were not
engaged by our planes, although on occasions they appeared
to be directing fire.
  Signals. 2.15 a.m. A white rocket bursting into two
green stars was followed by artillery fire.

John D. Crosthwaite

Head Qrs. 56th Divn.
14th June, 1917.

Captain,
General Staff.

SECRET.

War Diary Copy

56th DIVISIONAL TACTICAL PROGRESS REPORT No. 4
from 12 noon 14th June to 12 noon 15th June 1917.

On receipt of current copy of Tactical Progress Report, previous copy to be burnt.

PART I OPERATIONS.

Artillery. Our artillery fired on back areas and tracks throughout the night in addition to putting down S.O.S. barrages during the counter-attacks against the Division on our left.

Patrols. A patrol moved along the COJEUL VALLEY to about O.14.d.3.6. They could hear nothing of the enemy, but were forced to retire owing to hostile shelling. Another patrol moved along the North side of the CAMBRAI Road towards LANYARD TRENCH in which they could hear the enemy talking. The isolated pieces of trench in front of the right sub-section were patrolled and found clear of enemy troops.

Machine Guns. Our M.G's fired on their fixed S.O.S. lines during enemy counter-attack and the right group of guns who could see no movement on their barrage line, lengthened their fire into O.9.b.

Trench Mortars. Our L.T.M's opened rapid fire on the shell-holes in O.8.d during enemy counter-attack.

PART II INTELLIGENCE.

Hostile Artillery was active on left sub-section throughout the day, but damage was very small considering the amount of fire. About 2 a.m. JACKDAW and IBIS TRENCHES were heavily shelled by all calibre guns, but damage was slight. At 7-30 p.m. N.15.b was shelled with 5.9's and gas shells, but counter-battery work soon caused this to cease. During the night and early morning the VALLEY in N.15. and 16 was intermittently shelled by 5.9's from the direction of HAUCOURT. Field guns from the direction of VIS-EN-ARTOIS were active against O.7.a - O.13.c and O.19.d, whilst WANCOURT and the Cross-roads W of it were shelled with 5.9's and 8".

Hostile T.M's. GRANATENWERFER again reported on JACKDAW TRENCH.

Movement. Considerable movement was seen between BOIRY and BOIS DU VERT. Throughout the day many wounded men crawling and walking back towards BOIRY and stretcher parties were at work over the whole of this area. There is a Dressing Station at Q.29.b.7.2. Stretchers are carried here every day. Two stretchers and six bandaged men were seen to enter here from O.23.d.6.5.

General. Between 3-30 and 3-45 p.m. three hostile 'planes patrolled our line between O.20 central and O.8. central. They were flying very low and were not attacked by aircraft or anti-aircraft guns.

Enemy counter-attack. at 5-15 p.m. a Company Commander of the Battalion on the right observed the enemy concentrating E. of BOIS DU VERT. Our artillery was stood to and on the S.O.S. signal being received at 5-30 barrage fire was immediately laid down. At the same time M.G's, which had been warned, fired 7,000 rounds on the line across which the enemy's left could be seen moving and a further 4,000 as a barrage on the west face of the BOIS DU VERT. At 5-55 p.m. enemy was seen retiring from the South corner of BOIS DU VERT and rapid rifle fire was brought to bear on them.

Hostile movement in rear was reported as follows :-

5-30 p.m. in J.31 about 200 moving West.
6-5 p.m. another 100 in the same place.
6-15 p.m. Support troops moving S.W. in extended order in O.4.c. The troops in O.10.a advancing together with those in O.4.c were driven back by our artillery fire.
6-25 p.m. Enemy troops in O.4.c were reported to have changed direction to N. and N.W.; possibly in order to avoid the barrage which had been so effective in O.10.a.
6-40 p.m.) Parties of Germans, largest about 30, moving West
6-45 p.m.) on tracks leading from BOIRY.
6-50 p.m.)

7-30 p.m. Wounded & stretcher cases commenced entering BOIRY from West.

Observation points to the line by which supports moved up as J.31 - O.6 - BOIRY. They appeared to be sent forward from a very considerable distance in rear.

15th June 1917.

John D. Crosthwaite
Captain,
General Staff.

SECRET.

56th DIVISION TACTICAL PROGRESS REPORT No. 5.
from 12 noon 15th June to 12 noon 16th June 1917.

On receipt of current copy of Tactical Progress Report in the trenches, previous copy to be burnt.

PART I OPERATIONS.

Patrols. NO MAN'S Land in front of SPOOR LANE was reconnoitred and sites for two posts selected.-O.20.d.2.7 & 4.9.
Artillery. Fired on back areas and tracks throughout the night. At 2.30 a.m. the S.O.S. signal went up from the direction of BOIS DU VERT, the enemy having put down an intense barrage on the Bn. on our left, and heavily shelling CAMBRAI Road and FARM TRENCH. All batteries at once opened on their night lines and continued firing until 3 a.m. when the situation was cleared.
Lewis Guns. During the bombardment our L.Gs. kept up bursts of fire on the left front, and at dawn inflicted at least 20 casualties to small parties of Germans withdrawing from shell holes over the ridge in O.9.a.

PART II INTELLIGENCE.

GUEMAPPE and N.12.d. received a good deal of attention from 4.2's and 5.9's and MONCHY and CAVALRY FARM from 77 mm. during the afternoon. N.5.d. was continuously shelled from 9 to 11 a.m. with 5.9's from direction of I.30.d. SHRAPNEL Trench and TOOL Trench were heavily shelled with 5.9's between 8.45 and 9.15 a.m. O.19. was shelled intermittently throughout the morning, and N.16.a. and d. N.22.a. and b. throughout the night. From 4 a.m. to 12 noon N.30.a. and c. were shelled at intervals with 5.9's 4.2's and 77 mm.

Hostile T.Ms. Fired on APE Trench during the night.
Enemy Movement. Small parties of the enemy coming out of S.E. corner of BOIS DU VERT at 11.15 and 11.30 a.m. were engaged by our artillery.
Hostile Aircraft. Active, one patrolled our front line trenches between 4 p.m. and 5.30 p.m. Between 6 a.m. and 7 a.m. a 'plane flying low fired into TOOL TRENCH.
General. There is a mound of new earth in BOIS DU VERT at O.9.a.70.40. which might be a dugout or O.P.
White Very Lights were fired from LANYARD Trench between 1.30 and 2 a.m.

Head Qrs. 56th Divn.
16th June, 1917.

Lieutenant,
for Lieut-Colonel
General Staff

SECRET.   *War Diary*

56th DIVISION TACTICAL PROGRESS REPORT No. 6
from 12 noon 16th June to 12 noon 17th June 1917.

On receipt of current copy of Tactical Progress Report
in the trenches, previous copy to be burnt.

PART I, OPERATIONS.

Artillery. Our artillery fired on back areas and tracks during the night, STIRRUP Trench receiving special attention.

Patrols. Patrols were active over the whole front and obtained the following information. The shell holes along SADDLE LANE in O.14.b were held by the enemy. Flares were sent up from here and rifle fire was drawn. An M.G. in LANYARD TRENCH was active about O.14.b.7.1. Flares were fired from LANYARD TRENCH South of CAMBRAI Road. Four consolidated shell holes about O.14.d.1.5 were not occupied. No wire was found North of the River. Movement between the CAMBRAI Road and the River is difficult owing to the long corn. The positions of the new posts in front of APE TRENCH were marked and the routes to them taped out.

PART II INTELLIGENCE.

Hostile Artillery. During the afternoon trenches in O.8.a, N.10 LES FOSSES FARM and the crest of the WANCOURT RIDGE received attention. During the night the VALLEY in N.17 & 18 and the outskirts of WANCOURT were shelled with high bursting shrapnel from 4.2" guns. At 8 a.m. an 8" How. Battery firing at long range on an approximate grid bearing of 60° from N.11.c.50.65 fired about 200 rounds into the BROWN line just North of the CAMBRAI ROAD, and at the same time LES FOSSES FARM and LA BERGERE were shelled with about 150 5.9's by a battery on approximate grid bearing of 74° from N.11.c.50.65.

Movement. Movement throughout the day in O.9.b was continuous in small parties. Our artillery engaged this successfully. During the afternoon there was movement in J.31.c and d. One party of 50, another of 30 entered BOIRY from this direction. At 1-45 p.m. H.A. shelled BOIRY and a number of men ran from the village towards the East. There was also continuous movement along the road in O.6.b and O.5.d. In the evening the Germans were seen running along the road at O.21.b.7.2. This point is a busy one.

Aircraft. Hostile aircraft were active throughout the early morning. At 8 a.m. hostile balloons were observed on the following grid bearings from N.11.c.50.65; 37°, 43°, 101°, 122°.

H.Q. 56th Division.
17th June 1917.

Captain.
General Staff.

SECRET.

War Diary.

56th DIVISION TACTICAL PROGRESS REPORT No. 6̶7
from 12 noon 17th June to 12 noon 18th June 1917.

On receipt of current copy of Tactical Progress Report
in the trenches, previous copy to be burnt.

PART I OPERATIONS.
   Artillery. Our artillery fired sharp bursts about the BOIS DU VERT and STIRRUP LANE during the night.
   Patrols. Owing to artillery fire occasioned by counter-attack on our left, patrols North of the COJEUL obtained no information. South of the River on the night 16/17th posts have been established at the Eastern end of two isolated bits of trench at O.26.b.1.8. and O.26.b.2.9.
   Advance of the Line. A line of barbed consertina wire was erected from the COJEUL about O.14.d.4.1. to the railway about O.20.d.2.5. Four posts at O.20.b.3.7. - 4.3. O.20.d.4.9. - 3.7. were taped out behind this wire without interferance from the enemy. Work was continued on the posts at O.26.b.1.8 and 2.9. but the enemy who are holding the right angled trench about O.26.b.3.7. interfered with this work. Two attempts were made to dislodge him without success, and an attempt by the Germans to attack these posts was repulsed by L.G. and rifle fire.
   Enemy counter-attack. About 1 a.m enemy commenced a heavy bombardment of the Brigade on our left and TOOL Trench and HOE Trench. Our M.G. and L.Gs. fired on their S.O.S. lines and all available Lewis Guns opened fire to cover the front of the Battalion on our left.

PART II INTELLIGENCE.
   Hostile Artillery. Was quiet during the afternoon of the 17th. During the night it was very active chiefly with gas shells on back areas. Several salvoes were fired along the COJEUL VALLEY and JUNGLE ALLEY. At 8.30 a.m. trenches in O.20 shelled by howitzers.
   Hostile M.Gs. Fired at intervals during the night from the direction of ST.ROHART FACTORY.
   Hostile T.Ms. An occasional Granatenwerfer shell fell on APE and JACKDAW Trenches during the night.
   Movement. Normal on roads and back areas. Small parties were seen round St.MICHAELS Statue. Work is being carried out on the mound in J.31.d. Movement was seen at the dugout in O.9.a.7.0.
   Aircraft. Hostile 'planes patrolled our trenches on both banks of the COJEUL flying very low and dropping flares. They were not attacked by aircraft or A.A.guns and L.G. and rifle fire had no effect.

18th June, 1917
                                       John D. Crosthwaite
                                          Captain,
                                          General Staff.

   General. Portuguese troops have repelled several German raids during the current month. The attack on the 3rd Divn. this morning was carried out by 2 Coys. each of the 76th E.I.R. 162 I.R. and 163 I.R. The attack swept over LONG Trench but failed to mop it up. LONG TRENCH is still held by our troops and the majority of the enemy between LONG and HOOK Trenches have become casualties or surrendered. Prisoners report that the attack was carried out in complete disorder, that morale is bad as instanced by the fact that the men on their way up to their assembly positions threw away their bombs and managed to lose their M.G. ammunition. Another prisoner states that they had received orders to occupy no trenches and their dispositions are now by groups of 1 N.C.O. and 8 men pushed forward into shell-holes.

Re 56th Div. T.P.R. No. 8 dated 19.6.17, Points at which posts have been established should read :-

Post	"A"	O.20.b.3.7.
"	"B"	O.20.b.4.4.
"	"C"	O.20.b.5.0
"	"D"	O.20.d.3.7.

and not as stated.

War Diary Copy

SECRET.

56th DIVISION TACTICAL PROGRESS REPORT No. 8
from 12 noon 18th June to 12 noon 19th June 1917.

On receipt of current copy of Tactical Progress Report in the trenches, previous copy to be burnt.

PART I OPERATIONS.

Artillery. Our artillery was continuously active during the day and fired on allotted targets at night. The bombardment E. of the BOIS DU VERT was effective.

* S. of the CAMBRAI Rd.

Patrols. * Patrols report sounds of work in the direction of LANYARD Trench. Wiring was in progress W. of this trench and a covering party of 3 men was seen. Owing to the new work on the right Battalion front no patrols were out.

Advance of the line. Four posts, each of 3 fire bays and 2 traverses were dug as follows :-

```
"A" Post,  0.20.d.3.7,  4 ft. by 3 ft.     36 yard frontage.
"B" Post,  0.20.b.6.0,  3'6" by 3', 6"     50   "        "
"C" Post,  0.20.b.4.4,  4"6" by 3 ft.      36   "        "
"D" Post,  0.20.b.3.7,  4'9" by 3 ft.      36   "        "
```

ground; post "D" all chalk, remainder 2' of earth, then chalk. Each of these posts is now garrisoned by a N.C.O. and 8 men. The enemy has not interfered with them in any way.

INTELLIGENCE PART II.

Hostile Artillery. During the whole period hostile artillery has been very much below normal. During the night N.28.b and N.29.b were intermittently shelled by howitzers and GUEMAPPE received a few rounds from a H.V. gun. At dawn the railway cutting in N.24 was shelled with 5.9" and field guns. JACKDAW and TOOL trenches also received some H.E.

Hostile Patrols. Covering parties in front of the new posts saw several parties of the enemy each about 20 strong moving about No Man's Land during the night. Owing to the large working parties out no action was taken.

Movement. Several men were seen at different times at the S. end of SPUR Trench. In the early morning a party of 20 moving E. from CHERISY was dispersed by artillery fire. At the same time several stretcher parties were observed moving towards VIS-EN-ARTOIS from CHERISY. Our Lewis Guns opened fire on a small party of the enemy crawling back from shell holes near POLE Trench. Movement was seen in LANYARD Trench at 0.14.b.8.2. Sentries reported sound of work from shell holes in 0.8.d.2.3. Small parties reported during afternoon in 0.5,6 & 11

Aircraft. A hostile 'plane which flew very low over our lines at 3-45 a.m. was driven off by L.G. and rifle fire.

General. At 8-40 p.m. hostile artillery was observed shooting short in front of the BOIS DU VERT. Green rockets were sent up and the range lengthened. Hostile A.A. guns were observed at 2-45 and 3-45 p.m. firing from behind the crest in J.31.b and at 6 p.m. an A.A. Battery was seen to fire from J.31.d.2.3

John D. Crossthwaite
Captain.
General Staff.

H.Q. 56th Division.
19th June 1917.

From the Division on our left. The 5 posts in continuation of LONG Trench, N. of GREEN LANE, which were driven in by yesterday's counter-attack, were all re-established last night.

SECRET.

56th DIVISIONAL TACTICAL PROGRESS REPORT No. 9
from 12 noon 19th June to 12 noon 20th June, 1917.

On receipt of current copy of Tactical Progress Report
in the trenches, previous copy to be burnt.

PART I OPERATIONS.
Artillery. Our artillery carried out usual harassing fire.#
Trench Mortars. Our L.T.Ms. active against the line of shell holes East of TOOL TRENCH in O.8.d.
Patrols. Touch was gained with the enemy in the Southern portion of LANYARD Trench.
Advance of the Line. Work was continued on the advanced posts in O.20.b. and d. without interference by the enemy.

PART II INTELLIGENCE.
Hostile Artillery - much quieter than usual, only light calibre shells were reported on trenches. FOSSE FARM and SPEAR LANE were intermittently shelled during the afternoon. 20 rounds from a 4.2" gun fell in N.10.c. and N.16.a. Between 5 and 6 p.m. 100 field gun shells fell about the WANCOURT LINE in N.10. Between 9.30 and 10 p.m. about 80 5.9's fell in O.8.a. About midnight 500 4.2" gas shells fell in the WANCOURT AREA. O.19.d. was shelled by field guns at intervals during the morning.
Hostile M.Gs. Were reported active from LANYARD Trench firing across the valley aginst BUCK Trench.
Movement. Movement was seen at the following points during the period :-
  A two horsed wagon with white flag moving N. along road in O.30.d. and a. and then E. along the CAMBRAI Rd.
  Individual movement about TRIANGLE WOOD, and N. of it throughout the period.- about the dugouts O.23.b.7.3. - in QUARRY Trenches at O.21.d.8.5. - about dugouts at O.29.d.1.2.- men inspecting telephone wires on track in O.21.c.- continual movement around OCEAN WORK - Truck on light railway at O.23.d.1.9. - part of 7 men digging about O.21.b.7.1. - Individual movement on road in O.5.d. and O.6.c.- party of 6 moving West from mound J.31.d.4.3. - party of 8 left trench at O.6.c.5.3. into J.31.d. - wiring party at O.5.c.4.0. - train of 18 trucks moving East on railway in J.29.c. - digging in trench at O.4.d.5.8. - 8 men entered trench at O.6.c.6.0. - 1 man left house at O.22.d.72.73. - At 7 p.m. when our artillery fired a few rounds on line of shell holes East of TOOL Trench 6 men left the shell hole at O.8.d.35.40. and disappeared about 20 yards away in different direction.
  Movement on BELLONNE - ESTREES Road 3.40 p.m. 4 parties of about 40 led by man on horseback followed by two wagons going East. 6 p.m. 3 or 4 parties averaging about 50 going East. 10.15 a.m. a party of 50 moving East.
Balloons. At 11.45 a.m. two balloons on grid bearings of 69° and 101° from N.24.d.9.1. In the afternoon at 3.25 one on bearing of 103°.
Light Signals. Hostile artillery fired short in front of TOOL Trench and 5 Green Lights were sent up from the line of shell holes at O.8.d.

June 20th 1917.
Captain,
General Staff.

and fired on much of the movement reported in PART II.

SECRET.

War Diary Copy

56th DIVISIONAL TACTICAL PROGRESS REPORT No. 10.
from 12 noon 20th June to 12 noon 21st June, 1917.

On receipt of current copy of Tactical Progress Report
in the trenches, previous copy to be burnt.

PART I OPERATIONS.
   Artillery. Harassing fire has continued during the period on enemy's tracks and trenches.

PART II INTELLIGENCE.
   Hostile Artillery. Hostile artillery has been very quiet during the last 24 hours. TOOL Trench shelled with light H.E. between 2 & 2.30 a.m. APE, BOAR, JUNGLE ALLEY, EGRET Trench, received slight attention between 8.15 a.m. and 10 a.m. During the afternoon of the 20th a few rounds from 5.9" Hows. fell in N.17.a. and N.29.d. and a few 4.2's and 77 mm in N.17.c. GORDON ALLEY and N.11.a. & b. During the night there was slight shelling in N.16.a. & d. N.15.d. N.21.b. by 4.2's and 77mm. There has been intermittent shelling of N.11.c. this morning with 5.9's fired in salvoes of two. O.19.d. GORDON ALLEY have been slightly shelled with 4.2's and 77mm during the morning. From 7 a.m. to 8.30 a.m. N.27.a. shelled with 5.9's at rate of about one round per minute.
   A 77 mm battery which was seen firing from O.11.a.6.6 yesterday opened fire at 8 p.m. five guns were in action. Shells falling N.W. of MONCHY.
   Hostile T.Ms. L.T.Ms shells fell on APE, BOAR and BISON Trenches between 3 and 3.20 a.m.
   Movement. Odd men were seen walking between Western Corner of LONG WOOD and BOIRY. 12 noon party of men seen to leave BOIRY at . O.5.b.D5.10. and proceed across the open to embankment O.6.b.4.5. 12.35 p.m. six men from embankment P.1.a.70.35. to trench O.6.b.85.80. Between 1 p.m. and 4 p.m. considerable amount of individual movement about these embankments and mound J.31.c. 1 p.m. Ambulance Wagon flying Red Cross Flag on road in O.30.a. S.E. of ARRAS-CAMBRAI Road proceeded to Dressing Station in O.30.d.20.85. After halting for 10 minutes it returned to road junction O.24.c.7.1. and then moved along ARRAS CAMBRAI Road in S.E. direction. Occasional movement of transport on DURY - HENDECOURT Road P.31. and P.32. Also on road to P.16 and P.22. 5.10 a.m. four men on road in O.5.d. moving N.W. 6.45 p.m. five men on road O.6.a.50.95. - they disappeared behind Copse in O.5.b.95.70. 7.55 a.m. slight movement in OCEAN WORK O.29.b. 9.15 a.m. Ambulance again seen at Dressing Station O.30.d. 20.85. 10.5 a.m. four men left trench O.6.c.5.1. and disappeared in trench at O.5.c.8.9. 11.30 a.m. one man crawled out of LANYARD Trench O.14.b.80.35. and got into a shell hole a few yards behind the trench.
   Hostile Aeroplanes. Flew at a low altitude over our lines at intervals between 4 a.m. and 7 a.m. Lewis Gun fire succeeded in driving them off. While over our lines several RED and GREEN Lights were dropped over points in our trenches, which were immediately ranged on by hostile artillery.
   Hostile Balloons seen to-day.-

From 2.45 p.m.	Bearing from	O.P. N.24.d.9.1.	- 64°	Grid N.
" 3.45 "	" "	O.P. N.24.b.80.15	67°	" "
" 11.30 a.m.	" "	" "	64.32	" "
" 11.30 a.m.	" "	" "	N.24.d.9.1. 104°	" "
			101.30'	" "
			92.30'	" "
			74°	" "
			64°	" "

   This latter ascends from vicinity of . TORTEQUENNE.
   General. Green lights still appear to mean "Lengthen range"

[signature]
Captain,
for General Staff.

21.6.17.

SECRET.

War Diary Copy

56th DIVISIONAL TACTICAL PROGRESS REPORT No. 11
from 12 noon 21st June to 12 noon 22nd June, 1917.

On receipt of current copy of Tactical Progress Report in the trenches, previous copy to be burnt.

PART I OPERATIONS.

Artillery. At 1-50 p.m. three hostile batteries were observed from O.19.a to be active. A section of a 77 mm battery and a section of 4.2" battery, firing from the hollow in O.12.d, were silenced by our 4.5's and 18-pdrs., shooting at extreme range. The third hostile battery thought to be 4.2's was observed to be shooting from emplacements at O.6.d.7.5, which could be clearly seen. A line was at once run out from the Brigade Headquarters to a 6" Siege Battery near by and a successful shoot was then carried out with direct observation. Several direct hits on emplacements were scored and one shell fell amongst the retreating detachments with good effect.

During the night our fire as usual.

Patrols. A patrol from the left sub-sector dispersed a party by L.G. fire working in LANYARD Trench about O.15.a.O.8.

PART II INTELLIGENCE.

Hostile Artillery. During the afternoon WANCOURT Ridge and railway cutting were heavily shelled by 77 mm and 4.2 H.V. guns at irregular intervals.

At 1-15 p.m. six 8" armour piercing shells were reported to have fallen in N.14.a. Between 8-45 and 9 p.m. about 150 5.9's fell in N.16.a. Between 10-15 and 11 p.m. about 300 4.2's were fired into N.11.b from the direction of VIS-en-ARTOIS. Between 2-15 a.m. and 3 a.m. H.E. barrage was put down on APE, SPOOR and BOAR Trenches, which, during the last 15 minutes, spread to JACKDAW and IBIS Trenches.

Hostile Trench Mortars. Between 2 a.m. and 4 a.m. a T.M. was active on JACKDAW and APE Trenches, which appeared to be firing from S.E. end of SPOOR Trench.

Hostile Machine Guns. A gun was firing during the night from approximately O.8.d.5.5. Occasional bursts of fire were opened on RAKE Trench from about O.21.c.7.6. Two M.G's in O.15.a and O.20.a opened short bursts of fire down the COJEUL RIVER Valley about 3-30 a.m. Trenches in O.21.c were swept with occasional bursts from a gun firing from ST. ROHART's FACTORY.

MOVEMENT. 1-10 p.m. A party of men with full packs on DURY-HENDECOURT Rd. P.25 and 26.

1-15 p.m. 24 men with full pack moving West along PEACH Trench P.25.d to L'ESPERANCE P.26.d.

4-20 p.m. 4 men unloading a wagon halted at dump O.6.c.5.1.

7-50 p.m. A stretcher-party moving N.E. along track in O.28.d.

6-35 a.m. Train and ten trucks moving East in J.27.d.3.5.

7-30 a.m. A number of men appeared to be cutting grass in field N.E. of road in O.5.d.

9-0 a.m. Working party in OSTRICH Trench O.30.b.05. Considerable movement round Mound in J.31.d.4.3 70. and on road in O.5.d and O.6.a.

Enemy Aircraft. Between 4-15 a.m. and 4-30 a.m. an E.A. flew low over our trenches in right sub-sector, several rockets bursting into red and green were fired with no apparent result. It was eventually driven off by M.G. and L.G. fire.

General. A prisoner belonging to 458 I.R. was captured in SPOOR Trench O.20.d.45.30. He was one of a party estimated from 6 to 8 men seen withdrawing just before daybreak from the enemy's side of the bombing block in SPOOR Trench at O.20.d.45. The party was dispersed by our L.G.'s. The prisoner, who was 30. wounded, was heard groaning, found, and brought into our lines, but died soon after. Other bodies were seen and attempts to recover them will be made tonight.

/Hostile Balloons

- 2 -

Hostile Balloons, were seen as follows:-
    From O.P. N.24.b.80.15 Grid bearing 64-32'
      " " N.24.d.9.1.   Grid bearing 104 degs.
                               "   "   101-30'
                               "   "   92-30'
                               "   "   74 degs.
                         TORTEQUENNE Area 64 degs.

     Green lights were observed at 10-18 p.m. - 10-45 p.m. - 10-50 p.m. and 1-15 a.m. On the last occasion they were followed by hostile shelling.

                                                        H. F. Malleun

22nd June 1917.
                                                        Lieutenant,
                                                 for General Staff.

SECRET.

56th DIVISIONAL TACTICAL PROGRESS REPORT No. 12
from 12 noon 22nd June to 12 noon 23rd June, 1917.

On receipt of current copy of Tactical Progress Report
in the trenches, previous copy to be burnt.

PART I OPERATIONS.

Artillery. Enemy's front line trenches and shell holes were dealt with during the day. Enemy's trenches S.E. of VIS-EN-ARTOIS were heavily shelled during the evening.

Patrols. NUT TRENCH was found to be occupied - no wire was met in O.20.b. or O.21.a. The bank running from O.20.b.6.9. to O.21.a.0.9. was examined. It contained what appeared to be open M.G. positions, but these were not occupied. An enemy post in the bank at O.20.b.9.9. opened rifle fire on the patrol. LANYARD TR. in O.15.a. is strongly held.

PART II INTELLIGENCE.

Identifications. Prisoner was captured near SPOOR TR. last night. He was of the 7th Coy. 458th I.R. (normal).

Hostile Artillery. Usual intermittent shelling of the front line system, with special attention to TITE'S COPSE, TOOL, CURLEW, BISON and APE Trenches, and KESTREL C.T. LA BERGERE received a good deal of attention during the day. About midnight COJEUL VALLEY between WANCOURT and HENINEL shelled by 5.9's.

Hostile T.M.s. JACKDAW received T.M. shells from about O.21.c.1.4. at 11 p.m. A T.M. in SPOOR Trench was again active on APE and JUNGLE. TOOL and PLOUGH Trenches were also targets.

Hostile M.Gs. The M.G. at O.14.d.45.80. again fired on BUCK Trench during the night. COJEUL VALLEY was swept by M.Gs. from the BOIS DU VERT and ST. ROHART'S FACTORY. The gun at O.14.b.60.45. was again active. An M.G. fired on one of our 'planes from the Southern end of BOIS DU VERT.

Movement. Was seen in small parties at the following places :-
  Ruined house in HAUCOURT at O.24.c.05.48.
  Road at O.17.a.3.1.
  Road through O.29.b. and d. running N. & S.
  VIS Trench at O.17.c.1.9.
  OX Trench at O.29.c.5.5.
  VILLAGE TRENCH - O.22.b.1.4.
  Dugout at P.1.a.8.4.
  ORIX Trench - OCEAN WORK.
  Dugout at O.29.b.67.18.
  From Trench at O.5.b.35.05 to CIGARETTE COPSE.
  LANYARD TR. at O.14.b.8.3.
  Road in O.5.d. and O.6.c. on several occasions.
  Mound at J.31.d.4.3.
  GALLEY WOOD.

An engine and four trucks was seen going S.W. on the railway at P.2. Engine and 9 trucks seen going S.W. in J.27.c. A RED CROSS Wagon was seen at the Dressing Station at O.30.d.2.9. A two-horsed wagon stopped for a quarter of an hour at MOULIN d'AMIENS P.28.a.20.35. for a quarter of an hour and then went N. Several motor lorries were seen moving S.W. on the ETAING-ETERPIGNY Road. Several wagons have drawn up to the dump at O.6.c.4.1. at different times. Six men were seen examining telephone wires from house at O.22.d.6.9. to VILLAGE Trench O.22.a.9.1. Working party on DROCOURT-QUEANT LINE at P.27.a.87.75. A mound in QUARRY TR. at O.21.d.8.8. has been considerably increased.

Light Signals. On several occasions last night Green Rockets were sent up from LANYARD TR. when enemy Hows. fired short.

Aircraft. Inactive except between 9 and 10 a.m. when they were subjected to A.A. and M.G. fire.

Information from Prisoner. Went out with 2 others to find a German who they could hear crying for help. His companions were wounded - prisoner lost his way and was captured by a working

/party.

party.

<u>Method of Holding Line.</u> The Bn. has all four Coys in the line - all in shell holes - 2 coys. 150 yards in rear of the other 2. Each Coy. is divided into 12 to 16 groups of an N.C.O. and 8 men each. Each group hold 3 or 4 shell-holes near one another.
<u>Work.</u> No work is being done nor any wire being put up.
<u>Company Strength.</u> About 120.
<u>Losses.</u> Prisoner's Coy. has had about 10 casualties since the 18th.

* <u>Hostile Artillery.</u> Between 1.15 and 3.15 p.m. 200 4.2's were fired on N.11.b. and N.5.d.   During the night N.16.a. N.22.c. and d. and N.29.a. were intermittently shelled. This morning N.29.a.5.0. was shelled with 4.2's. The battery which bombarded N.11.b. yesterday was firing on a true bearing of 98° from N.11.c.50.65. The time of flight from report of gun to burst of shell was about 18 secs.

23rd June, 1917.

Captain,
for Lieut-Colonel,
General Staff.

56th DIVISIONAL TACTICAL PROGRESS REPORT NO. 13
from 12 noon 23rd June to 12 noon 24th June, 1917.

On receipt of current copy of Tactical Progress Report in the trenches, previous copy to be burnt.

PART I OPERATIONS.

Artillery. Our artillery was active throughout the period on trenches and movement. At 8-45 a.m. enemy front line system was heavily shelled in retaliation for hostile shoot on EGRET Trench.

Patrols. The shell holes in O.8.d and O.14.b were found to be occupied.

Work. The trench from the junction of JACKDAW and SPOOR Trenches between APE Trench and the posts in O.20.b and d was worked on last night. Average depth 2' 6". Work was much interrupted on the right portion of this line by hostile T.M. and artillery fire. Good progress was made with M.G. nests.

PART II INTELLIGENCE.

The Cross-roads in N.29.a – N.16.b and N.11.b and d were intermittently shelled during the afternoon. During the night N.16.a and N.12.a received attention. From 10 p.m. to 10-20 p.m. the CAMBRAI ROAD in O.7 and O.13 was heavily shelled by 4.2's. Between 11 and 11-30 p.m. heavy timed shells burst over the CAMBRAI ROAD near TILLOY. Hostile artillery was active on our front line system during the night, JUNGLE, BOAR, KESTREL, CAVALRY and LOCK Trenches receiving special attention. During the morning COPSE in O.19.d – O.20 and N.29.b were shelled. At 8-30 a.m. LES FOSSES FARM was shelled by 5.9's with aeroplane observation.

Hostile M.G's. M.G's were again active during the night against BUCK Trench, firing from LANYARD Trench. Fire also came from ST. ROHART FACTORY and the BOIS DU VERT.

Hostile T.M's. A hostile T.M. in SPOOR Trench fired on BISON and the party digging new trench. From 11 p.m. to 2 a.m. TOOL and PLOUGH Trenches were bombarded by T.M's probably from STIRRUP LANE.

Movement. Was seen at the following points:-

in afternoon. On Railway at O.23.d.8.1 From CAMBRAI Road to OLIVE Trench At P.31.b.45.25 in PEACH Trench Near dug-out at O.27.d.95.65 A carrying party at the dump at O.6.c.5.1.

Along Trench at O.10.b.1.1 By a dug-out in TRIANGLE WOOD at O.21.d.75.75.

Two men disappeared into shell-holes in rear of LANYARD Trench at O.15.a.4.7.

Thirty men marching in fours S.E. on road at P.28.c.35.95.

Men drilling in a field in P.2.a.

Motor and Horse Transport on road at P.21.b.90.65

Large parties of men and Motor Transport moving N.W. on ETAING – SAILLY Road during the evening. Our artillery were put on to several fleeting targets in O.5.d and O.6.c

in morning. Small parties in GREEN LANE entered LONG WOOD.

Two men entered LANYARD TRENCH from FACTORY trench In trench O.22.b.1.4 Two parties of 10 men each carried timber to HILLTOP WORK.

Two engines moving east on railway in J.28.d.

Party of 50 moving South on road in P.28.c.

Hostile Aircraft. at 2 p.m. a hostile plane over our lines was driven off by A-A fire. From 6 a.m. many enemy planes were up, but they did not cross our lines. The plane observing the shoot on FOSSES FARM was driven off by one of our scouts.

Light Signals. At 9-45 p.m. ten green lights from the BOIS DU VERT were followed by field gun fire on our front line.

General. Gun flashes are reported at 9-30 p.m. on true bearings 116° – 120° and 139° from N.11.c.50.65 and 108° from O.10.c.3.3.

24th June 1917.

Captain,
General Staff.

SECRET.

56th DIVISION TACTICAL PROGRESS REPORT No. 14, from 12 noon 24th June to 12 noon 25th June 1917.

On receipt of current copy of Tactical Progress Report previous copy to be burnt.

PART I OPERATIONS.
  Artillery. We fired during the night on suspected T.M. Emplacements in O.8.d. and O.14.b.
  M.Gs. Harrassing fire was maintained during the night on tracks in O.15.b. LANYARD TR. and CHALK PIT West of St.ROHART FACTORY. Hostile Aircraft was fired on on several occasions.

PART II INTELLIGENCE.
  Hostile Artillery. During the afternoon LA BERGERE, GUEMAPPE N.33.b. and N.39.a. were lightly shelled. Our front and support lines received attention during the night. During the night and this morning a 10 cm. gun fired intermittently into N.16.a. and c. and N.22.a. and b. on a sound bearing of 68° grid, from N.11.c.50.65. During the afternoon a 4.2" battery was seen firing on true bearing of 74° from N.24.b.55.25. The shells were falling in GUEMAPPE. N.15.b., N.11.a. and N.5.c. were shelled at intervals during the morning and N.34.b. and N.28.b. continuously with 5.9's
  At 8.10 a.m. an A.A. gun was seen firing from J.31.b.75.15.
  An A.A. battery of 2 guns was seen firing on a true bearing of 91° from N.24.d.9.1. It appears to be West of DURY-HENDECOURT Road in P.26.
  Hostile M.Gs. Active from St.ROHART FACTORY, LANYARD TR. and BOIS DU VERT during the night.
  Hostile T.Ms. A T.M. apparently firing from STIRRUP LANE was active during the night, the shells dropping short of PLOUGH TR. APE and JACKDAW Trenches received attention from 10 p.m. to 2 a.m. from the T.M. in SPOOR Trench. Approximately 100 rounds accompanied by aerial darts fell every half hour.
  Movement.
    Afternoon 24.6.17.   Ambulance at Dressing Station O.30.d.25.80.
                          Party of 20 men on road at P.21.b.50.65.
                          Continual movement of men and vehicles in REMY.
                          Motor Lorries seen on road P.14.d., also a Red Cross Wagon.
                          Usual individual movement on road in O.5.d. and O.6.a. and round the mound J.31.d.4.3.
    Morning 25.6.17.   12 men left trench in O.5.b. and proceeded to Trench in P.1.b. Motor lorry proceeding to St.SERVINS FARM, from ARRAS-CAMBRAI Road O.24.c.7.1. Train travelling from SAILLY-EN-OSTREVENT in N.E. direction. Party of men on road at J.31.d. moving W. A one-horsed limber left ST.ROHART and went towards VIS-EN-ARTOIS.
                          3 Motor Lorries on road from ETAING to SAILLY-EN-OSTREVENT
                          4 motor lorries and 4 wagons on road from REMY VIS-EN-ARTOIS.
                          Engine and 5 trucks moving W. in O.11.c. which after shunting at O.11.c.77. returned in direction of ETAING.
                          Continual movement on Road from VIS-EN-ARTOIS between ETAING and SAILLY-EN-OSTREVENT Road in O.5.c. and d. and dump at O.6.c.4.1.
  General. Smoke seen at ETAING from 6 p.m. to dusk. An explosion was observed at 1.30 p.m. at HAUCOURT O.23.c. central. At 11.15 p.m. the enemy was observed to be signalling with a red lamp on 90° grid from N.11.c.50.65.

N.F. Malleson
Lieut.
for General Staff.

25.6.17.

SECRET.

**56th DIVISION TACTICAL PROGRESS REPORT No. 15.
from 12 noon 25th June to 12 noon 26th June 1917.**

On receipt of current copy of Tactical Progress Report in the trenches, previous copy to be burnt.

PART I OPERATIONS.

Artillery. In addition to normal fire on enemy trenches and movement, hostile T.Ms. were silenced by bursts of fire at 10.30 p.m. and 4 a.m.

Machine Guns. Night firing was carried out on ST.ROHART FACTORY, QUARRY in O.15.c. and tracks in O.15. A party of 8 men who were moving up to occupy the shell holes W. of LANYARD TR. were dispersed by L.G. fire.

Trench Mortars. A destructive shoot was carried out on enemy post in SPOOR TR. in conjection with L.G.fire. The extreme E. end of SPOOR TR. was blocked with 30 rounds rapid and 70 rounds were expended in searching the remainder of the trench.

PART II INTELLIGENCE.

Hostile Artillery. Between noon and 2 p.m. about 75 5.9's fell in N.11.a. and N.5.c. Between 12.30 and 3.30 p.m. N.28.b. was heavily shelled by 5.9's. During the night 4.2 H.V. guns fired intermittently on WANCOURT and GUEMAPPE. The whole of the front line and the new line in O.20. received attention. At 5 a.m. H.V. guns fired on N.10.d. and 4 H.V. guns were active against N.22.a. from 9 a.m.

Hostile M.Gs. Were active from BOIS DU VERT, LANYARD TR. HILL TOP WORK and TRIANGLE WOOD, but no accurate locations were obtained.

Hostile T.Ms. A T.M. near LANYARD TR.fired on PLOUGH TR. during the night. Another firing from near HILL TOP WORK was active against APE, BOAR and BISON Trenches.

Movement. Seen at the following places in small parties :-

Afternoon 25.6.17. Small party in LANYARD TRENCH in O.15.a.
Digging party in Trench at O.5.b.5.1.
30 men moving N.E. on road in O.12.d.
4 men in BOIRY TR. at O.4.d.6.8.
Carrying party at dump at P.1.b.4.6. It disappeared behind the mound in J.31.d.
Man leading two horses approached the mound in J.31.d.
A man observing from ST.ROHART FACTORY.

Morning 26/6/17. 6 men entered trench at O.16.d.5.6. from N.E.
Several small parties moving N.W. on track in O.16.a.
Small working party at O.9.d.55.10.
Small parties moving between VIS-EN-ARTOIS and QUARRY TRENCH in both directions.
Party digging in STIRRUP TR. at O.15.a.65.95.
Parties carrying timber have been observed throughout the period going up to the mound in J.31.d.

At 4.25 p.m. 3 large columns of black smoke were seen rising from behind BELLONNE CHURCH.
4.30 p.m. About 60 horses were grazing 1 mile S. of SAILLY.
7. 0 p.m. Party about 150 strong moving East along BELLONNE - ESTREES ROAD.
6.15 a.m. Train moving East in J.26.c.
7.30 a.m. 4 motor lorries moving N.E. on LONG LANE in O.12.a.
10.30 a.m. 3 aeroplanes rose from SAILLY.

Light Signals. During our T.M. fire on SPOOR TRENCH golden rain rockets were answered by T.Ms.

Aircraft. Hostile activity increased towards the evening, and single aeroplanes constantly patrolled our lines. At 8.30 p.m. a long reconnaissance of the ground W. of MONCHY was carried out. Hostile A.A. fire was very heavy during the period.

Gun flashes. Were observed during the night on grid bearings of 117° and 122° from N.11.c.50.65. At 10.50 a.m. two A.A. guns were seen on a true bearing of 62° from N.24.b.80.15.

26th June, 1917.

John T. Crosthwaite
Captain,
General Staff.

SECRET.

56th DIVISION TACTICAL PROGRESS REPORT No. 16,
from 12 noon 26th June to 12 noon 27th June 1917.

On receipt of current copy of Tactical Progress Report
in the trenches, previous copy to be burnt.

PART I OPERATIONS.

Artillery. Occasional bursts of fire on enemy's trenches. Our H.A. active during the evening on enemy's rear positions. About 10 p.m. our field artillery silenced a hostile T.M. firing from about LANYARD TR. The mound in J.31.d. received some attention.

Trench Mortars. Our L.T.Ms. fired on shell holes West of LANYARD TR. in reply to enemy bombardment of TOOL TR.

Machine Guns. Harassing fire was maintained during the night on LANYARD TR. ST.ROHART FACTORY and the trenches in O.15.b. Usual fire against enemy aircraft.

General. Talking and work heard in enemy's post in SPOOR TR.

PART II INTELLIGENCE.

Hostile Artillery. Less active than usual. LES FOSSES FARM and LA BERGERE were shelled intermittently throughout the day. The shells appeared to be coming from the direction of VITRY. Between 8 p.m. and 10 p.m. WANCOURT was shelled with 4.2's from the direction of SAILLY-EN-OSTREVENT. At 12.15 a.m. the enemy shelled TOOL TR. CAVALRY FARM and the COJEUL VALLEY with 4.2's from the direction of BOIS DU SART and JIG SAW WOOD. Between 8 a.m. and 10.30 a.m. the new trench, APE, JACKDAW, BOAR, BISON and IBIS received a good deal of attention with 4.2's and 77 mm.

Hostile M.Gs. The enemy M.Gs. in BOIS DU VERT, ST ROHART FACTORY and NARROW TR. were active during the night.

Hostile T.Ms. Active on ST.ROHART FACTORY and LANYARD TR. A hostile L.T.M. is suspected to be about the railway in O.21. between NUT and NARROW Trenches.

Hostile Aircraft. Very active about 4 a.m. and 8 p.m. when several reconnaissances at a low altitude were made. Regularly at these hours a hostile 'plane reconnoitres their line, dropping lights at intervals to their infantry.

Movement. About 300 Germans seen marching on road J.33.a.3.2. in direction of ETAING. at 5.45 p.m.

   1.10 p.m. Party of 11 left trench at O.29.c.25.10. and disappeared into dugouts O.30.b.2.1.
   3.30 p.m. A pair horsed wagon on road in O.10. moving N.W. was unloaded by 8 men at O.10.b.40.15. and the load carried and dumped about O.4.d.4.6.
   4. 0 p.m. G.S.wagon on road in O.12.a. moving towards BOIRY. Stopping at O.5.d.20.75. it turned along the same road.
   4.10 p.m. Individual movement in a trench about O.5.c.2.7.
   4.25 p.m. Six men left OLGAR TR. at O.28.d.1.1. and walked along road in S.W. direction to OEUS TR. O.34.a.45.60.
   5.15 p.m. Four men with stretcher left ORIENT LANE at O.34.b.20.55. and disappeared into trench at O.34.b.50.75.
   5.30 p.m. Movement round dugouts O.23.d.93.
Between 6.30 p.m. and
   7.30 p.m. Large parties of stretcher bearers, each party being led by a man carrying a Red Cross Flag were seen on road at O.28.b. and d. moving N.E.
   7.50 a.m. Movement in trench O.10.c.8.1.
   8.30 a.m. Digging in progress in trench O.29.b. 10.35.
   9.15 a.m. A party of about 120 men wearing packs and carrying rifles moving towards CHERISY from the DURY - HENDECOURT Road were dispersed by our artillery.

    There has been considerable movement of troops and transport on road from ETAING to ETERPIGNY, also on the ETAING SAILLY-EN-OSTREVENT Rd. There has been the usual movement on the road in O.5.d. and O.6.c. and round the mound in J.31.d.

General. A searchlight was seen grid bearing 109° from N.11.c.50.65 Gun flash observed true bearing 69° 44' from O.24.b.80.15. Considerable amount of work has been done in trenches between HILL SIDE WORK and HILL TOP WORK.

27.6.17.

J.K.Maitland
for Captain,
General Staff.

56th DIVISION TACTICAL PROGRESS REPORT No. 17.
from 12 noon 27th June to 12 noon 28th June 1917.

On receipt of current copy of Tactical Progress Report
in the trenches, previous copy to be burnt.

PART I OPERATIONS.

Artillery. Registration fire was carried out this morning.

Patrols. The enemy post in O.26.b.3.8 (opposite E. and F posts) is reported to be occupied at night. Work was in progress in this post between midnight and 1 a.m. Wire has been erected in front of NUT Trench about O.26.b.6.7. Another patrol reports enemy working in NUT Trench in O.20.b. Our wire in front of posts A, B, and C is reported to be good. The enemy holds shell hole positions South of the ARRAS - CAMBRAI Road about O.14.d.5.7. Enemy working parties were heard in shell holes about O.8.d.5.9 and O.8.d.4.8; L.G. and Rifle Grenade fire was brought to bear on them. Two hostile patrols were seen opposite our left sub-sector.

Hostile Activity. At about 2 a.m. this morning the enemy attacked E. and F. posts. The attack on F. post was made from a bank just South of the post. The garrison was forced to retire and an immediate counter-attack was organised, but the posts were re-occupied without resistance. The attack on E post was beaten off by L.G. fire.

Trench Mortars. Our L.T.M's opened a shoot on shell holes West of LANYARD Trench in retaliation for enemy T.M. bombardment of TOOL Trench.

Machine Guns. During the night harassing fire was maintained on ST. ROHART's FACTORY, Roads and tracks in O.15.c and d, STIRRUP LANE and tracks in O.9.c. Hostile aircraft was engaged by our L.G's and M.G's.

Aircraft. Active during the period. At 7 p.m. an encounter took place behind the enemy's lines and two machines were seen to come to earth; one which appeared to be British landed about P.25 central.

INTELLIGENCE PART II.

Hostile Artillery.
The trenches in N.4.c and d and N.10.a were heavily shelled by 5.9's at intervals during the afternoon; also the area around WANCOURT TOWER. O.10.b was intermittently shelled during the day by a 5.9 battery, firing from about O.12.d. From 11 a.m. till 12 noon the trenches in O.25.b were shelled intermittently by 77 mm's. At 4-50 p.m. a hostile battery was seen firing on a grid bearing of 95° from M.24.d.9.1. At 10 a.m. and 10-30 a.m. an anti-aircraft gun was seen firing from about J.31.c.1.6.

Hostile Machine Guns. Active from ST. ROHART FACTORY, NUT Trench approximately O.21.c.15.75, HILL SIDE WORK and BOIS DU VERT.

Hostile Trench Mortars. A Trench Mortar fired from about the junction of NUT and NARROW Trenches. The T.M's in BOIS DU VERT and ST. ROHART FACTORY were also active during the night.

Movement. (Afternoon)
27-6-17. Four men working in Trench O.7.c.10.95.
Seven men on road O.30.c.3.4. Disappeared into OSTRICH Trench, O.30.c.00.85.
Movement in OBUS and OLGA Trenches.
Party of 50 men walking in a North Easterly direction across open at P.31.d and b.
Five trucks drawn by a motor-engine travelling South West in J.32.b.
A train of 12 trucks moving North West on railway in J.27.d.
Movement in Wood about O.12.a.8.4.
Thirty men on track in J.31.d, moving N.E.
Considerable movement of small parties on road in O.30.d in both directions.
(Morning). Red Cross wagon at Dressing Station in O.30.d.3.8
28-6-17. Movement in OCEAN WORK.
Usual movement on the ETAING - SAILLY en OSTREVENT Road, roads in O.5.d and O.6.c, Mound J.31.d, and Road between VIS-EN-ARTOIS and REMY.

H.F. Malleson

28th June

SECRET.

56th DIVISION TACTICAL PROGRESS REPORT No. 18.
from 12 noon 28th June to 12 noon 29th June, 1917.

On receipt of current copy of Tactical Progress Report
in the trenches, previous copy to be burnt.

PART I OPERATIONS.

   Artillery. The line of shell-holes in O.14.b. & O.8.d. were
shelled. In view of the suspected relief of the 76th R.I.R. tracks
East of BOIS DU VERT were searched during the night. Registration
was carried out during the day.
   M.Gs. Owing to the suspected relief harassing fire was maintained
on the tracks in O.9.b. and c. Cross Road O.9.c.99. LANYARD TR.
during the night. About 2 a.m. hostile artillery commenced to
search for our M.G. positions with 77 and 105 mm. guns.
   T.Ms. Our L.T.Ms. carried out a shoot on the trench at O.26.b.38.
about daybreak.
   Patrols. Patrols moved 300 yards E. of FARM TR. and though several
shell-holes were observed which showed signs of recent occupation
no touch was gained with the enemy. The ground E. of TOOL TR.
from the CAMBRAI Rd. to O.14.b.16. was patrolled and no sign of
the enemy was seen.

PART II INTELLIGENCE.

   Hostile Artillery was less active than usual during the night.
RAKE, FARM, EGRET, DUCK and the new trench in O.20.b. received
attention. From 5 to 6.15 p.m. 5.9's shelled N.25.a. and b. at
the rate of 2 rounds per minute. At 8.50 p.m. N.10.b. was shelled
with 5.9's from the direction of O.12.b.
   Hostile M.Gs. Enemy M.Gs. have been less active during the last
24 hours. The following locations were obtained O.9.a.6.1.
O.8.d.40.85; O.9.c.05. ST.ROHART FACTORY and HILL SIDE WORK.
   Hostile T.Ms. 2 T.Ms. from about O.9.c. 15.75. and O.15.a.30.45
were active on TOOL TR. at intervals during the night.
   Hostile Sniping. Movement in JACKDAW TR. drew fire from enemy
snipers.
   Movement.
      Afternoon 28.6.17. Movement in small parties was seen at the
following places.-
         From OX. TR. to the Sunken Rd. in O.28.d.
         In OCEAN WORK.
         Party of men moving along the new trench in O.16.b. and d.
         Near FACTORY TR.
   Morning 29.6.17
         On road in O.30.d.
         Two stretcher parties near Dressing Station in O.30.d.
         Party left track at O.28.d. and went into OBUS TR.
         In OX. TR.
         A telephone linesman on Ridge in O.15.a.
         In VIS TR.
      Considerable movement throughout the period near CORNER COPSE
and on the tracks in O.5.d. and O.6.c. Very little movement
near the mound in J.31.d. The ETAING-SAILLY Rd. was being much
used.
      2.55 p.m. For 3 minutes flashes were seen from a house at
            J.27.c.1.9. No message could be picked up.
      3. 0 " 30 horses grazing in P.1.c. were led away towards
            ETAING.
         Between 4.30 and 6.30 p.m. three cyclists, 8 lorries
and several parties of about 20 were seen moving in both directions
on the BELLONNE TORTEQUENNE Rd.
   General. Smoke was seen at the following places :-
         House in BOIRY O.5.a.8.1.
         In REMY O.9.c.8.1.
         In O.16.a. puffs of black smoke followed by small
            explosions.
         ST.ROHART FACTORY - A flash followed by a puff of
            smoke at 4.35 p.m.
         At 2 p.m. during our shelling of VIS-EN-ARTOIS a
            fire broke out and was still burning in the evening.

Work. Has been noticed at the following places :-
   HILL TOP WORK. O.34.a.75.05.
   OCEAN WORK. O.29.b.2.7.
Light Signals. Opposite the right sub-section Green Lights still appear to mean lengthen range.
Aircraft. Our 'planes were very active during the day over of our the enemy lines. 2/'planes flew down our line at 6 p.m. at about 400 ft. Hostile aircraft were active this morning early.

John T. Crosthwaite

29th June, 1917.

Captain,
General Staff.

SECRET

56th DIVISION TACTICAL PROGRESS REPORT No. 19.
from 12 noon 29th June to 12 noon 30th June 1917.

On receipt of current copy of Tactical Progress Report
in the trenches, previous copy to be burnt.

PART I OPERATIONS.

Artillery. Registration was carried out yesterday. Enemy's communications were heavily bombarded between 6.30 and 7.30 p.m.

Patrols. A patrol from the Left Sub-Sector discovered and dispersed with L.G. fire an enemy working party in shell-holes in O.8.d.

Machine Guns. Harassing fire was maintained during the night on HILL TOP and HILL SIDE WORK.

PART II INTELLIGENCE.

Hostile Artillery. Our front line was intermittently shelled with 4.2's and 77 mm. during the day. N.10.b. and N.11a. and N.17 received attention during the day with 5.9's and 8". N.28. central was shelled with 5.9's from about O.30. central between 12 noon and 1.30 p.m. N.35.a. received about 20 rounds of 10.5 cm. at about 2.15 p.m. Occasional shelling of GUEMAPPE during the afternoon with 5.9's and again this morning between 11 and 11.15 a.m. TOOL, HOE, SADDLE, BOAR, BISON & LION Trenches were lightly shelled during the night.

Hostile M.Gs. Active from BOIS DU VERT and ST. ROHART FACTORY during the night.

Hostile T.Ms. Active from BOIS DU VERT and LANYARD Trench. SPOOR and JACKDAW Trenches received some attention during the night. T.Ms. appear to frequently change their positions.

Hostile Aircraft. At 2 p.m. 5.30 p.m. and 8 p.m. hostile 'planes flying at a low altitude swept our trenches with M.G. fire. They were driven off with L.G. and rifle fire.

Movement.
  Afternoon 29.6.17.
    Large number of horses grazing about P.3.a. & c.
    Individual movement in VIS trench at O.17.a.05.90.
    Slight movement in OSTRICH Trench.- O.30.a.25.10. On road in O.20.d. and in OX Trench O.29.c.45.60.
    Train moving N. on railway in J.29.a. Train observed moving towards ETAING, returning about 15 minutes later.
  Morning 30.6.17.
    Five men entered OSTRICH Tr. O.29.d.45.35. followed a few minutes later by 5 other men. They were all in full marching order. Considerable movement during yesterday afternoon and evening between SAILLY-EN-OSTREVENT - ETAING & ETERPIGNY. Heavy traffic principally moving in a Northerly direction was observed on the BELLONNE TORTEQUENNE Rd. Usual movement near mound J.31.d. Roads in O.5.d.and O.6.c. and OCEAN WORK. Slight movement at ST.ROHART FACTORY.

New Work. Observed at the following points -
  J.32.d.6.2. a party of men seen digging.
  ST.ROHART FACTORY - party carrying timber.
  Shell-holes in O.8.d.
  Trench O.6.a.1.5.
  OCEAN WORK O.29. OX Trench O.29.c.70.15.

Smoke and Fires. Seen at the following places -
  Smoke at P.13.b.7.8.
  The Chimney at ETERPIGNY was smoking during the afternoon and evening.
  At 3 p.m. a fire was observed burning near the Church in SAILLY-EN-OSTREVENT.

General. At 7.40 p.m. an Anti-aircraft gun was observed firing on a true bearing of 61° from N.24.b.80.15.

H.F. Walleson
for. Lieutenant,
General Staff.

30th June, 1917.

SECRET.   Copy No. 26

56th DIVISION ORDER No. 101.

Reference attached Maps A and B.   6th June, 1917.

1.   56th Division (less Artillery) is to relieve the 61st Division (less Artillery) in the line, the relief to be completed before daylight on 11th June.

2.   (a) 169th Infantry Brigade will take over the whole of the Divisional front under arrangements to be made direct with the Brigadier General Commanding 184th Infantry Brigade (H.Q. N.10.d.57)
    (b) Two Battalions 168th Infantry Brigade will move to the WANCOURT LINE on the evening of 11th inst., and will then be at the disposal of Brigadier-General Commanding 169th Infantry Brigade for use in case of emergency.

3.   On the night 9th/10th June the present Divisional boundaries are being changed, and will become as shown on attached Map B.
    To avoid a double relief, one Battalion 169th Infantry Brigade will, therefore, be relieving a Battalion of 14th Division (VII Corps) on that night, under arrangements to be made by Brigadier-General Commanding 184th Infantry Brigade.

4.   Two Sections (8 guns) of 193rd Div. M.G.Coy. are placed at the disposal of Brigadier-General Commanding 169th Infantry Brigade; the O.C. these Sections will report to Brigadier-General Commanding 169th Infantry Brigade on arrival in the TELEGRAPH HILL Area.

5.   West of ARRAS the following distances will be maintained on the march :-

    250 yards between Battalions.
    100 yards between Companies or Sections of transport.
East of ARRAS :-
    200 yards between Platoons.

6.   The following communication trenches may be used in common:-

    PICK TRENCH - by 56th Div. & Left Div. VI Corps.
    KESTREL LANE - by 56th Div. & Left Div. VII Corps, until another route can be made by VII Corps.
    KESTREL LANE will be maintained by 56th Divn.

7.   The 3rd & 12th Divisional Artilleries will support 56th Division.
    The C.R.A. 56th Division will assume command on completion of the relief.

8.   The Anti-Aircraft protection of

    (a) "F" Dump - L.32.b.
    (b) FAUBOURG DUMP - L.30.a.

by two Vickers or Lewis Guns will be taken over by 61st Divn. from 6 p.m. 10th inst.
    O.C. 193rd Div. M.G.Coy. will arrange to hand over all instructions to incoming reliefs.

9.   The C.R.E. will arrange to take over details of work from the C.R.E's 14th & 61st Divisions respectively for the Sectors to be taken over from those Divisions.

/10.

10. The A.D.M.S. will make arrangements direct with the A.D's M.S. 14th & 61st Divisions for the relief of the Medical Units.

11. The A.P.M. will arrange for the relief of the Police of 14th & 61st Divisions in the area to be taken over.

12. Moves of Units not mentioned in this Order or relief table will be carried out under the Orders of the A.A. & Q.M.G.

13. Railhead will be at ARRAS on 10th inst.

14. General Officer Commanding 56th Division will assume Command of the Line at 10 a.m. on 11th inst.

15. Div. H.Q. will close at HABARCQ at 10 a.m. on 11th inst. and open at ARRAS, 15, Rue de la Paix, at the same hour.

16. ACKNOWLEDGE.

B Pakenham
Lieut-Colonel,
General Staff.

Issued at 9 pm

Copy No. 1. 167th Infantry Brigade.
2. 168th Infantry Brigade.
3. 169th Infantry Brigade.
4. 1/5th Cheshire Regiment.
5. 61st Division.
6. 14th Division.
7. 3rd Division.
8. VI Corps H.A.
9. VI Corps Artillery.
10. No. 12 Squadron, R.F.C.
11. C.R.A.
12. C.R.E.
13. A.P.M.
14. 193rd Div. M.G.Coy.
15. 56th Div. M.G.Officer.
16. 56th Div. Signals.
17. 56th Div. Train.
18. 56th Div. Gas Officer.
19. D.A.D.O.S.
20. 4th Aust. Div. Supply Col.
21. No. 2 Amm. Sub Park.
22. A.D.M.S.
23. A.D.V.S.
24. "Q"
25. A.D.C.
26. War Diary.
27. File.

RELIEF TABLE to accompany 56th DIVISION ORDER No. 101.

Serial No.	Date. June.	Unit.	From	To	Remarks.
1.	8th.	"A" Battalion 169th Inf. Bde. 169th M.G.Coy.	AGNEZ-LES-DUISANS.	TELEGRAPH HILL AREA.	(a) On arrival come under the orders of B.G.C. 184th Inf.Bde. (b) M.G's.(6) of 14th Div. in front line system will be relieved on night 10th/11th, remainder (5) on night 9th/10th (c) No restrictions as to time - route via DAINVILLE -BEAURAINS.
2.	9/10th	"A" Bn.169th Inf.Bde.	TELEGRAPH HILL Area.	Front line S. of COJEUL RIVER.	In relief of "A" Bn. 43rd Inf. Bde. 14th Div. Relief to be completed by 6 a.m. 10th inst. when B.G.C. 184th Inf. Bde. assumes command. 14th Div. is arranging to move "A" Bn. 169th Inf.Bde. during the day to NEPAL Trench, whence the relief will be carried out by night.
3.	9th	169th Inf.Bde.(less 1 Bn.)	AGNEZ-LES-DUISANS.	TELEGRAPH HILL Area.	Via DAINVILLE - BEAURAINS. Not to enter area before 9 pm.
4.	9th	416th Fld.Coy.R.E.	GOUVES.	2 Secs. N.20.b.68) 2 Secs. N.10.d.57) approx.	To march under the orders of 169th Inf.Bde.
5.	9th	2 Secs.193rd Div. M.G.Coy.	SIMENCOURT.	TELEGRAPH HILL Area.	To March under the orders of 169th Inf. Bde.
6.	9th	41st Inf.Bde. 14th Div.	TELEGRAPH HILL Area.	BEAURAINS.	Via DUISANS - March at 9 p.m.
7.	10th	2 Coys.5th Cheshire Regt.(Pioneers) 2 Coys.5th Cheshire Regt. (Pioneers)	GOUVES. ARRAS.	ARRAS. WANCOURT Line about N.16.b.33.	During the day. Move to be made by Platoons at not less than 10 minutes intervals, and to be complete by 9 p.m. See Note at end.

(2)

Serial No.	Date. June.	Unit.	From.	To.	Remarks.
8.	10/11th.	169th Inf.Bde.(Less 1 Bn.)	TELEGRAPH HILL Area.	Line.	In relief of 184th Inf.Bde. who will leave front line Machine Guns in line until night 11/12th inst.
9.	10/11th.	184th Inf.Bde.	Line.	TILLOY Area.	On relief by 169th Inf.Bde.
10.	10th.	168th Inf.Bde. 512th Fld.Coy.R.E. 193rd Div.M.G.Coy. (less 2 Secs.)	SIMENCOURT. " "	TELEGRAPH HILL Area N.8.d.88. ACHICOURT.	168th Inf.Bde. to arrive in area by 8 p.m. Via BEAUMETZ - ACHICOURT - BEAURANS - under the orders of B.G.C. 168th Inf.Bdo.
11.	10th	183rd Inf.Bde.	TILLOY	SIMENCOURT.	Not to leave TILLOY before 7 p.m.
12.	11th	167th Inf.Bde.	GOUVES & MONTENESCOURT.	ACHICOURT & ARRAS	In relief of 182nd Inf.Bde.- H.Q. ACHICOURT. Via DAINVILLE. Move to be completed by 9 a.m.
13.	11th	H.Q. 56th Divn.	HABARCQ.	ARRAS.	Via ST.POL - ARRAS Rd. To arrive at 10 a.m.
14.	11th	H.Q. 61st Divn.	ARRAS.	WARLUS.	To be clear of ARRAS at 10 a.m.
15.	11th	2 Bns.168th Inf.Bdo.	TELEGRAPH HILL Area	WANCOURT Line.	Not to arrive before 9 p.m. Will come on arrival under orders of B.G.C. 169th Inf.Bdo.
		2 Coys. 1/5th Cheshire Regt. (Pioneers) in ARRAS 2 Secs. 512th Fld.Coy.R.E. at N.9.c. 2 " " " " N.12.a.22.			will be relieved from work under C.E. Corps on 10th inst. under arrangements to be communicated later.

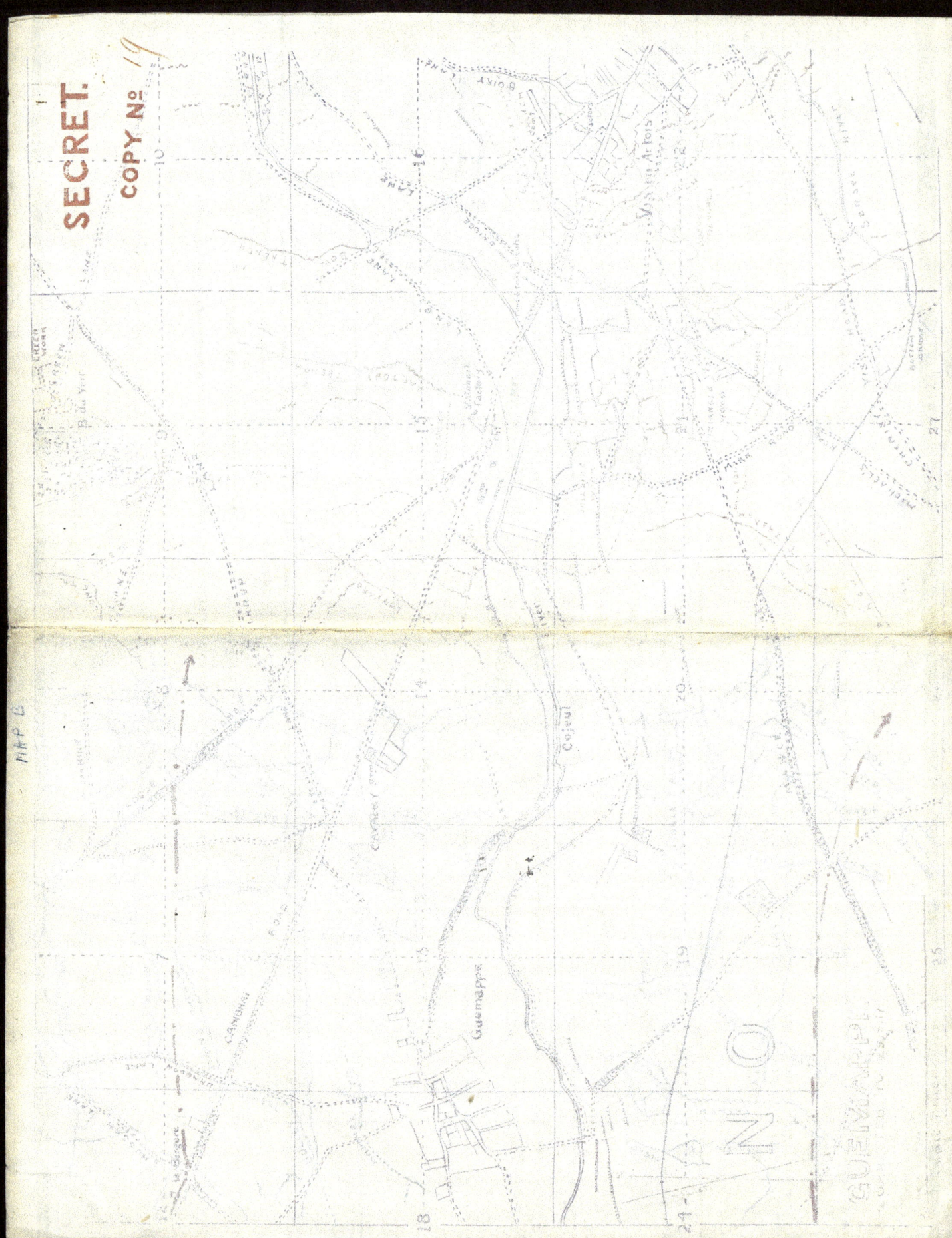

SECRET   *War Diary Copy*   Copy No. 26

56th DIVISION ORDER No. 102.

7th June 1917.

1. An attack is to be made at a date and time to be notified later with the object of capturing HOOK Trench and LONG Trench so as to obtain a more favourable position from which the BOIS DU VERT can be attacked at a later date.

2. The attack is to be carried out by troops of the 3rd Division.

3. The Artillery bombardment with the object of shaking the enemy's nerve and destroying his defences, is to commence on the 8th June. Separate Artillery Instructions have been issued.

4. The line to be consolidated will run roughly as follows:-

   O.8.b.1.1. - LONG Trench - O.2.b.45.10 - thence back to TWIN Trench.

5. As soon as this line has been captured strong patrols are to be pushed forward to gain ground, especially the mound in O.2.d. and to cover the work of consolidation.

6. The attack will be carried out as a surprise without a barrage. Heavy Artillery covering fire will however commence on selected points and localities at Zero plus 2 minutes.

7. 169th Infantry Brigade will co-operate by manning TOOL Trench, and arranging to bring heavy rifle and Lewis Gun fire at Zero hour on to the hostile occupied system of shell-holes extending from approximately O.8.d.11 to O.8.b.42, so as to prevent the enemy bringing enfilade rifle or machine gun fire to bear on the attacking troops of 3rd Division.

8. Details of Artillery and M.G. co-operation will be communicated later.

9. A contact aeroplane will fly over the area at Zero plus 30 minutes, and will call for flares by sounding a Klaxon Horn or firing White Lights.
   This contact aeroplane is only intended to co-operate with 3rd Division, and its calls will not be responded to by 169th Infantry Brigade troops.

10. The B.G.C. 167th Infantry Brigade will detail an Officer to report to the General Staff Officer of VI Corps in charge of the Corps Dropping Ground at N.2 Central at Zero minus 1 hour. No ground signals are to be put out at this station until Zero.

11. ACKNOWLEDGE.

B. Pakenham
Lieut-Colonel,
General Staff.

7th June, 1917.

Issued at 9 pm

Copy No.					
1. 167th Inf.Bde.	10. No.12 Squad.R.F.C.	19. D.A.D.O.S.
2. 168th Inf.Bde.	11. C.R.A.	20. 4th Aust.D.S.C
3. 169th Inf.Bde.	12. C.R.E.	21. No.2 Amm.Sb Pk
4. 1/5th Ches.Regt.	13. A.P.M.	22. A.D.M.S.
5. 61st Division.	14. 193rd Div.M.G.Cy.	23. A.D.V.S.
6. 14th Division.	15. 56th Div.M.G.O.	24. "Q"
7. 3rd Division.	16. 56th Div.Signals.	25. A.D.C.
8. VI Corps H.A.	17. 56th Div.Train.	26. War Diary.
9. VI Corps Arty.	18. 56th Div.Gas O.	27. File.

SECRET.

56th Divn. G.S/424.

167th Infantry Brigade.
168th Infantry Brigade.
169th Infantry Brigade.
1/5th Cheshire Regt.
3rd Division.
C.R.A.
C.R.E.
193rd Div. M.G. Coy.
56th Div. Signals.
War Diary.
File.

---

1. With reference to 56th Division Order No. 102 of 7th June, para 7, the hour at which 169th Infantry Brigade will open heavy rifle & Lewis Gun fire on the hostile system of shell holes <u>will be at Zero plus 2 minutes</u> instead of at Zero.

2. An officer of Divisional Headquarters will synchronize watches at 3rd Div. H.Q. at 10 a.m. & 10 p.m. on the day previous to the attack. The correct time will then be sent round by Special Despatch Rider to C.R.A. and B.G.C. Infantry Brigade in the line.

B. Pakenham

Head Qrs. 56th Divn.
10th June, 1917.

Lieut-Colonel,
General Staff.

56th Divn. G.S/440.

SECRET.

167th Infantry Brigade.
168th Infantry Brigade.
169th Infantry Brigade.
1/5th Cheshire Regt.
3rd Division.
C.R.A.
C.R.E.
193rd Md. M.G.Coy.
56th Div. Signals.
War Diary.
File.

With reference to 56th Division Order No. 102 of 7th June.

   (a) The Operations therein referred to will be carried out on Thursday, 14th June.

   (b) Zero hour will be notified later.

2. With reference to 56th Division G.S/424 para. 1 last line for Zero plus 2 minutes read Zero plus 1½ minutes.

3. ACKNOWLEDGE.

Head Qrs. 56th Divn.
12th June, 1917.

Lieut-Colonel,
General Staff.

SECRET

56th Division. G.3/439.

167th Infantry Bde.
168th Infantry Bde.
169th Infantry Bde.
1/5th Ches. Regt.
3rd Division.
C.R.A.
C.R.E.
193rd Div. M.G. Coy.
56th Div. Signals.
War Diary.
File.

In continuation of this office No. G.3/440 of 12th June 1917.

Zero hour will be 7-20 a.m.

ACKNOWLEDGE.

H.Q. 56th Division.
13th June 1917.

Lieut.-Colonel,
General Staff.

SECRET. *War Diary* Copy No. 20

56th DIVISION ORDER No. 103

11th June, 1917.

1. The two Battalions 168th Infantry Brigade & 168th Bde. M.G.Coy. now quartered in ARRAS will move on 13th inst. into BEAURAINS CAMP.

2. Remainder of 168th Infantry Brigade & Brigade H.Q. will remain as at present located.

3. The new area will not be entered before 10 a.m. 13th inst.

B Pakenham

Lieut-Colonel,
General Staff.

Issued at

Copy No. 1. 167th Infantry Brigade.
2. 168th Infantry Brigade.
3. 169th Infantry Brigade.
4. 1/5th Cheshire Regiment.
5. C.R.A.
6. C.R.E.
7. A.P.M.
8. 193rd Div. M.G.Coy.
9. 56th Div. M.G.Officer.
10. 56th Div. Signals.
11. 56th Div. Train.
12. 56th Div. Gas Officer.
13. D.A.D.O.S.
14. 4th Aust.Div.Sup.Column.
15. No.2 Amm. Sub Park.
16. A.D.M.S.
17. A.D.V.S.
18. "Q"
19. A.D.C.
20. War Diary.
21. File.

SECRET.   War Diary Copy   Copy No 26

56th DIVISION ORDER No. 104

14th June 1917.

1. It is possible that the enemy may at any time carry out a withdrawal to the QUEANT - DROCOURT Line.
   In the first instance he would probably hold the intermediate line BOIRY NOTRE DAME - REMY.

2. Close touch must be maintained with the enemy by constant patrolling and a careful watch kept on his movements, so that immediate advantage may be taken of such a withdrawal.

3. As soon as it is definitely known that the enemy is retiring or has retired, the following action will be taken :-

   (a) <u>By the Brigade in the Line.</u>

   (i) Push forward at once without awaiting orders.

   (ii) Inform Div. H.Q., Brigades on flanks and Support and Reserve Brigades of the action taken.

   (iii) Arrange for the garrisoning of our present front system until the Support Brigade can take it over, using the two attached Battalions of the Support Brigade for the purpose.

   (b) <u>By the Brigade in Support.</u>

   (i) Remainder of Brigade will "Stand to" at once, and will be sent forward to the WANCOURT Line, as soon as the B.G.C. Brigade in the line reports that he is moving forward troops from it.

   (ii) Brigade H.Q. will move forward at once to N.16.a.18 (old Brigade H.Q. of right Brigade) and will take over the defence of the present line when it is vacated by the Brigade in the line.

   (iii) Report of action to Div. H.Q.

   (c) <u>Reserve Brigade.</u>

   Will "Stand to" ready to move in accordance with orders to be issued by Div. H.Q.

4. The first objective in the advance will be the following line :-

   NARROW Trench (where touch will be gained with the left Division, VII Corps) - TRIANGLE WOOD - HILLSIDE WORK - ST.ROHART FACTORY - high ground South of the BOIS DU VERT, N. of which touch will be gained with left Division, VI Corps.
   Further objectives will be communicated by Div.H.Q.

   At each advance each Brigade in rear will move forward to occupy ground vacated by the Brigade in its front.

5. Each objective, when gained, will be consolidated, and strong fighting patrols will be pushed out to gain and keep touch with the enemy.

/6.-

6. (a) Brigadier Generals Commanding Infantry Brigades will have their plans prepared for this operation.

   (b) The C.R.A. will submit to Div. H.Q. plans for moving forward artillery in support and will have positions reconnoitred.

   (c) The C.R.E. will forward plans for repair of roads, pushing forward dumps, etc.

   (d) The A.D.M.S. will forward plans for moving forward Dressing Stations as necessary.

   (e) O.C. Signals will forward plans for maintaining signal communication.

   The plans from each of the above will be forwarded to Div. H.Q. by 19th inst.

7. All preparations must be made by each Infantry Brigade for communication with aeroplane contact patrols, "S.O.S." Signals etc. in the event of its becoming the leading Brigade.

8. Div. H.Q. will in the first instance, remain in ARRAS.

9. ACKNOWLEDGE.

B Pakenham
Lieut-Colonel,
General Staff.

Issued at

Copy No. 1. 167th Infantry Brigade.   15. 56th Div. M.G.Offr.
        2. 168th Infantry Brigade.   16.   "   Signals.
        3. 169th Infantry Brigade.   17.   "   Train.
        4. 1/5th Cheshire Regt.   18.   "   Gas Officer
        5. 3rd Division.   19. D.A.D.O.S.
        6. 18th Division.   20. 4th Aust.Div.Sup.Col.
        7. 50th Division.   21. No.2 Ammn. Sub.Park.
        8. VI Corps H.Arty.   22. A.D.M.S.
        9.   do.   Arty.   23. A.D.V.S.
       10. No.12 Squad. R.F.C.   24. "Q"
       11. C.R.A.   25. A.D.C.
       12. C.R.E.   26. War Diary.
       13. A.P.M.   27. File.
       14. 193rd Div.M.G.Coy.

SECRET.   Copy No. 26

56th DIVISION ORDER No. 105

17th June, 1917.

1. 168th Infantry Brigade will relieve 169th Infantry Brigade in the Line on the night 20th/21st June; relief to be completed before daylight 21st June.

   Details of relief will be arranged direct between Brigadiers concerned.

2. The 2 Battalions of 167th Infantry Brigade attached to 169th Infantry Brigade will be relieved by 2 Bns. 167th Infantry Brigade, under arrangements to be made between B.G's C. 167th and 169th Infantry Brigades, as convenient, but this relief will not be made on the same night as the relief of the line.

3. 167th and 168th Brigade M.G.Coys. will be at the disposal of B.G.C. 168th Infantry Brigade to relieve 169th and 193rd M.G.Coys.

   Machine Guns in advance of the Divisional Reserve Line (EGRET - LION - RAKE & SPADE Trenches) will not be relieved until the night 21st/22nd June.

4. Command will pass at 10 a.m. 21st June.

5. Progress and completion of relief to be reported to Div. H.Q.

6. ACKNOWLEDGE.

B. Pakenham

Lieut-Colonel,
General Staff.

Issued at
Copy No. 1. 167th Infantry Brigade.
2. 168th Infantry Brigade.
3. 169th Infantry Brigade.
4. 1/5th Cheshire Regt.
5. 3rd Division.
6. 18th Division.
7. 50th Division.
8. VI Corps H.Arty.
9. do. Arty.
10. No. 12 Squad. R.F.C.
11. C.R.A.
12. C.R.E.
13. A.P.M.
14. 193rd Div. M.G.Coy.
15. 56th Div. M.G.Offr.
16. " Signals.
17. " Train.
18. " Gas Officer.
19. D.A.D.O.S.
20. 4th Aust. Div. Sup.Col.
21. No. 2 Ammn. Sub Park.
22. A.D.M.S.
23. A.D.V.S.
24. "Q"
25. A.D.C.
26. War Diary.
27. File.

SECRET.   Copy No. 25

56th DIVISION ORDER No. 106.

26th June, 1917.

1. On the night 1st/2nd July the 37th Infantry Brigade, 12th Division will take over from 168th Infantry Brigade the front North of the following line :-

    GORDON ALLEY from its junction with the front line to its junction with ARRAS-CAMBRAI Road (inclusive to 56th Division) - thence the Grid line between squares O.7. and O.13 produced westwards.
    Details of relief will be arranged between Brigadiers concerned.

2. Machine Guns of 37th Infantry Brigade will relieve Machine Guns of 168th Infantry Brigade N. of above boundary on the night 30th June/1st July under arrangements to be made direct between Brigadiers.

3. The 2 Battalions, 167th Infantry Brigade now attached to 168th Infantry Brigade will be withdrawn from the WANCOURT LINE during the night 1/2nd July under arrangements to be made by the B.G.C. 168th Infantry Brigade, and will proceed to BEAURAINS CAMP.

4. During the 1st July and night 1st/2nd July the B.G.C. 168th Infantry Brigade will arrange to relieve 167th M.G.Coy. by guns of 168th M.G.Coy.

5. H.Q. of 168th Infantry Brigade will be established at N.16.a.18 by 10 a.m. 2nd July.
    As the 37th Infantry Brigade is at the same time taking over a portion of 12th Division front North of our present boundary, the B.G.C. 168th Infantry Brigade will give the B.G.C. 37th Infantry Brigade facilities for establishing necessary signal communications and for command of 37th Infantry Brigade front.

6. Orders regarding the redistribution of Artillery necessitated by the above changes will be issued later.

7. ACKNOWLEDGE.

                                                              B.Pakenham
                                                                Lieut-Colonel,
                                                                 General Staff.

Issued at 9pm

Copy No.			
1.	167th Infantry Brigade.	14.	56th Div. M.G.Officer.
2.	168th Infantry Brigade.	15.	" Signals.
3.	169th Infantry Brigade.	16.	" Train.
4.	1/5th Cheshire Regt.	17.	" Gas Officer.
5.	12th Division.	18.	D.A.D.O.S.
6.	50th Division.	19.	4th Aust.Div.Sup.Column.
7.	VI Corps H.Arty.	20.	No.2 Amm.Sub Park.
8.	do. Arty.	21.	A.D.M.S.
9.	No.12 Squad R.F.C.	22.	A.D.V.S.
10.	C.R.A.	23.	"Q"
11.	C.R.E.	24.	A.D.C.
12.	A.P.M.	25.	War Diary.
13.	193rd Div.M.G.Coy.	26.	File.

SECRET. *War Diary* Copy No. 25

56th DIVISION ORDER No. 107.

29th June, 1917.

1. At 12 noon on 2nd July, 56th Division will be transferred to VII Corps; the inter-Corps boundary between VII and XVII Corps will then be that described in para. 1 of 56th Divn. Order No. 106 of 26th inst., produced as far West as the ARRAS-BOIRY ST.RICTRUDE Road, with the exception that GORDON ALLEY has now been made inclusive to XVII Corps.

2. 56th Division (less Artillery) will be relieved between 2nd and 4th July 1917, by 50th Division in accordance with attached relief table.

3. 9th Divisional Artillery will continue to cover the front taken over and will come under the command of G.O.C. 50th Division on conclusion of the relief. Supply railhead will be BOISLEUX AU MONT from July 3rd.

4. The relief of the 168th Infantry Brigade will be completed by 8 a.m. on 4th July.

    The Battalions on the left bank of the COJEUL RIVER and the Machine Guns and Trench Mortars on the right bank will be relieved by 151st Infantry Brigade on the night 2nd/3rd July.

    The Battalions on the right bank of the River, and the Machine Guns and Trench Mortars on the left bank will be relieved by 151st Infantry Brigade on the night 3rd/4th July.

    Details will be arranged direct between Brigadier Generals Commanding 168th and 151st Infantry Brigades.

    The Command will pass on the completion of the relief.

5. 50th Division is arranging for 1 Coy R.E. and 2 Coys. Pioneers to move to about N.15 and N.14 respectively on 1st July in order to take over work in the line from 2nd July (inclusive).

    C.R.E. will arrange to hand over to C.R.E. 50th Division all necessary details of work in the area for which he is responsible.

6. The A.D.M.S. will arrange direct with A.D.M.S. 50th Divn. for the relief of Medical Units so that they may march with their respective Brigade Groups.

7. Moves of units not mentioned in the attached relief table will be arranged by the A.A. & Q.M.G.

8. Brigade Groups will be formed as shewn in the footnote to the relief table for the purposes of marching and billeting in accordance with this Order.

9. Progress & completion of reliefs will be reported to Div. H.Q. by wire.

10. General Officer Commanding 50th Division will assume Command of the line on completion of the relief.

11. Div. H.Q. will close at ARRAS at 10 a.m. on 4th July, and open at the CHATEAU, LE CAUROY, at the same hour.

/12.

12. The following distances will be maintained on the march West of ARRAS :-

    250 yards between Battalions.

    100 yards between Companies or Sections of Transport.

    ACKNOWLEDGE.

B. Pakenham

29th June 1917.
                                                Lieut.-Colonel.
                                                General Staff.

Copy No. 1.   167th Infantry Brigade.
        2.   168th Infantry Brigade.
        3.   169th Infantry Brigade.
        4.   1/5th Cheshire Regt.
        5.   12th Division.
        6.   50th Division.
        7.   VI Corps H. Arty.
        8.   VI Corps Arty.
        9.   No. 12 Squadron, R.F.C.
       10.   C.R.A.
       11.   C.R.E.
       12.   A.P.M.
       13.   193rd Div. M.G. Coy.
       14.   56th Div. M.G. Officer.
       15.   56th Div. Signal Coy.
       16.   56th Div. Train.
       17.   56th Div. Gas Officer.
       18.   D.A.D.O.S.
       19.   4th Aust. Div. Sup. Col.
       20.   No. 2 Amm. Sub Park.
       21.   A.D.M.S.
       22.   A.D.V.S.
       23.   "Q".
       24.   A.D.C.
       25.   War Diary.
       26.   File.
       27.   VII Corps.

RELIEF TABLE TO ACCOMPANY 56th DIVISION ORDER No. 107.

Serial No.	Date. July.	Unit.	From	To.	Route.	Remarks.
1.	1st & 2nd.	151st Inf.Bde.	50th Div. Area.	Neighbourhood of HENIN.		No restrictions.
2.	2nd.	169th Inf.Bde. Group.	ACHICOURT & BEAURAINS.	GOUY.	WAILLY - BEAUMETZ.	No restrictions.
3.	Night 2/3rd.	2 Bns. 151st Inf. Bde.	As in Serial No. 1.	Line.	"	In relief of 2 Bns. 168th Inf.Bde. on left bank of COJEUL.
4.	"	2 Bns. 168th Inf. Bde.	Line.	ACHICOURT.	"	On relief by 2 Bns. of 151st Inf.Bde.
5.	3rd	169th Inf.Bde. Group.	GOUY.	GRAND RULLECOURT SUS ST. LEGER. SOMBRIN.	FOSSEUX - EARLY.	No restrictions.
6.	3rd	1/5th Ches. Regt. (Pioneers). 193rd Div.M.G.Coy. 416th, 512th Fld.Coys R.E. 513th Fld.Coy.R.E. (less 2 Soctns.)	Present billets. " " "	GOUY.	WAILLY-BEAUMETZ.	No restrictions. Under the Command of O.C. 1/5th Cheshire Rt. (Pioneers).
7.	Night 3/4th.	151st Inf.Bde. (less 2 Bns.)	As in Serial No. 1.	Line.		In relief of remainder of 168th Inf.Bde.
8.	"	168th Inf.Bde. (less 2 Bns.)	Line.	ACHICOURT & BEAURAINS.		On relief by 151st Inf. Bde. H.Q. at ACHICOURT.
9.	4th.	1/5th Ches. Regt. Pioneers. 193rd Div.M.G.Coy. 416th, 512th and 513th Fld.Coys.R.E.	GOUY. " "	GRAND RULLECOURT. SARS-LEZ-BOIS SOMBRIN.	FOSSEUX - EARLY. " "	No restrictions. Under the orders of O.C. 1/5th Cheshire Rt. (Pioneers)

Serial No.	Date. July.	Unit.	From.	To.	Route.	Remarks.
10.	4th.	167th Inf. Bde.Group.	TELEGRAPH HILL Area & BEAURAINS.	GOUY.	AGNY-WAILLY - BEAUMETZ.	
11.	4th.	168th Inf. Bde.Group. (Dismounted portion)	ACHICOURT & BEAURAINS.	LIGNEREUIL LIENCOURT DENIER.	By bus.	Under arrangements to be made by A.A. & Q.M.G.
12.	4th.	168th Inf. Bde.Group. (Mounted portion)	do.	do.	DAINVILLE - WANQUETIN - AVESNES.	Will be clear of DAINVILLE by 9. 0. a.m.
13.	4th.	Div.H.Q.	ARRAS.	LE CAUROY.		No restrictions.
14.	5th.	167th Inf. Bde.Group.	GOUY.	IVERGNY - BEAUDRICOURT.	FOSSEUX-BARLY SUS ST.LEGER.	No restrictions.

N O T E.

Composition of Brigade Groups.

```
167th Infantry Brigade.      168th Infantry Brigade.      169th Infantry Brigade.
167th M.G.Coy.               168th M.G.Coy.               169th M.G.Coy.
167th T.M.Battery.           168th T.M.Battery.           169th T.M.Battery.
No. 2 Coy. Train.            No. 3 Coy. Train.            No. 4 Coy. Train.
2/1st Field Ambulance        2/2nd Field Ambulance        2/3rd Field Ambulance.
```

LOCATION TABLE.

JUNE

	16	17	18	19	20	21	22	23	24	25	26	27	28	29	30
Div. H.Q.	ARRAS														
167th Inf. Bde.															
H.Q.	TELEGRAPH HILL														
1st Ldn. Rgt.	L. RESERVE														
3rd " "	R. RESERVE														
7th Mx. "															
8th " "	TELEGRAPH HILL										L. RESERVE				R. RESERVE
168th Inf. Bde.															
H.Q.	ACHICOURT									LINE Nº d 36					
4th Ldn. Rgt.	ACHICOURT					L. SUPPORT					ACHICOURT				
12th "	DESURANDS CAMP					R	L	R	L		ACHICOURT Rgt				
13th "	ACHICOURT					L	R	L	R		DESURANDS CAMP				
14th "						R. SUPPORT					ACHICOURT				
169th Inf. Bde.															
H.Q.	LINE Nº d 36										R. SUPPORT				L. SUPPORT
2nd Ldn. Rgt.	L. SUPPORT	L	R	R	R	R	R	R	R		L	L	L	L	R
5th Ldn. Rgt.	R	R	R	R	L	L	L	L	L		R	R	R	R	
9th "	L	L	L	L	R	R	R	R	R		L	L	L	L	
13th "	R. SUPPORT	R	R	R	L	L	L	L	L		R	R	R	R	
Div. Arty.															
H.Q.	ARRAS														
280 Bde.	detached to VII Corps.														
281 "															
Pioneers															
HQ. + 2 comp	LINE. Nº 6 X														
2 comp	TELEGRAPH HILL Nº 6d 5½														

LOCATION TABLE.

JUNE	1	2	3	4	5	6	7	8	9	10	11	12	13	14	15
Div. H.Q.	HABARCQ										ARRAS. 1st R. de la Paix				
167th Inf. Bde. H.Q.	MONTENESCOURT									TELEGRAPH HILL	R.Reserve				
1st Ldn. Rgt.	GOUVES									SUPPORT AREA	R.Reserve				
3rd " "	MONTENESCOURT										R.Reserve				
7th M.K. "											TELEGRAPH HILL				
8th "															
168th Inf. Bde. H.Q.	SIMENCOURT									MONTENESCOURT ACHICOURT					
4th Ldn. Rgt.	SIMENCOURT									MONTENESCOURT ACHICOURT					
12th " "										MONTENESCOURT ARRAS					
13th " "										GOUVES	ARRAS				
14th " "										MONTENESCOURT ACHICOURT			Beaurains Camp		
169th Inf. Bde. H.Q.	AGNEZ les DUISANS								TELEGRAPH HILL		LINE M6 & 36				
2nd Ldn. Rgt.	Detached to VII Corps								SUPPORT AREA		L. SUPPORT				
5th Ldn. Rgt.	AGNEZ les DUISANS								SUPPORT AREA		R. SUPPORT				
9th " "										R	R				
13th " "										R	R				
Div. Arty. H.Q. 280 Bde.	BEAUMETZ										ARRAS				
281 Bde.	Detached to VII Corps														
Pioneers HQ & 2 coys.	GOUVES									TELEGRAPH HILL M6 & 36					
2 coys	ARRAS									LINE					

56TH DIVISION

GENERAL STAFF

JAN - JUN 1917.

This seems to be a "duplicate copy" of 56 Div Gs diary for April 1917.

THE NATIONAL ARCHIVES (TNA): TERMS AND CONDITIONS FOR THE SUPPLY OF COPIES OF RECORDS

Copyright

1. <u>Most public records in TNA are in Crown Copyright</u>
There are no restrictions on the use of copies for non-commercial research or private study. Copies, and copies of those copies, may be made and used for education purposes. This covers both teaching and preparation for teaching and/or examination by either teacher or student. Applications for permission to use copies for publication (including web-site publication), exhibition or broadcast or any other purpose must be addressed to TNA Image Library, The National Archives, Kew, Richmond, Surrey TW9 4DU. Email: image-library@nationalarchives.gov.uk

2. <u>Copies of Public Records in privately owned (ie not Crown) Copyright</u>
There are no restrictions on the use of copies for non-commercial research, private study or education (as defined above) within the limits set in UK Copyright Law. Applications for permission to use copies for publication (including web-site publication), exhibition or broadcast or any other purpose must be addressed to the current owner(s) of the Copyright in the original document. Anyone wishing to reproduce the material in transcript, translation or facsimile is responsible for identifying the current owner and for obtaining any permission required. An application must also be made to TNA Image Library (address as above) for use of the copy.

3. <u>Copies of non-public records and of published Copyright works held in TNA</u>
These are supplied subject to the customer completing a declaration form and observing the conditions it contains. Any infringement of these conditions may result in legal action. Any use other than for non-commercial research, private study or education, if approved by the copyright owner, may also require the permission of the Image Library.
TNA Copyright Officer will provide further information on request.

Supplying copies

4. Prices quoted on estimates are valid for three months.

5. Orders for copies placed in person at one of TNA's Record Copying counters are accepted on the following conditions:
   a) TNA may cancel the order if the copying process paid for subsequently proves to be unsuitable, e.g. if it may damage the document or fail to produce good copies. If an order is cancelled for such reasons TNA will offer to refund the payment and if feasible will provide an estimate for completing the work by an alternative copying process.
   b) TNA may cancel the order and refund payments if markers are found to be missing, documents are incorrectly marked up, or customers' instructions are unclear.
   c) If the customer's calculation of the number of copies required proves to be an under-estimate TNA will complete the order but will retain the copies until the balance of payment has been received. If it proves to be an overestimate TNA will refund customers where the balance exceeds £3.00 (or £6.00 for overseas customers).

6. TNA will securely package copies supplied by post and will not accept liability in the event of damage or loss in transit. It can, however, arrange insurance cover at an additional cost if customers request it when they place their order. Such cover will usually be provided by a lower rate international recorded delivery unless otherwise requested by the customer.

7. Customers are advised to seek advise from their Internet Service Provider before placing any order for electronic images to be delivered electronically. Customers should note that digital images are supplied in compressed jpeg format via a link to TNA DocumentsOnline site unless specified otherwise and CD images in tif format. AO images can only be requested on CD-ROM.

8. TNA will normally aim to provide 'research' quality copies, i.e. sufficient to convey written or graphic information in the original document. There can be no guarantee that it will be able to do so or that the copies will be suitable for any other purpose, e.g. if the original documents are of poor quality. Higher quality copies or copies suitable for other purposes can be supplied if requested when placing an order. Customers are advised to discuss their requirements with TNA staff to ensure the most suitable process can be recommended.

9. Image sizes:
   a) Photocopies and digitally scanned images: TNA will normally produce copied images, which are approximately the same size as the originals. Photocopies will normally be printed onto sheets of paper of the appropriate size in the A2 to A3 range (within preservation guidelines and at the discretion of the operator) and charges will be based on the size of the paper. In the case of digitally scanned copies the images will normally be printed onto paper approximately the same size as the original and charges will be based on the size category into which the paper falls (i.e. AO to A1, A1 to A2, A2 to A3, A3 to A4. TNA can supply images of sheets of paper of different sizes if customers request it when they place their order.
   b) Prints from microfilm: images will normally be printed onto A3 size paper and may be larger or smaller than the original documents.
   c) Photographs or transparencies can be supplied in the specified dimensions. These will normally be required if a copy is for publication. The Image Library provides such images at the rates indicated in the appropriate leaflet.

Deemed Acceptance

10. TNA will display these terms and conditions at all points of sale. Customers will be deemed to have accepted the terms and conditions in completing an order form, submitting a counter order or accepting documents by any means.

RSDY drive/PSdev/PSDP/SSP self service copying/Terms and Conditions - 2.7.2003

WAR DIARY
or
INTELLIGENCE SUMMARY.
(Erase heading not required.)

Army Form C. 2118.

Place	Date	Hour	Summary of Events and Information	Remarks and references to Appendices
BEAURETZ-LES-LOGES	1st April		Some hostile shelling of BEAURAINS and tracks in rear otherwise quiet. 51st Division Instructions, Dress and Equipment issued. 167 and 168 Inf Bdes relieved 169 Bde in the line during the evening.	APPENDIX II APPENDIX IX
"	2nd		No change. Considerable movement was seen behind the enemy lines during the afternoon, parties digging an advanced trench was seen by the enemy and heavily fired on. 51st Divisional Instructions "Tanks" issued	APPENDIX III
"	3rd		Quiet day on the whole. Hostile artillery shelled our front line and BEAURAINS. 168 Bde carried out an inter-battalion relief. Instructions from Corps received that zero day would be April 8th + that there would be a few days bombardment commencing up not. Bombardment commenced. The enemy's retaliation has not been heavy. 51st Division Operation Order No 19 issued — Orders to Attack —	Appendix I
"	4th		The following Instructions were issued — Signal Communications — Flags — Tanks (No 2) — Contact Aeroplane Signalling Instructions — Concentration and Assembly — Signal Instructions No 2 for Cable Cells etc. Also Orders re Signal Time to commencement of bombardment — Instructions issued from VII Corps for Patrols to examine hostile wire at front line — Brigades informed	Appendix II

Army Form C. 2118.

WAR DIARY
or
INTELLIGENCE SUMMARY.
(Erase heading not required.)

Instructions regarding War Diaries and Intelligence Summaries are contained in F. S. Regs., Part II. and the Staff Manual respectively. Title pages will be prepared in manuscript.

Place	Date	Hour	Summary of Events and Information	Remarks and references to Appendices
BEAUMETZ - LES - LOGES	5 April		W day: Our Artillery continued their wire cutting and bombardment. Our reported cut in several places. The Hun has not been active. Information received from patrols stating the Brown line has not been held. 51st Division Order No 50 issued accordingly. 167 Brigade carried out an internal relief.	APPENDIX I
"	6th		Instructions received from VII Corps post-poning Z day for 24 hours.	
"	7th		X day. - Wire cutting and bombardment continued and good progress made. 51 Div. Instructs "Operation" issued. Zero hour received + issued.	APPENDIX II
"			Q day. Progress was made with wirecutting + destructive fire, and enemy reply was very slight. During the night, 1st LONDON regt attempted to occupy NEUVILLE MILL but was unsuccessful. Heavy artillery dealt with the enemy during the day.	
"	8th		At dusk, 1st LONDON regt attacked NEUVILLE MILL but after obtaining a footing were driven out again with loss of 5 Officers and 50 ORs.	
"			Y day. Move and concentration took place during the night - Battalion returned + Battle replies were dug in ready for Rendezvous except for Reserve which were dug in railway embankment ACHICOURT. Div HQ opened at the railway embankment AGNY.	

6-

Army Form C. 2118.

WAR DIARY
or
INTELLIGENCE SUMMARY

(Erase heading not required.)

Instructions regarding War Diaries and Intelligence Summaries are contained in F. S. Regs., Part II. and the Staff Manual respectively. Title Pages will be prepared in manuscript.

Place	Date	Hour	Summary of Events and Information	Remarks and references to Appendices
AGNY.	April 9th.	a.m. 7.30	Zero hour. Assault commenced.	
		7.52	12th and 13th Londons reported through German front line with little opposition or casualties. Hostile artillery barrage slight. 14th Division on our left crossed crest of TELEGRAPH HILL and advancing in good order.	
		8.0	3rd Londons reported in southern portion of NEUVILLE VITASSE.	
		8.5	8th Middlesex and 12th Londons had been held up by uncut wire, but were now advancing. 3rd and 13th Londons progressing well through the Village. German barrage behind the infantry all the time.	
		8.10	168th Brigade reported assaulting troops had crossed PINE LANE and LEAF TRENCH on the whole Brigade front.	
		8-8.30	F.O.Os reports show that progress of infantry through NEUVILLE VITASSE is steadily progressing.	
		8.27	One Tank was approaching the Sugar Factory.	
		8.40	One Tank North and one South of NEUVILLE VITASSE going well.	
		8.55	168th Brigade message timed 8.12 a.m. reported 13th Londons on the BLUE LINE. 12th Londons had been held up by wire in front of BINE LANE, but were now approaching GRASS LANE TRENCH. 14th Division in touch with our left. Tank moving round the North of NEUVILLE VITASSE was on fire. Barrage in NO MAN'S LAND had stopped.	
		8.50	Batteries started to move to forward positions.	
		9.6	Enemy shelling NEUVILLE VITASSE heavily.	
		9.20 to 9.50	Heavy hostile barrage in M.11., 12 and 24.	
		9.30	Div. M.G.Officer ordered to move forward.	

Army Form C. 2118.

WAR DIARY
or
INTELLIGENCE SUMMARY

(Erase heading not required.)

Instructions regarding War Diaries and Intelligence Summaries are contained in F.S. Regs., Part II. and the Staff Manual respectively. Title Pages will be prepared in manuscript.

Place	Date	Hour	Summary of Events and Information	Remarks and references to Appendices
	April 9th	a.m. 10.5	168th Brigade report right flank of 12th Londons in touch with 13th Londons in MOSS TRENCH, with left flank thrown back owing to right Brigade 14th Division being held up by wire about ACORN LANE.	
		10.0	167th Brigade report 3rd Londons in BLUE LINE, but 8th Middlesex held up by pocket of Germans at M.19.a.6.4.	
		10.10	C.R.A. reported leading Batteries had reached the forward position. Two tanks in action on N.19.b.7.3. N.19.b.3.6. firing heavily due East. Hostile barrage now heavy on M.24 and between MERCATEL and NEUVILLE MILL.	
		10.20	168th Brigade report Reserve Coy. 13th Londons, was moving South through the Village to help the 8th Middlesex. 1 Coy. 12th Londons report themselves in the BLUE LINE.	
		10.30	Scouts of 13th and 14th Londons report wire between MOSS and TELEGRAPH HILL TRENCH passable and the latter weakly held. 14th Londons in assembly area ready to move.	
		10.45	Capture of BLUE LINE by 12th Londons confirmed.	
		10.55	167th Brigade report their Support and Reserve Battalions moving up according to programme. G.O.C. ordered 167th Brigade to extend the left of the 3rd Londons and join up with 13th Londons along the BLUE LINE using their Reserve Coy to do this.	
		11.20	167th Brigade report 3rd Londons on BLUE LINE and 1st Londons and 7th Middlesex pushing through towards second objective.	
		11.30	VII Corps asked to send a Contact 'plane to clear up the situation about N.19.a.6.4.	
		11.35	168th Brigade report 14th Londons had left their forward assembly area.	
		11.45	Situation at N.19.a.6.4. cleared up, and 8th Middlesex moved to the BLUE LINE - 68 prisoners and 4 Machine Guns captured here.	
		p.m. 12.15	30th Division on our right reported the BLUE LINE had been crossed under a heavy barrage	

Army Form C. 2118.

WAR DIARY
or
INTELLIGENCE SUMMARY
(Erase heading not required.)

Instructions regarding War Diaries and Intelligence Summaries are contained in F.S. Regs., Part II and the Staff Manual respectively. Title Pages will be prepared in manuscript.

Place	Date	Hour	Summary of Events and Information	Remarks and references to Appendices
	April 9th	p.m. 12.35	4th Londons placed at disposal of 167th Brigade.	Appendix IA
		12.45	9th Londons placed at disposal of 167th Brigade.	Appendix IB
		12.50	Wire received from VII Corps that time table must be strictly adhered to, and Brigades warned to carry this out leaving Supports at points that were holding out.	
		1.50	14th Division seen moving through N.15. Left flank of 30th Division had heavy losses from Machine Gun and shell fire, but were still advancing.	
		3.0	G.O.C. instructed 167th Brigade to form strong point at N.21.a.2.0 defensive flank facing S.E. along LION LANE.	
		3.5	168th Brigade report that 14th Londons had taken the COJEUL SWITCH 1 Machine Gun and 100 prisoners.	
		3.10	Seven Guns of 193rd Machine Gun Coy. in position covering our left flank.	
		3.20	F.O.O. reports left of 30th Division held up outside its objective.	
		4.15	14th Division report themselves on the line N.9.c.50.25 N.15.d.35.50 with their right in touch with 14th Londons, but no troops on the right of them.	Appendix IC
		4.20	G.O.C. ordered 167th Brigade to push forward 3 Coys. of 4th Londons to support of 7th Middlesex and work forward and get in touch with 14th Division N.21.b.	
		4.40	G.O.C. again told 167th Brigade to get in touch with 14th Division using the 4th Londons.	
		4.50	168th Brigade report that 14th Londons had gone right forward over their objective leaving only a few Platoons in the COJEUL SWITCH. 13th Londons being sent forward to clear up the situation.	
		5.20	167th Brigade report a pocket of Germans in IBEX TRENCH.	

Army Form C. 2118.

WAR DIARY
or
INTELLIGENCE SUMMARY

(Erase heading not required.)

Instructions regarding War Diaries and Intelligence Summaries are contained in F. S. Regs, Part II. and the Staff Manual respectively. Title Pages will be prepared in manuscript.

Place	Date	Hour	Summary of Events and Information	Remarks and references to Appendices
	April 9th	p.m. 5.30	168th Brigade ordered 13th Londons to occupy BACK and CARD Trenches, and 14th London to withdraw and reorganise, leaving out posts to cover consolidation.	
		5.35	F.O.O. reports Germans still holding out at M.20.b.0.3. and our troops digging in about N.20 central.	
		5.50	14th Division ordered bombardment of BROWN LINE to continue till 6.45 and then lift. G.O.C. agreed to prolong this barrage across our front and ordered 167th Brigade to move up 8th Middlesex in rear of 4th Londons ready to assist in this attack.	
		6.30	167th Brigade ordered 7th Middlesex to take IBEX TRENCH and push up LION LANE to night, and then to push out its left and gain touch with 4th Londons.	APPENDIX IV
		6.50	G.O.C. ordered 5th Londons to move up and replace 9th Londons if they moved.	
		7.30	14th Division report their attack on BROWN LINE had failed. Situation evening 9th April - see Situation map.	
			Prisoners passed through Prisoners' Cage during the day total 12 Officers, 72 N.C.Os. 538 O.R. from the 162nd, 163rd and 76th Infantry Regiments.	
		10.40	Corps Order received. Assault on the WANCOURT LINE to take place at 8 a.m.	Appendix
	10th a.m. ---		VII Corps informed of the Situation of 56th Division and informed that assault at 8 a.m. not possible. The situation was not likely to be cleared up before daybreak.	
		12.15		
		1.10	VII Corps informed 56th Division would be in a position to carry out assault about 12 noon.	
		1.30	VII Corps Order for the assault was amended and the assault is not now to take place until 14th and 56th Divisions report that the situation has been cleared up on their front.	
		2.20	O.O.No.81 issued detailing 167th Brigade with 9th Londons attached to carry out the assault on WANCOURT LINE.	APPENDIX I

Army Form C. 2118.

WAR DIARY
or
INTELLIGENCE SUMMARY
(Erase heading not required.)

Place	Date	Hour	Summary of Events and Information	Remarks and references to Appendices
	10th	a.m. 7.45	During the night and early morning bombing parties of the 7th Middlesex and 1st Londons had made good the whole of the COJEUL SWITCH LINE as far South as LION LANE, but Germans were still holding out in the small system of trenches about 21.a.2.2. North of the SUNKEN ROAD. 14th Londons had established touch with 14th Division about N.15.d.5.8. and posts were being established along the WANCOURT LINE.	Appendix IE
		9.16	One Battalion 169th Brigade placed at the disposal of 167th Brigade to replace 9th Londons.	Appendix IF
		10.45	VII Corps Order extended the scope of the attack and ordered the troops after the capture of the BROWN LINE to continue their advance to the GREEN LINE, 56th Divn. occupying the high ground in N.21.d. and N.22.c. in support of 14th and 30th Division. Assault commenced at 12 o'clock.	
		p.m. 1.55	167th Brigade report that the advance was continuing with bombing parties down NEUVILLE VITASSE TRENCH and ZOO TRENCH. Left of 9th Londons held up by M.G.fire at junction of LION LANE and ZOO TRENCH. 8th Middlesex held up at cross roads N.20.b.7.5. by M.G.fire. 3rd Londons were late getting to position - T.Ms. being pushed forward to clear up the situation.	
		1.20	14th Division report they had captured BROWN LINE and wished to go forward to WANCOURT.	
		2.10	It is now clear that 14th Division had lost direction and their right flank is about N.18.c.9.1. leaving a large gap between their right and our left.	
		3.45	F.O.O. reports THE EGG now clear and our infantry advancing up the slope without opposition. In spite of continued reports from all sources that the WANCOURT LINE had been captured, the situation in the evening as definitely ascertained is shewn on Situation Map. 14th Division advance on WANCOURT had been held up by M.G.fire from HILL 90.	Appendix IG Appendix IH
		8.15	VII Corps ordered 56th Division to make good HILL 90 in order to assist the advance of the 14th Division.	
		9. 8	This task was allotted to 167th Infantry Brigade.	

Army Form C. 2118.

WAR DIARY
or
INTELLIGENCE SUMMARY

(Erase heading not required.)

Instructions regarding War Diaries and Intelligence Summaries are contained in F.S. Regs., Part II. and the Staff Manual respectively. Title Pages will be prepared in manuscript.

Place	Date	Hour	Summary of Events and Information	Remarks and references to Appendices
	10th	p.m. 11.52	VII Corps informed that it would be impossible for us to establish ourselves on HILL 90 during the night.	
	11th	a.m. 12.45	Prisoners passed through Cage during the day 10 Officers 25 N.C.Os. 219 O.Rs.	Appendix I
		8.0	167th Brigade ordered to capture NEPAL TRENCH between the COJEUL SWITCH and the 14th Division commencing 5.30 a.m. and to carry HILL 90 as soon as possible.	
		8.40	167th Brigade report the junction of WANCOURT LINE with the COJEUL SWITCH was captured at 5 a.m. and counter attack beaten off.	Appendix 5
		8.45	8th Middlesex bombing parties making progress North and South from N.21.d.05.00.	
		9.10	169th Brigade warned to prepare to relieve 167th Brigade during the day.	
		9.30	NEPAL TRENCH between N.27.a.8.5. N.27.b.1.9. was captured.	
		10.15	14th Division report that attack on WANCOURT was stopped at outset by M.G. fire from HILL 90.	
		11.55	1st London bombing parties commenced clearing trenches in N.27.b.	
		p.m. 12.30	VII Corps O.O. ordering 56th Division to take the place of 30th Division and advance from HENINEL in touch with the 14th Division.	
		1.0	One Tank is placed at our disposal for this.	
		1.30	8th Middlesex report they had joined up with the 1st Londons in NEPAL TRENCH.	
		4.80	167th Brigade reported post had been established at junction of HENINEL and USK Trenches.	
			9th Londons have posts established at N.28.c.05.40 N.28.c.7.7. The HINDENBURG LINE clear of Germans as far as COJEUL River. 9th Londons also hold THE COT and C.T. towards HENINEL as far	Appendix 5

Army Form C. 2118.

WAR DIARY
or
INTELLIGENCE SUMMARY

(*Erase heading not required.*)

Instructions regarding War Diaries and Intelligence Summaries are contained in F.S. Regs., Part II. and the Staff Manual respectively. Title Pages will be prepared in manuscript.

Place	Date	Hour	Summary of Events and Information	Remarks and references to Appendices
	12th	4.30 a.m.	18th Manchesters of the Division on our Right, arrived at junction of COJEUL SWITCH and WANCOURT LINE preparatory to moving down COJEUL SWITCH LINE and attack trenches South of the River during the night.	Appendix IK
		4.47	169th Brigade warned to relieve 167th Brigade to-night.	
		9.15	Orders issued for 169th Brigade to consolidate HILL 90 to form a defensive flank towards WANCOURT and push patrols into HENINEL and when 30th Division have occupied HINDENBURG LINE to occupy the high ground in N.35.a. and 29.d.	Appendix IL
			For Situation see Situation Map.	APPENDIX IV
		12.50	Prisoners captured during the day 7 N.C.O. 62 O.Rs. of the 86 & 31st Reserve I.R. Relief of 167th Brigade by 168th Brigade in Support Brigade Area complete.	
		7.0	Our attack started at 5.15 a.m. and enemy resistance was overcome and after stiff bombing 2nd and 5th Londons got connection in N.28.d. Enemy were then seen withdrawing from HENINEL in large numbers and leading Coy. 2nd Londons immediately pushed into the Village. High ground in N.22.d. was consolidated and strong points made. 30th Division on our right crossed the COJEUL RIVER and reached high ground along the COJEUL SWITCH.	
		9.40	2nd Londons established posts from N.29.a.8.4. N.29.b.1.8. and in touch with the 30th Divn. on its right N.29.c.5.4. HENINEL clear of the enemy.	
		10.30	Patrol of 2nd Londons occupied the Line N.29.d.2.0 29.d.8.9. where view of the country beyond was obtainable. Patrol also occupied the Line N.29.a.0.5. 29.a.4.9. joining up with 30th Division on our right.	Appendix IM
		11.15	Patrol of 5th Londons entered WANCOURT and found it unoccupied, and posts were established at N.24.a.4.1.	
		11.55	14th Division report patrols in WANCOURT, and one Battalion moving North and one South of the Village trying to establish themselves on the GREEN LINE.	
		p.m. 1.0	VII Corps ordered the advance to be continued to the SENSEE RIVER	Appendix IN

2449 Wt. W14957/M90 750,000 1/16 J.B.C. & A. Forms/C.2118/12.

Army Form C. 2118.

WAR DIARY
or
INTELLIGENCE SUMMARY
(Erase heading not required.)

Instructions regarding War Diaries and Intelligence Summaries are contained in F. S. Regs., Part II. and the Staff Manual respectively. Title Pages will be prepared in manuscript.

Place	Date	Hour	Summary of Events and Information	Remarks and references to Appendices
	12th	p.m. 4.30	169th Brigade Headquarters ordered to move to the vicinity of HENINEL.	Appendix O
		5.10	VII Corps ordered the GREEN LINE to be consolidated and Strong Reconnaissance sent forward towards SENSEE River.	Appendix P (APPENDIX N)
			56th Division ordered to make all preparations to advance from the GREEN LINE the next morning For situation see SITUATION MAP.	
			Prisoners of the 86 and 84 Reserve I.R. were taken during the day.	
	13th	a.m. 12.5	VII Corps O.O. received ordering 56th Division to move forward on CHERISY, keeping in touch with the Division on either flank and taking advantage of their progress on the high ground.	Appendix Q
		12.50 p.m. 1.0	169th Brigade ordered to carry this out, forming defensive flanks where necessary. Situation. Crest of the ridge from M.35.b.0.6. to within 20 yards of WANCOURT TOWER consolidated. 2 Battalions entrenches in depth with 6 M.Gs. The advance of the 50th Divn. has been held up by M.G. fire from West of GUEMAPPE, and now hold line M.24.c.5.3. N.18.c.3.0 The advance of the 30th Division along the COJEUL SWITCH Line failed to make ground.	
		5.45	Evening Report - Situation unchanged. Hostile M.G. fire from direction of GUEMAPPE and snipers, causing us some casualties. Shelling only occasionally and with light guns.	APPENDIX IV
			Situation - see Situation Map.	
		6.30	VII Corps Order received for General Advance in conjunction with the VIth Corps. Zero hour at 5.30 a.m.	Appendix R
		6.40	169th Brigade warned that they would be required to carry out the attack and gain the line of the SENSEE RIVER.	APPENDIX L
		10.10	O.O.No.82 ordering 169th Brigade to carry out the attack issued.	
			Prisoners of the 84th, 86th and 99th R.I.R. were captured during the day.	

Army Form C. 2118.

WAR DIARY
or
INTELLIGENCE SUMMARY

(Erase heading not required.)

Instructions regarding War Diaries and Intelligence Summaries are contained in F.S. Regs., Part II. and the Staff Manual respectively. Title Pages will be prepared in manuscript.

Place	Date	Hour	Summary of Events and Information	Remarks and references to Appendices
	14th	a.m. 6.50	169th Brigade reported the attack had started at 5.30 a.m. with approximately 500 yards gap between our left and 50th Division.	
			Enemy blew up WANCOUR TOWER during the night. Enemy barrage was quick in opening and heavy.	
		7.15	Enemy counter attacked our left flank strongly from spur in N.19.c. where the gap had been left driving back our front wave. Supporting waves pushed forward again but heavy enfilade fire prevented the attack making ground.	
			169th Brigade wire timed 6.15 a.m. reported the attack appeared to go well over the Crest, and it subsequently appeared that a point O.31.c.2.7. was reached and a post established there, but it was withdrawn later as it was so far in the air.	
		8.0	169th Brigade report the attack on either flank had not/made ground and the situation on the whole Corps front was as before Zero.	
		8.40	168th Brigade ordered to move 2 Battalions forward in the COJEUL SWITCH LINE North of the WANCOURT LINE.	
		9.5	169th Brigade report that as long as the Divisions on our right flank were unable to advance it was useless to try and push the attack on the Divisional front.	Appendix IS
		10.50	Situation on Divisional front was very involved. Portions of 3 Battalions 56th Division, 2 Battalions 50th Division being mixed up in N.30.a.	
		11.20	14th Londons placed at the diposal of 169th Brigade.	
		11.55	Division on our right reported strong German counter attack developing along the COJEUL SWITCH LINE. 169th Brigade ordered to be ready to take this attack in the flank should it develop and to secure Crest Line East of HENINEL strongly.	Appendix IT
		p.m. 12.25	169th Brigade ordered 14th Londons to consolidate on HILL 90 as second line of resistance.	Appendix V

Army Form C. 2118.

WAR DIARY
or
INTELLIGENCE SUMMARY
(Erase heading not required.)

Instructions regarding War Diaries and Intelligence Summaries are contained in F. S. Regs., Part II. and the Staff Manual respectively. Title Pages will be prepared in manuscript.

Place	Date	Hour	Summary of Events and Information	Remarks and references to Appendices
	14th	p.m. 12.30	VII Corps order that general advance should not be pressed owing to situation on the left.	Appendix IV
		12.45	Division on our left reported enemy counter attacking and advancing against GUEMAPPE on a frontage of 1000 yards - strength estimated one Brigade.	Appendix IV
		1. 0	168th Brigade informed of this attack and ordered to occupy COJEUL SWITCH with a defensive line facing N.E.	
		1.40	F.O.O. reported enemy occupying trench in N.36.c. in strength and that our artillery fire had been observed to cause many casualties.	
		2.10	169th Brigade reported that the attacking waves are in shell holes 400 yards S.E. of the Sunken Road N.29.d.7.9. Officer of the 50th Division in charge.	Appendix IX APPENDIX XIV
		2.15	168th Brigade warned to be in readiness to relieve 169th Brigade to-night.	
		3.30	168th Brigade ordered to relieve 169th Brigade during the night, and 167th Brigade to relieve 169th Brigade in Support Brigade Area during the next day. Situation - See Situation Map.	
		9. 0	VII Corps order leading Divisions to seize every opportunity of making ground on their front with the object of reaching the Line of the SENSEE RIVER by the night of April 16th	Appendix IV
	15th	a.m. 5.30	Relief of 169th Brigade by 168th Brigade complete.	
		p.m. 4.25	A quiete day was passed in consolidating the ground gained. G.O.C. instructed 168th Brigade to establish themselves in the bombing trenches at N.30.c. and d. during the night, and to join up their right flank with the 21st Division.	
	16th	a.m. 10.20	168th Brigade reported that 14th Londons had reached bombing trenches in N.30.c. and d. and found them about 2 feet. deep and full of water and had withdrawn.	Appendix IV

Army Form C. 2118.

WAR DIARY
or
INTELLIGENCE SUMMARY

(Erase heading not required.)

Instructions regarding War Diaries and Intelligence Summaries are contained in F. S. Regs., Part II. and the Staff Manual respectively. Title Pages will be prepared in manuscript.

Place	Date	Hour	Summary of Events and Information	Remarks and references to Appendices
	16th p.m.	6.55	Strong hostile barrage commenced creeping up the COJEUL VALLEY indicating a counter attack on GUEMAPPE against WANCOURT and possibly further South. 188th Brigade ordered to stand to on Hill 90.	
		7.50	German counter attack did not materialize. 188th Brigade ordered to Stand down.	
		8.15	VII Corps cancelled the order for advance to Line of the SENSEE RIVER, and said it would suffice if the leading Divisions could work forward to the Line T.6 central 0.31.c. 0.19 central in the next three days. Quiet day on the whole front.	
		8.30	168th Brigade reported heavy barrage on the whole front as well as on the front of the Division on our left and that they expected to be attacked. Support Brigade ordered to stand to.	
		8.55	50th Division reported that Germans had recaptured WANCOURT TOWER and had also got into the Brigade on our right, but had been driven out again.	Appendix AA
		9.5	167th Brigade ordered to place 1 Battalion at the disposal of 168th Brigade on HILL 90.	
			50th Division attempted to retake the Tower during the night but failed.	
	17th a.m.	9.12	Arrangements made for the slopes East of WANCOURT TOWER to be swept by M.G. and artillery fire, while 50th Division counter attacked. 50th Division again attacked at midday and retook the TOWER.	
		5.10	Evening Report - considerable artillery and M.G. activity both sides of the COJEUL VALLEY, and HILL 90 heavily shelled.	
			O.O. No. 83 issued ordering 167th Brigade to relieve 168th Brigade in the line with 2 Battalions 169th Brigade at their disposal.	APPENDIX I
		7.10	VII Corps Order for further advance received, such not to take place before 22nd.	
		7.35		

Army Form C. 2118.

WAR DIARY
or
INTELLIGENCE SUMMARY
(Erase heading not required.)

Instructions regarding War Diaries and Intelligence Summaries are contained in F. S. Regs., Part II. and the Staff Manual respectively. Title Pages will be prepared in manuscript.

Place	Date	Hour	Summary of Events and Information	Remarks and references to Appendices
AGNY	18th	9.35 a.m.	168th Brigade reported that the enemy were sending up our S.O.S. signal opposite our front.	Appendix I BB AA
		11.0 p.m.	50th Division report that information from a German prisoner points to hostile attack on WANCOURT TOWER about 1 p.m. All preparations were made for this eventuality. 168th Bde relieved as detailed in Appendix I BB	
		12.30	VII Corps Order for the relief of 56th Division by 30th Division by 20th inst. received.	APPENDIX I
		2.30	O.O. No 84 for relief issued.	
	19th		During the evening the relief of 1/67 Bde in the support area carried out. A quiet night in the front line. 167 Bde were by bus to Pt POMMIER area. The command of the line was handed over and Div HQ opened at COUIN	
COUIN	20th	3pm am 12.30	168 Bde relief in the line complete. 169 Bde were relieved in the reserve area during the day and entrained for the SOUASTRE area direct.	
	21st		168th Bde proceeded to COUIN area by bus.	
	22nd		Spent in completing the relief for the area.	
	23rd		Owing to attacks of Corps bombardment 167/168 proceeded by buses to the HARLEY area ... 169 Bn ... area concentrated — SOUASTRE	

Army Form C. 2118.

WAR DIARY
or
INTELLIGENCE SUMMARY
(Erase heading not required.)

Instructions regarding War Diaries and Intelligence Summaries are contained in F. S. Regs., Part II. and the Staff Manual respectively. Title Pages will be prepared in manuscript.

Place	Date	Hour	Summary of Events and Information	Remarks and references to Appendices
COUIN	24th		Orders received from XVIII Corps that division would move up so as to be in position to support VI or VII Corps as required. O.O. No 85 issued.	APPENDIX I
	25th		168 & 169 Bdes moved by route march to GOUY and WANQUETIN during the afternoon. 167 Bde moved by bus to HARARCQ area.	
HAUTEVILLE	26th	3pm	Div. HQ closed at COUIN and opened at HAUTEVILLE.	
	12.30am		Orders received for division to move to WARLUS area and to come under orders of VI Corps. Orders issued.	APPENDIX I
	2pm		Div. HQ opened at WARLUS. Bdes moved by route march — in order attached	
	3pm		G.O.C. at C.S.O. attended conference at VI Corps HQ and received orders to relieve 15 Division in the line	
	6pm		B.G.G.S. 168 & 169 Bdes attended conference at Div. HQ	
	8.45pm		O.O. No. 86 issued with orders to relief – the line	APPENDIX I
WARLUS	27th		167 Bde relieved 15 Div reserve brigade by midnight.	

2449 Wt. W14957/M90 750,000 1/16 J.B.C. & A. Forms/C.2118/12.

WAR DIARY or INTELLIGENCE SUMMARY

Army Form C. 2118.

Place	Date	Hour	Summary of Events and Information	Remarks and references to Appendices
WARLUS	28th	1pm 9.30	164 Bde relieved 167 Bde and the were became support area. 166 Bde moved into divisional reserve in ARRAS	
	29th	1am 10am 2pm 2.30 3pm	Relief in the line by 167 Bde complete. Dw HQ opened at Rue de la PAIX, ARRAS. O.O No. 87 issued giving warning orders for a general attack on 3rd May and ordering 167 Bde to take over night outposts the divisional front. G.O.C. & G.S.O. attend a Conference called in confirmed that in Dw HQ ARRAS. Evening report - Quiet day	APPENDIX I
	30th	5am 1pm 5pm	Relief of outpost line by 167 Bde by 164 Bde in night outposts completed. Mornings report - Quiet night. O.O No. 88 issued with orders for the attack on the 3rd May. Evening report - Quiet day	APPENDIX I

www.ingramcontent.com/pod-product-compliance
Lightning Source LLC
Chambersburg PA
CBHW081402160426
43193CB00013B/2091